DAISY'S DIARY

Octavia Johnstone Douglas,
painted by her brother Sholto

Carleton Salkeld in his
Hussars Uniform

DAISY'S DIARY

A HONEYMOON JOURNEY TO THE FAR EAST

Octavia Salkeld

Introduction by Isobel Wybergh

Edited by Diane Mortimer

TITUS WILSON, KENDAL

1993

ISBN 0 9522424 0 0

Cover: Octavia, painted by her brother Sholto
(photography: Jean Knight, Solway Studio)
Back: The twins on their eightieth birthday

Edited and published by Diane Mortimer, DKM Publishing, Caldbeck
First printed in 1993 and reprinted in 1998 by Titus Wilson, Kendal

CONTENTS

ILLUSTRATIONS

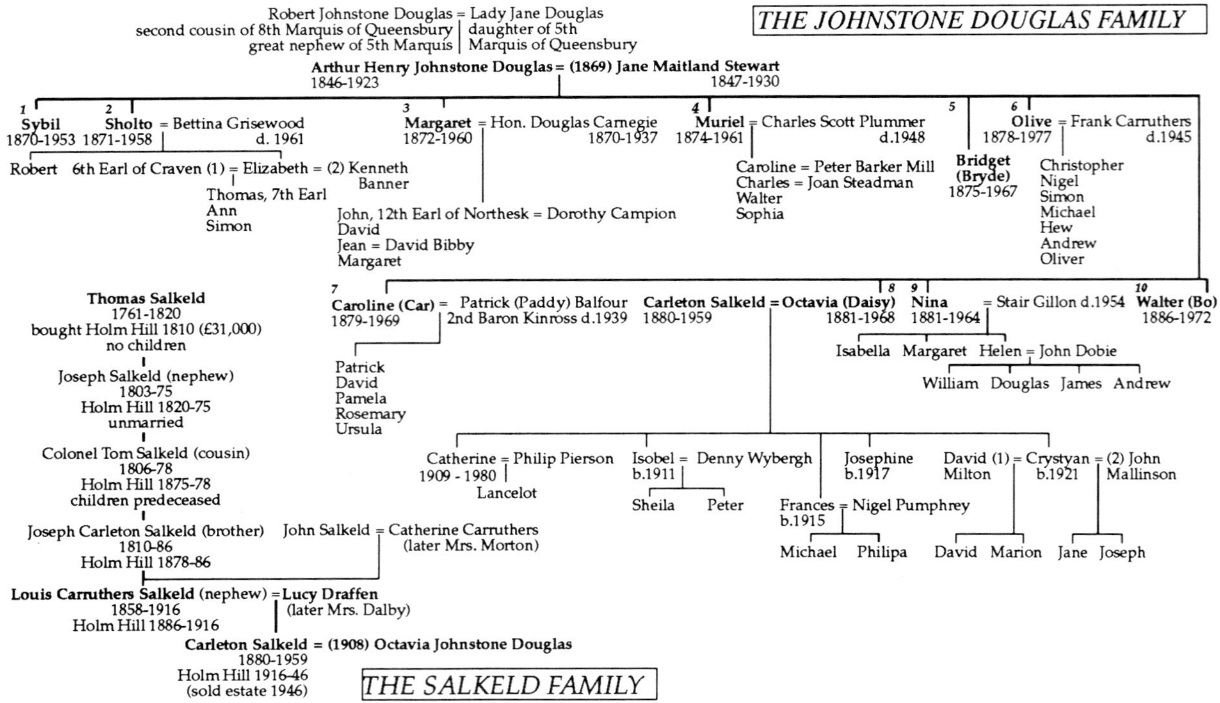
THE JOHNSTONE DOUGLAS FAMILY
Robert Johnstone Douglas = Lady Jane Douglas
second cousin of 8th Marquis of Queensbury
great nephew of 5th Marquis
daughter of 5th Marquis of Queensbury
Arthur Henry Johnstone Douglas = (1869) Jane Maitland Stewart
1846-1923
1847-1930
1 Sybil 1870-1953
Robert
2 Sholto = Bettina Grisewood
1871-1958
d. 1961
6th Earl of Craven (1) = Elizabeth = (2) Kenneth Banner
Thomas, 7th Earl
Ann
Simon
3 Margaret = Hon. Douglas Carnegie
1872-1960
1870-1937
John, 12th Earl of Northesk = Dorothy Campion
David
Jean = David Bibby
Margaret
4 Muriel = Charles Scott Plummer
1874-1961
d.1948
Caroline = Peter Barker Mill
Charles = Joan Steadman
Walter
Sophia
5 Bridget (Bryde)
1875-1967
6 Olive = Frank Carruthers
1878-1977
d.1945
Christopher
Nigel
Simon
Michael
Hew
Andrew
Oliver
7 Caroline (Car) = Patrick (Paddy) Balfour
1879-1969
2nd Baron Kinross d.1939
Patrick
David
Pamela
Rosemary
Ursula
Carleton Salkeld = 8 Octavia (Daisy)
1880-1959
1881-1968
Catherine = Philip Pierson
1909 - 1980
Lancelot
Isobel = Denny Wybergh
b.1911
Sheila
Peter
Frances = Nigel Pumphrey
b.1915
Michael
Philipa
Josephine
b.1917
David (1) = Crystyan = (2) John
Milton
b.1921
Mallinson
David
Marion
Jane
Joseph
9 Nina = Stair Gillon d.1954
1881-1964
Isabella
Margaret
Helen = John Dobie
William
Douglas
James
Andrew
10 Walter (Bo)
1886-1972
Thomas Salkeld
1761-1820
bought Holm Hill 1810 (£31,000)
no children
Joseph Salkeld (nephew)
1803-75
Holm Hill 1820-75
unmarried
Colonel Tom Salkeld (cousin)
1806-78
Holm Hill 1875-78
children predeceased
Joseph Carleton Salkeld (brother)
1810-86
Holm Hill 1878-86
John Salkeld = Catherine Carruthers
(later Mrs. Morton)
Louis Carruthers Salkeld (nephew) = Lucy Draffen
1858-1916
Holm Hill 1886-1916
(later Mrs. Dalby)
Carleton Salkeld = (1908) Octavia Johnstone Douglas
1880-1959
Holm Hill 1916-46
(sold estate 1946)
THE SALKELD FAMILY

Introduction

If you had been a passenger travelling from Waterloo Station to Southampton on 12 October 1908, you might have seen among your fellow travellers a Honeymoon couple, my father Carleton Salkeld aged 29 and his newly wedded wife my mother aged 28.

They were embarking on a journey to the Far East in a German Coaling boat; sailing via the Bay of Biscay, the Mediterranean, the Red Sea, Ceylon, China and the Yangtse River, Japan, Korea, Siberia, Russia, Berlin, Brussels and Home! It was indeed a formidable itinerary, and would have been adventuresome enough today with all the advantages of modern air travel, but a second class Coaling Ship was rather a different matter! It took them nearly six months to complete and turned out to be a unique experience, a mixture of intense interest and enjoyment and considerable real hardship. Unfortunately for my mother, she was in her own words a "Rotten Sailor" and suffered from bouts of excruciating sea sickness.

In spite of this she succeeded in recording their experiences in the remarkable Diary that follows. This is accompanied by almost daily letters to her beloved twin sister Nina to whom she expressed herself more freely and with whom she shared all her most intimate thoughts and feelings.

First let me introduce my parents and a few of the other people who figure most prominently in the Diary.

My father was the only son of Louis Carruthers Salkeld and Lucy Marion (née Draffen) of Holm Hill, Dalston (now Lime House School) near Carlisle in Cumbria. He was educated at Eton and Sandhurst. He served in the South African War in the 10th. Hussars. He retired from the Army early in the century but joined the Cumberland and Westmorland Yeomanry with whom he served in the 1914-18 War. There are some interesting exhibits in the Yeomanry Museum in the base of the Norman Pele Tower at Dalemain, near Ullswater, which were pointed out to me by the present owner Robert Hasell McCosh. The first one is a silver cup presented by Mrs. Salkeld (my mother) in 1909 and won by Corporal Graham for general efficiency. The second, two telegrams sent on August 4th and 5th respectively and ordering the mobilisation of the Regiment at the beginning of the 1914-18 War, and signed by Major Salkeld Adjutant.

My parents first lived at Wreay Syke, south of Carlisle, and then at Calthwaite Hall. After my grandfather's death in 1916 we moved to Holm Hill. My father retired from the Army to run the Estate. He was a keen sportsman and organised shooting parties from Holm Hill. He was also a dedicated fisherman, and some of his happiest days were spent salmon fishing in the Highlands at Drumruinie Lodge near Ullapool,

Ross-shire - where my grandmother rented a Shooting Lodge. In the Second World War 1939-45 he did sterling work in the Special Constabulary in Cumberland. Another of his hobbies was an absorbing interest in railways. He would often be seen talking to the engine drivers in Carlisle Station, and not infrequently gave luncheon parties for their benefit.

He served on the Committee of the Carlisle Infirmary before it was taken over by the Welfare State. He was a familiar figure on the wards and a favourite with the staff. In 1946 he sold Holm Hill and bought a house in Wetheral. In his garden there he grew flowers for the Infirmary and arranged them personally in the staff dining hall. It was his dream to do something permanent for the nursing staff. This was realised when through his efforts £8000 was raised to build a recreation hall for their use. This resulted in "The Salkeld Hall" which is still in use. It was a proud day for him when it opened.

Young hunters grazing at Holm Hill, Dalston, the home of the Salkeld family 1810-1946

Carleton's parents, Louis and Lucy Salkeld, in the porch at Holm Hill

My mother, Octavia Johnstone Douglas, known to her family and friends as "Daisy" and the author of the diary, was one of a large family of eight girls and two boys. Their father, Arthur Johnstone Douglas, was Agent to Lord Mansfield and lived at Comlongon Castle, Dumfriesshire. He was the second cousin of Sholto, the eighth Marquis of Queensbury - of the fairy tale castle Drumlanrig near Thornhill, Dumfriesshire, and Bowhill, Selkirk - both houses filled with rare pictures, furniture and china collected by earlier generations of the Montagu, Douglas and Scott families.

Comlongon Castle, near Ruthwell in Dumfriesshire, where Daisy and her family grew up

In spite of his connections, Arthur (my grandfather) was not a rich man so the family were brought up most frugally with much passing down of clothes, which comes out in the diary. The twins suffered the most from this strict regime, and used to tell us of how, when oranges and apples were passed round, they were given half each! There was of course no central heating at Comlongon and the house was far from warm. Most likely this contributed to the fact that they nearly all suffered from arthritis in their later years.

My grandfather was a keen hunting man, and many of his family inherited his enthusiasm for the sport. In 1886 he had a real break and spotted a National winner in "Old Joe", whom he saw jump a fence while out hunting at Westward near Wigton. He bought the horse for £300 and had him trained. Great were the rejoicings when he won the race mainly due to his jumping ability and staying power. My mother never tired of telling us (though she was only five years old at the time) of how the local men made a triumphal arch at the gate to Comlongon - the horses were removed from the carriage and they entered the shafts themselves and pulled my grandfather up to the front door, where hospitality was dispensed to all. She remembered running round the dining room table with her twin sister and shouting, *"Three chairs for Old Joe!"*

My grandfather was a broad-minded, tolerant man, who believed in encouraging his family to develop their talents as they wished. They were beyond doubt an extremely gifted family in a wide range of creative activities - amateur dramatics, song recitals, writing magazines and stories, and not least painting. My eldest uncle, Sholto, was a painter of no mean stature. His most famous picture was of seven of his sisters, which won him acclaim in 1902 when it was shown at the Royal Academy Exhibition at Burlington House in London. My youngest uncle, Walter, was a professional singer and a pupil of the famous Polish tenor Jean de Reszke. He studied with him in his studio in Paris and became a much valued member of his staff. It was Jean's wish that after his death my uncle would found, in his memory, a school of singing in London for young singers in this country. So in due course the Webber Douglas School in Clareville Street, South Kensington was launched and is still in existence. The emphasis now is more on drama than on singing.

'The Seven Sisters' painted by their brother Sholto - his most celebrated work, exhibited at the Royal Academy in 1902. The eighth sister Madge was already married and away from home.

My mother Octavia and her twin sister Nina were the youngest of the eight girls. They also inherited the family flair for art, and were also passionately fond of horses and dogs, which comes out in the diary and is also shown in their delightful portraits of their own and other people's pets. They learnt a lot from their older brother Sholto, who encouraged them to develop their talent. While young, they stayed at home and were educated by their governess Miss Lamphier, of whom they were very fond.

The next stage took them to Brussels where they studied art at L'Atelier Blanc Garin, Rue de la Porte from 1902-3. They also attended the Slade School in London. This was rather an advanced move for those days on my grandfather's part. It was more usual for girls from their background to remain at home until hopefully the right man came along.

The twins owed much to Margaret Broadhurst, a distant cousin and a kind and generous lady, who had lost her husband in tragic circumstances - Harry shot himself in a fit of depression. He left her Houghton House, Carlisle, and as she had no children of her own, she opened her heart and her home to many young people, including the twins who were allowed to ride her many fine horses and enjoy their hunting with the Cumberland packs to the full. She is referred to in the Diary as "Mog", or she and Harry as "H & M".

Later on in her married life at Holm Hill, where they lived after my grandfather's death and the birth of her five daughters, my mother became a pioneer in the Girl Guide Movement. In the early 1920s she ran a Brownie Pack and a Guide Company at Holm Hill which is still remembered today by many of its former members. Frequently they say to me, "We'll never forget your mother"! She succeeded Lady Rochdale as County Commissioner in 1919, a position she held for 16 years. Both Lord and Lady Baden Powell were visitors at Holm Hill in the early days of the Guide Movement.

It might be helpful to readers to add a few explanatory notes about people referred to in the Diary by their Christian names or sometimes nicknames.

For example, "Spookie" was the seventh sister Caroline, who married Lord Kinross in 1903 and lived in Edinburgh. Eleanor Chance (married name Calthrop) was the only sister of Sir Robert Chance of Morton Hall, Carlisle and manager of Ferguson Brothers. "At Alice" was a sister of the 10th Earl of Northesk and Douglas Carnegie who married Madge Johnstone Douglas, my mother's sister (D and M in the letters). The "Co Mother" was Lady Northesk and the mother of Douglas Carnegie. "Shosh" was Sholto. "Ollie" was Olive, another of their sisters, who married Colonel Frank Carruthers of Dormont, near Lockerbie.

Finally, what can one say about the truly remarkable relationship between the twins? They were beyond doubt identical both in looks and tastes. Perhaps this is what prompted them to call themselves DayNin as a contraction of their names. My aunt called my father T.B. or "Twin Brother". My mother was the stronger character of the two, my aunt a gentler person altogether. They were however utterly devoted to each other and kept up a correspondence which lasted all their lives. When my mother married in 1908 it was a sad wrench for my aunt who did not get married herself until 1919 when she married Stair Gillon, a barrister in Edinburgh who eventually inherited Abbey St. Bathans, Duns, Berwickshire - his son-in-law John Dobie still lives in one of the houses on the estate.

During the 1914-18 War my aunt became Divisional Director of the WRNS, for which service she was awarded the OBE. She died in 1964, four years before my mother. She left two daughters, Isabella and Helen (who married John Dobie). They were very special cousins to us, unfortunately both of them have died. My aunt's death was naturally a great grief to my mother. Frequently we heard her say: "What I miss most are the letters from my twin sister".

On her return from an adventurous trip in a houseboat up the rapids of the Yangtse Gorges, my mother wrote to her twin to share the glad news of her pregnancy. When "Young Salkeld" was born on 24th July 1909, "HE" turned out to be a "SHE" - my eldest sister Catherine. Then followed four more daughters: Isobel, Frances, Josephine and Crystyan. This was a big disappointment for my father, who longed for a son. But as my mother would have said: "Que voulez-vous ?"

For those readers who may be understandably concerned about my mother's extreme views on both Germans and class - her prejudices can best be explained by her upbringing and the time in which she lived when both these views were commonly held.

Isobel Wybergh
1993

Postscript

The five daughters have expressed the same enterprising spirit as their parents, each in their own way.

Catherine (who died in 1980) trained at the Webber Douglas and became a stage and radio actress. Isobel (Belle) also trained at the Webber Douglas and is a singing teacher to this day, and also a Church of England Lay Preacher. Frances has created a renowned garden in Hampshire, open to the public every Sunday in the summer. Josephine (Jophe) has owned several successful racehorses, and has become involved in sheep farming in the Borders. Crystyan was a highly regarded GP until her career ended as the result of a tragic riding accident. All except Jophe married and had children, and now grandchildren.

Lance Pierson (Daisy's Grandson)

Editor's Note

Octavia's Diary was always intended - as she makes clear in her letters to her sister, Nina - to serve the dual purpose of describing the journey for anyone in the family who was interested and also to serve as a permanent record for Octavia herself. This caused tensions, not only for Nina when faced with the embarrassment of having to pass the diary on, but also for Daisy: "I must say I wish I c$^{d.}$ write it to you alone but it is the best plan don't you think to do it so that anybody can read it?" (22.10.08) Sometimes the Diary was written up later, when travel or sea-sickness prevented Daisy's regular, and lengthy, sessions of diary and letter writing. It was written on sheets of self-ruled blue paper, each section being stitched together at the top left-hand corner before despatch to Nina. The instalments were accompanied by private letters, mostly written on headed notepaper from the ship or hotel, which were addressed to Nina herself and often gave a slightly different perspective from the 'official' version. Sometimes a letter was sent before the relevant diary section. These letters, without their envelopes, were kept by Nina, Daisy retrieving the Diary.

The trip was arranged through Thomas Cook, who had started tours to the Far East in the late 1800s. In order to have the opportunity of stopping at several ports on the way out, they sailed with the Nord Deutscher Lloyd shipping company of Bremen. The return journey was made on the Trans-Siberian Railway which had been completed six years earlier. Octavia and Carleton also had the security of a wide circle of friends and contacts who had gone to the Far East in the diplomatic service, the army and navy or in business, particularly with Jardine Matheson. Political problems in China did cause the couple some concern: "I hope they're not going to have any fuss in China to prevent us going there. News here is of the scantiest -" (20.11.08) but they had few qualms about the discomforts of embarking on a house boat with a Chinese crew, only one of whom spoke any English. Local contacts, however, provided an accompanying safety boat.

The diary and letters are printed with the letters inserted into their places between the diary sections. The assumption has been that Nina would have read her private letter first! Duplications are cut. The spelling and punctuation have been left as in the original; Octavia expressed her irritation at Carleton's corrections (letter to Nina, 8 February 1909)! In her dating of Pompeii, she has confused the dates of foundation and destruction, putting 600 B.C. instead of A.D. 79 - an understandable mistake when on a 2 hour guided tour of excavations covering a very wide area even in 1908. At other sites, she expresses scepticism about the knowledge of guide or guidebook!

Unfortunately, as happened with so many albums, the photographs so carefully collected on the trip have gone astray, but members of the family still treasure some of their souvenirs, such as the Chinese vases bought on the trip to the Yangtse Gorges.

Diane Mortimer

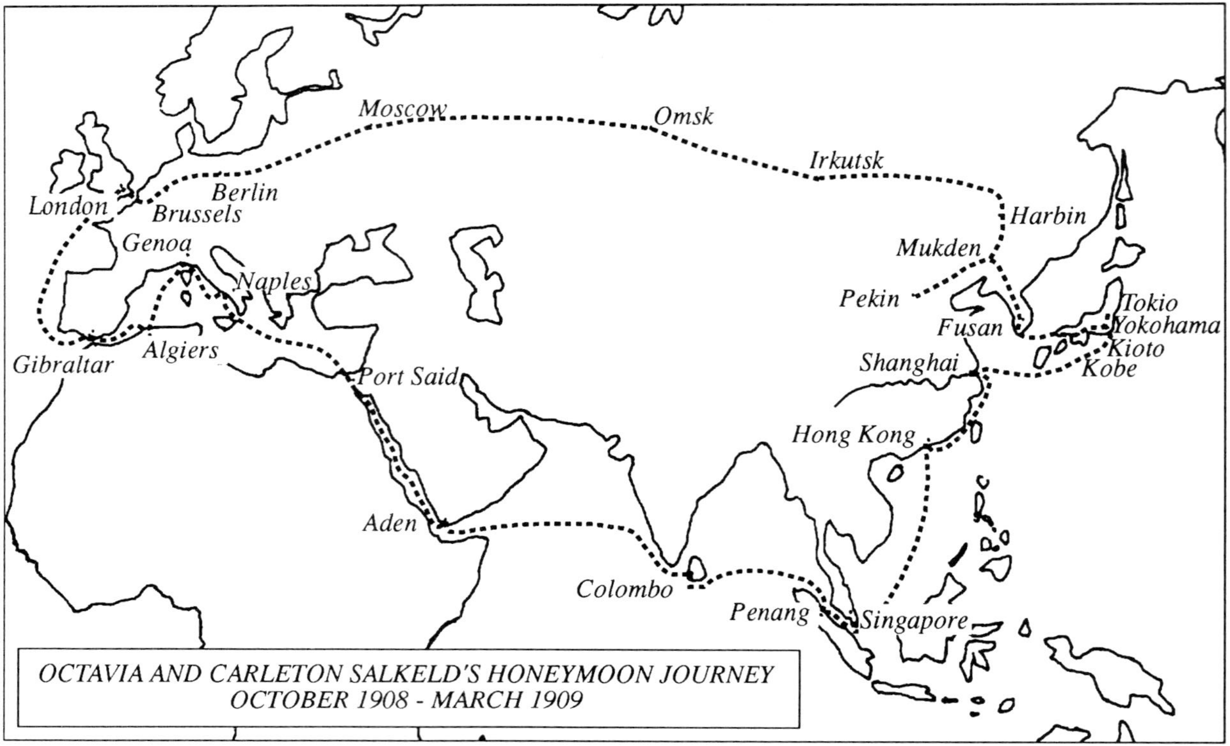

OCTAVIA AND CARLETON SALKELD'S HONEYMOON JOURNEY
OCTOBER 1908 - MARCH 1909

Prologue

13.10.08

Am writing this going to Southampton. Your letter this morning was A1. Enjoy Paris to the full my child. Bless the Broadies! I am quite happy about you now. As you say yourself Paris will give you a splendid change & you will feel bolstered up for hunting & work - The "send off" at Waterloo was very painful. I was thankful you weren't there. A lot of missionary people were going so heaps of people (men cheifly) were at the station - sang hymns ("they generally gie them a bit of a shout" as the guard said when we asked what was up) One poor wretched woman was in an awful state seeing her husband off - Poor devil I was sorry for her but wish she hadn't come. My next letter will be more interesting & lets hope better written! Bless you my own child. make these 6 months happy & profitable ones if you possibly can -

Always your own

D

Best love to the Piglet. Bless its heart - Best love from the T.B.

Daisy, Nina and Piglet

Carleton and Daisy before setting off on their honeymoon trip

Carleton "the T.B." ("Twin Brother") escorts "DayNin" (Daisy and Nina)

1

Southampton - Gibraltar - Algiers - Genoa - Naples

Göben

16.10.08

Well, my child, comment ça va-t-il. Here I sit writing to you on the deck of the Göben - Its a terribly lazy life - You must read the diary first I think & then I can make comments - well, now you've read it! Wasn't it beastly my being sea-sick? It was just misery but thank heaven I think its over now tho' I'm not going to try myself too much in case it s[d.] return! Our cabin is perfectly tiny & its for that reason as much as anything that I don't get up to breakfast. We simply c[dn't] dress together in it. C. was a perfect angel when I was badly - I didn't know anybody c[d.] have been so attentive - or so patient, for there is always something irritating about somebody being ill for no earthly reason - The life interests me very much as being something so absolutely new but I think one will get very sick of it soon - We get to Gibraltar tomorrow morning at 6 o'clock & stay till 10 - Rather a bad hour but still. I am looking forward to it enormously (not only for being on "terra-firma" again, in fact I think that is rather a pity as it will be awful if I have to begin all over again after landing!) I am lying on a deck chair - one of those nice cane ones - we were told they provided them on this line but they dont so these are only borrowed till Gibraltar when we will have to buy some of our own - dressed in my Bertie tweed, felt hat, tied on with my brown scarf, Helen's tennis shoes, & my blue coat wrapped round my "lower limbs" I bought 4 excellent cushions at Harvey & Nicol which make these chairs luxuriously comfortable - The people aren't very entertaining - mostly curious looking Germans & the English are "no class" at all tho' perfectly harmless in every way - There are a good many children on board who skip about & make things lively - they're quite nice to watch provided one has not got to look after them - There are 2 small ones who live just opposite us so that they might almost be in our cabin & the row they make in the mornings is something awful. C. swears furiously at them but it does no good - You don't know how glad I am to think that you are in Paris & therefore entirely distracted, for otherwise I'm afraid you'd be wearying very much for a letter - I will send this to Rosehill Cottage so you will get it as soon as you arrive there - It was so nice seeing Douglas & Madge, & the Co Mother at Southampton. They were all so interested & excited. Madge will be able to tell you what the ship is like - Now I'm going to write the diary up to date. It all had to be written yesterday for before that I was incapable of sitting up let alone holding a pen! Bless you my child - The joy of getting a letter from you at Algiers will be great & I do hope & trust it will be a really happy one - Best love from the T.B.

Ever yr own Twister -

Whatever happens don't let my diary get lost but I have told Mum you will send it to her at once & of course any of the rest of the family who like may see it -

Diary

1908

October 13th Tuesday - Started from 64 Lowndes Sq. at about 1/4 to 9 & went from Waterloo to Southampton in the 9-25 Special N.D.L. train. Some missionary people were being seen off at Waterloo so there was a good deal of hymn-singing ("giving them a shout" as the guard expressed it!) & affected leave-takings. At Southampton they took ages looking at all the tickets & then the train steamed right on in to the Docks. Here Douglas & Madge, & the Co Mother were waiting to see us off. It was about 1/2 an hour before we really got started, band playing, handkerchiefs waving etc:. Our cabin is perfectly minute but anyhow we have it to ourselves. Unfortunately there are a lot of children on board & one tiny baby & the noise they all make is fearsome. The times for meals are weird in the extreme - Breakfast 8-9. Lunch 12-1. Coffee 3 - Dinner 6-7 & Coffee again at 9. We had lunch almost immediately we started, rather curious German food. There are a lot of people on board, mostly English but a good many Germans too & as of course the stewards & sailors are all German so an incomprehensible jabber goes on all around - We had unpacked & were having a bit of a snooze on our bunks when suddenly there was a tremendous commotion on board & the boat stopped. We dashed up on deck & were told there was a man over board. They threw him a buoy to which he clung & then took a perfect age to lower a boat. However at last he was rescued & we continued on our way. We have since learned that the man is Dutch, was once a ship's doctor & has gone wrong in the head poor thing. He apparently threw himself overboard on purpose tho' when in the water he swam for his life. They are now keeping him in the hospital where he still has suicidal designs - I believe he will be put off at Genoa - This all happened at about 1/2 past 5 so all the excitement was over by dinner time at 6. I had some soup, refused the fish & then for some insane reason had to fly from the room! I felt perfectly alright lying down so ventured to return to dinner but had to beat another hasty retreat. There was no reason to be sea-sick as it wasn't the least rough & I'm afraid I'm just a rotten bad sailor. About 10 o'clock we ran into a fog & had to stay there for about 2 hours hooting madly so that was the 2nd excitement in the first day -

Oct. 14th Wednesday - Had an excellent night's rest tho' the children next door & the swabbing of decks woke us very early - I didn't feel at all like breakfast so C. went to his alone - in the most robust health! - I got up, with difficulty, soon after & spent the whole day lying full length on a deck chair feeling pretty miserable & counting the days to Columbo! C. was most attentive & made me very comfortable & with reading "Life & Sport in China" & dozing at intervals the day passed in the most wonderful way - We stayed up on deck till quite late - It was rather nice in the pitch dark & seeing the lights of other boats - There is a band on deck composed of the stewards - rather painful! They play in the afternoons & evenings which I s^d. think was rather hard work poor things after waiting - There are a lot of German Naval Officers on board & one comic little spruce soldier, who strut about in their uniforms - We had a whole heap of sea-gulls following us the first day & about 5 the second. Up to midday today 288 mls.

October 15th. Thursday - Another splendid night! Yesterday afternoon & last night spent going thro' the Bay of Biscay! Mercifully it was quite smooth or I don't know what w^d. have happened to me! I was quite miserable tho' as it was. I had breakfast in bed again & got up on deck to see the coast of Portugal away in the distance. I am miles better & beginning to enjoy life once more tho' I haven't quite the courage to go down to meals yet! C. is as strong as a horse & goes & samples the German food whenever the bell rings! There is a horse on board - Such a nice person, tho' I must admit I have not spoken to him since Southampton. He lives in a box lashed on to the lower deck & as this is reached by a flight of steps I think I won't go & see him just yet! Also C. tells me that being German he can't converse properly, neither does he care for apples! As I write the band is discoursing sweet music & 2 German men gravely waltzing round & round on the deck! They all look at such a very loose end poor things & never seem to do anything but loaf & talk, they don't ever sit & read. I am not the only person on board that disgraced myself yesterday I am glad to say! I do trust this is the end of it as now I am as right as rain - Its a glorious day & with big coats on we are sitting up on deck in perfect comfort. The band played at about ½ past 8 last night & after they had played some time - winding up with "Mumbling Mose" - somebody played "The Washington Post" with great brilliance on a perfect tin-kettle of a piano; this didn't end the concert for somebody else produced a gramophone to the bray of which I finally went to sleep - Did 322 miles up to midday today -

October 16th. Friday - Feeling ever so much better today & even ventured on a bath! Not a very nice proceeding in salt water as one comes out all sticky & horrid however its better than nothing - Some people left a tin biscuit box lying about on the deck & what was my surprise to see it came from "Robert Oughton Dumfries & Carlisle"! I must certainly try & get into conversation with them & find out who they are. Their name is Singer & the man is Captain but that conveys nothing to me tho' I feel I know the woman's face & C. says she was staring at me! We have been steaming along quite close to the coast of Portugal & with C.'s glasses can see the country quite plainly - The coast consists of great high cliffs, sort of grey in colour with here & there a strata of red - sandstone I s^d. think - The country is very bleak & bare & flat with no trees - There are any amount of villages built on slopes & little cottages dotted about all over the place, all pure white - most dazzling in the sun - It doesn't look a very interesting country - We passed Cape St. Vincent at 4-10 - There is a great big light-house there which we c^d. see beautifully - We pass any amount of ships coming & going but so far nothing very big - We got into a shoal of porpoises this afternoon! Huge great things jumping about, splashing & playing in the most engaging manner! We went & spoke to the horse, such a nice person who I am sure thoroughly understood & appreciated our attentions in spite of him being a German! He is going to Columbo & I am afraid will be very bored before the end of the voyage as he never gets out of his box where he stands with his head stuck out of the window, most friendly to all passers by - We bought books in London about China & Japan - Large & fat ones so we are well provided with literature - C. has just gone off to the Baggage Room to get suitable clothes for Gibraltar - They allow one so very little in ones cabin - & anyhow there's no room for more! - but let one go every evening to get anything out - Went to dinner tonight! Most successful, tho' the German food is comic in the extreme - One course called "Farced Roast" & proved to be German Sausage in slices cooked with some kind of brown looking sauce & eaten with stewed prunes & salad - I did <u>not</u> "partake" tho' C. did - without fatal results - marvelous to relate.

(*Insert in pencil:* I don't think the horse really appreciates us at all as I have since tried him with sugar - with no effect - He beamed at me when I addressed him in German! Ya Ya! CS.)

<u>October 17th Saturday</u> - Were woken this morning by the bell clanging wildly at ½ past 5 & got up at once. Had breakfast (my first in the saloon!) & hurried up on deck - We were approaching Gibraltar & it was perfectly lovely - On the right Africa with the sun just rising, on the left Spain, a wild barren looking country with hills towering up in the background & in front the Rock standing out a sort of glorious purple against a grey sky joined to Spain by what is called the "Neutral Ground" a very low strip of land with trees & houses on it where to get into Spain you have to pass thro' a great gate-way - I was <u>much</u> impressed with my first view of Gibraltar - A good many of the passengers landed here, some for good & others, like ourselves to see the place - The Göben stayed a good way out so a small tug came to take us off - Captain Edmeades was on the quay waiting for us with a small pony cart & a ripping little black Barb pony - We have none of us ever met but I felt sure it was him as it was one of the tallest men I've ever seen & we knew that he was next door to a giant! He drove us thro' the town & up the most fearsome hills to their little house which is right at the end of the rock - The streets are very narrow & very full & as the people never dream of getting out of the way unless you shout at them - & even then they don't take much notice - driving is rather perilous work! The cabs are curious things, rather like a 4-wheeled pony-carriage with a canopy & curtains, drawn by one or 2 ponies - more or less weedy - & the rest of the traffic consists of mule carts, & mokes with panniers & a great heavy man - as a rule - on their backs. Of course there are a great many British Khaki clad Tommies - We passed the Governor's House - still known as The Convent - it once was one - the public gardens, ever so many barracks, the hospital etc: till at last after about 20 mins: drive we got to the

Edmeades' house, a tiny little bungalow with 4 rooms & a kitchen in it! She seemed delighted to see us & gave us breakfast & took us over the house - it didn't take long! - We then went for a short walk as we had to be back at the tug by 10.30. It was a perfectly glorious morning & the views of Spain & Africa from the rock were quite lovely - Spain looked pretty wild & bare on the opposite side of the harbour with the town of Algeciras, on the coast, gleaming white in the sun & the "Queen of Spain's Chair", a hill, rising up behind it & behind that again ranges of distant blue mountains. Winnie Edmeades drove us back to the Quay <u>down</u> the hill! She & I sat in front - C & the groom behind - Going up so much as a slope, they very nearly broke the shafts they were such a weight but of course coming down it was better to have the weight at the back especially as the roads were as slippery as glass & as to the streets - of asphalt! - the pony $c^{d.}$ hardly stand! Again the people $\underline{w^{d.}}$ not get out of the way but we just managed not to run over them - more good luck than good guidance! The pony was a ripper & the best trotter up a hill I've ever met! There are some very fine old gate-ways leading to the different quarters of the town generally with the road turning at right angles to them - A veritable death-trap to any "exceeding the limit" - The flower season I am sorry to say was over & the rest of the vegetation parched brown as they have not had rain for ages & are praying for it, but all the same there were masses of a most glorious deep blue convolvulus & another lovely pale blue creeper called Plumbago also heaps of enormous white lilies $c^{d.}$ be seen over the wall of the Admiral's garden as we drove past - The market thro' which we drove was most interesting, there were great flocks of turkeys & poor little dead brown kids - not much bigger than hares - hanging in rows - When we got back to the tug we found it besieged by scores of natives selling fruit & beautiful work & all sorts of things to the passengers - We got on board the Göben & sailed again a little before 12 after a <u>most</u> pleasant 3 hours on shore - It was so nice knowing people there & therefore seeing the place to much more advantage than if we'd been on our own - I only wish we had had far longer to see all over the rock which they do allow English people to do under the very strictest supervision & enquiries - Sentries posted every few hundred yards all the way up - The "Galleries" excavated in the rock (the oldest of them by the Moors) must be most interesting but of course we had no time to see them tho' we $c^{d.}$ see the holes in the rock which serve as windows - In case of war it is there that the unfortunate women & children $w^{d.}$ be stowed! We steamed out of the harbour & came round the outside of the rock which is even more bare & desolate looking than the other side as there aren't even any houses there, only forts & a light-house & a summer cottage for the governor - On this side there is a sort of toboggan of sand from the very top of the rock right down to the sea & at the very foot of it a forlorn looking little village with just a very few trees - to make life bearable to the inhabitants, I $s^{d.}$ think - We left Gibraltar with a great night-cap of cloud over it, rather a pity as I s^{d}. like to have seen what it looked like from the Mediterranean. This evening C. was asked by one of the passengers if he w$^{d.}$ be on the Committee which they were forming to provide entertainment on the voyage! He said he w$^{d.}$ but carefully avoided being present at the meeting! The result is there is a long programme of concerts & dances stuck up on the stairs, something for every day nearly to Columbo - We do not intend to join in unless we can help it - We went to bed early having been up at such an unearthly hour but they started singing next door in the saloon so sleep was impossible - The poor dears can't sing nor the accompanist play so the result was painful in the extreme - We have made friends with such a nice English lady who is on her way to Hong Kong - She knows all the Jardine-Matheson lot & has been giving us much useful information about the climate etc: of China & Japan -

Damfer "Göben"

18. 10. 18

Well, my child, here is another installment of "the diary" - We will be at Algiers soon when I am simply longing for your letter & hope to have a real good one - I do hope you are enjoying yourself in Gay Paree at this moment, as much as I am enjoying myself in the blue blue Mediterranean with the still bluer hills of Africa to the south - A perfectly glorious day & the ship gliding along without the slightest motion, but all this is to go in today's diary, not yesterday's which is the one I am sending you. My dear, Gibraltar was fascinating. I shall never forget it unless I see so much more that I get confused! Algiers this afternoon is most exciting. Our Hong Kong lady friend is coming with us on the sort of "trip" which has been organised to go & see it - She is the only person with any pretentions to being a real person. The rest are hopeless especially the Germans but I don't expect we'd care for these much even in the 1$^{st.}$ class - The worst of it is the 2$^{nd.}$ class deck accommodation is so small & when everybody is spread out on a deck chair there is hardly room to move! They are all very comic to watch but the figures of the German women are something too awful! Dearie I am enjoying myself so enormously. Life is just teeming with interest. Let me know soon if you like my letters & diary & if I tell you the right kind of things. I'm afraid there must be a certain amount of description for my own future benefit so skip it if it bores you - My powers of composition are I find rocky in the extreme - haever - If you c$^{d.}$ see the little German officers! (Naval ones going out to China). Always in their uniform, spick & span little coves mostly with fierce moustaches & little imperials. It was too rediculous, as soon as we got to the Edmeades house & Winnie came out to welcome us, we all began to giggle & howl with laughter. I thought Winnie w$^{d.}$ have had hysterics & C. laughed till he was scarlet in the face & tears running down his cheeks! I dont know what it was but the whole situation seemed so comic! We went to church in the 1$^{st.}$ class saloon this morning. A curious experience & might have been impressive if the clergyman hadn't read at such a pace, sort of treading on the heels of the responses & see-

ing how much he c[d] get in in one breath - don't you know? Pon me word the German language is the ugliest & most utter gibberish that ever was - full of "aber" & "an" & "ich's" by the score - It irritates me so & yet the poor things cant help, it seems incredible that they really understand each other. I am sending you one of the breakfast menus which I think will amuse - There are pictures to all the Menus but as they are p.c's we cut them off & send them to people - The food is not good. I must send you a lunch & dinner menu at some future date - They eat stewed fruit with meat & have all kinds of curious looking filth that nothing w[d] induce me to eat! C. is much more courageous. Of course they do have quite good plain food too & now that I am perfectly well I don't mind a bit! Bien des choses ma petite. I am so looking forward to your letter.

Toujours à toi D

<u>October 18th Sunday</u> - Another perfectly glorious day - The Mediterranean as calm as a duck pond & as blue as blue - The coast of Africa looks lovely to the south, great high ranges of blue hills - We c[d] see Algiers from a long way off & at last got into the harbour, having waited outside for a pilot, amongst porpoises & little fishing boats at about 5 o'clock. The N.D.L. Company had organised a tour thro' the town for 7/6 a head which we joined going ashore as soon as the boat stopped in a N.D.L. tender - Algiers being French property is full of French people & one hears the French language on all sides - The harbour looked lovely as we went off in the tender - the sun just setting & a whole lot of fishing boats in besides many cargo boats of various nationalities & sizes being loaded by the natives accompanied by the wierdest shouts & noises - As we left the Göben a big Glasgow boat steamed out of the harbour. The first time we have seen a boat flying the British flag - except of course on the men of war in the harbour at Gibraltar - As soon as we got on shore the whole party were told to get into the string of cabs which were waiting ready. We had our Hong Kong lady friend with us so had a cab to ourselves - They are just ordinary landau sort of things drawn by 2 very weedy little arabs with French speaking drivers. Algiers is a most prosperous town & the streets thro' which we drove reminded me forcibly of Brussels - They are most up to-date with tramways & motors by the score all jumbled up with curious Arab carts & wagons drawn by sometimes as many as 6 mules with a Moor driving them cracking a great long whip. Other means of locomotion are some of the smallest donkeys I've ever seen, with panniers, rattly busses drawn by little Arab horses that look far too small & light for the work poor dears. It was quite dark when we got to the Botanical Gardens - which was our destination, but nevertheless we were requested to "décendez" so out we got & were conducted down great alleys of trees in the pitch dark! It was too ridiculous for words & we got the giggles! at the same time regretting that we c[d] see nothing - It was impossible to do any more sight-seeing in the dark so the party broke up - We

conducted Mrs. "Hong Kong" back to the quay & then went ourselves to the Hotel de la Régence on one of the principle "Places" where we had the most excellent dinner, much appreciated after the rather nasty German messes we got on board. Unfortunately, being Sunday, they were giving a popular "blood & thunder" drama at the Opera House as we wanted to go to the Opera but instead we went to the Casino - a Music Hall where some people that C. had once seen in London were performing. Some of the turns were quite good & of course all in French & very French at that! It was the most curious mixed audience with a very noisy gallery composed of Arabs of every caste, soldiers frenchmen & a' - We learnt in the Hotel that the Göben was not going to sail till tomorrow at midday as they were going to spend the night coaling so it was not necessary to go on board till quite late - The town by night was really very like Earl's Court - tho' it sounds very prosaic to say so! The Arabs were most fascinating with their brown faces & legs, dirty white clothes & things wound round their heads! We got back to the ship in a little boat rowed by a native standing up in the middle of the boat. It was most poetical with the stars shining & the 100's of lights reflected in the harbour! They were busy coaling when we got on board & everything inches thick in coal dust - Very hot at night as on account of the coal all the port holes had to be kept shut -

October 19th. Monday. Got up at about 7 for a hurried breakfast at half past to go on shore again & get the rest of our 7/6d. worth! - Mrs. "Hong Kong" did not come today so in our cab - drawn by 2 little greys - we had the 2nd. officer of the ship & a most voluable little German with a Kodak & a stick which he kept dropping out of the cab! We went to the Botanical Gardens again, Le Jardin d'Essai as it is called from the fact that it was started first of all by the french when they took possession in 1830 as an experiment to see which trees & flowers grew the best there. The trees are lovely & grown in long avenues - The gum trees are the biggest & very fine trees, then there are 2 different kind of palm trees, tall date palms & stumpy thick ones, banana trees - with bananas growing on them! another sort of banana tree or dragon tree, cocoa trees, orange trees & a few specimens of coffee trees - Unfortunately there were not many flowers out but the rose avenue must be lovely as they have them growing all in & out of the palms - There was one corner full of the homely dahlia & the most gorgeous bower of Plumbago & some other kind of blue creeper - It was very nice going there again in the daytime & the fact of going about in a troup with all these people didn't affect us much! We got into our cabs again & went for quite a long drive into the country getting higher & higher up the hill (Algiers is built on a hill) with the view getting more & more lovely till at last we stopped at an Inn place (where the Germans of course had beer!) & looked over the whole of the town & harbour - perfectly lovely - We cd. see the Jardin d'Essai & all the other places we had passed lying below us, the most interesting being a large open sandy place used as a cavalry parade ground, riding school & 4 times a year as a race course! When we passed it earlier in the day there were a lot of cavalry recruits at riding school. They looked so nice, most of them on white or grey horses - I noticed one having a horrid time, as his horse showed every sign of bolting & he had no stirrups & was not at all a "skillful" rider! Algiers is growing hard & the amount of houses in course of con struction is enormous. They first have to make a sort of terrace on the side of the hill carrying away the rubbish on the backs of mules. They were all working hard & seemed a most industrious people - Having "done" the modern part of the town, the country round about (where, by the way, I saw my first vine-yard!) & the suburbs - villas standing in their own lovely little gardens - about all which I c$^{d.}$ write pages more, but won't! - we were taken to the Arab Town which was the most interesting of all - We had to leave the cabs as they don't have any wheeled traffic there at all, considering that the streets are not more than 3 or 4 yards wide, very steep, with cobbles & sometimes steps & a gutter running down the middle. They were crowded, with Arabs of all sorts & every kind of costume going up & down & scores of children of all ages - They seem to do all their buying & selling in the streets & even sleep there - I never was in such a queer place in my life - It is quite beyond my powers of description but I shan't forget it in a hurry - nor the smell! We hadn't time to stay very long but as the Captain was of the party we stuck to him & knew we w$^{d.}$ be quite safe - no fear of being left behind! Before going on board again they took us to a Mosque, a very old one built before the coming of the French - It was a very curious place thickly carpeted, we were only allowed to go in on matting which was laid down for us - They don't have an altar or any special place of worship, it is just an empty hall built in arches with pillars - white both inside & out with thick red carpets & paths of matting leading to the different parts. Men were sitting about under the pillars quite motionless & the guide told us they were in the middle of some festival which lasts a month during which time they only eat early in the morning & at night, during the day they just sit in the mosque - "pour passer le temps"! Some of them were praying, bowing low with their foreheads on the ground. After this it was time to leave so back we went to the Göben - Algiers is a fascinating place tho' I don't think I'd like to live there always. The nicest things in it, to my mind are the pussies! Perfect rippers, fat & sleek & evidently very well taken care of - One in particular somewhat took my fancy - It was an orange one & had little pink ribbons tied in bows in its ears - slits apparently being made for the purpose! It was the most innocent sight as it sat there with a smile on its smug face! We left Algiers a little before 12 o'clock & after lunch had a good long sleep till "Kaffee" at 3, we hadn't had much sleep the night before what with getting on board so late, the weird shouts of the Arabs as they were coaling & then getting up so early this morning not to mention the extra noise which they made while swabbing the decks after coaling - this evening before going to bed we stood for some time right at the stern watching the sheet lightning which came in such huge & brilliant flashes that it lighted up the sea & sky for miles around & produced one of the most beautiful effects I've ever seen. There was also a lot of phosphorus in the water which had the most curious effect - Just in the wake of the ship there were great patches of it perhaps a foot across which looked exactly as if there was a brilliant electric light turned on just underneath while in the dark part of the water it appeared more like stars & what with the few stars, overhead - for it was a cloudy night - & the flashes of blue lightning at intervals the whole thing was most impressive -

October 20th Tuesday - A very cloudy morning with occasional heavy rain showers but the sea still as calm as can be - mercifully! There are quite a lot of little birds on board today, they must be migrating & are taking a rest on the Göben by the way - There is a robin amongst them - such a ripper, a sort of wag-tail, some sparrows & several of another species that we don't know but probably insect eating birds as they won't look at the bread which we all sprinkle for them on the deck by the loaf! I forgot to say that yesterday evening they had tug of war practice in anticipation of the sports which take place soon! It is to be an International one, English, Germans & French. C. has been chosen for one of the English team which is composed of the 4 largest men on the boat - a hefty lot who pulled 6 of the smaller men easily! The other passengers are all getting very friendly & gay amongst themselves, play games, dance & sing & make a hideous noise - One man - a Mr. Wetheral something to do with the post office in some town in India - is the ringleader!

Between Algiers & Genoa

20. 10. 08

Ma petite. A terrible disappointment yesterday in Algiers as we got no letters - Goodness knows why not unless perhaps because there was a Sunday but all the same if you posted when you were told to there ought to have been ample time & we can't understand it as we got nothing & other people did! Dear, dear the idiosyncracies of the post even follow one to the ends of the earth! I hope you'll get mine alright - It makes it so dificult to write - as we have so often before remarked - until one has heard from the other chap so that I am trusting in Providence to get a letter tomorrow - We arrive at Genoa at dawn not leaving again till 11 o'clock the following day so we shall have heaps of time to see all that there is to see - Algiers yesterday was just ripping - It reminded me so of Brussels - the french part & the Arab part of course was something totally different to anything I've ever seen - Its fearfully difficult to describe in writing, I've spent the whole morning trying to do so in the diary but tho' it may to some extent describe the look of the place & people it can't de-

scribe my feelings of it all - so teeming with interest & the strangeness of it all sort of eating into one - Dear me but travelling is interesting & what my brain will be like before we get home goodness knows! I hope it won't be too jumbly - When I'm writing about it I feel it is so difficult to keep coherent, all the impressions I have of the places seems to pour out without any relation to each other - but perhaps it doesn't give you this impression - I hope not anyway Its beastly not knowing where you are or what you're doing but presumably you're at Rosehill Cottage so I will send this there anyway & you must curse the posts & not me if you never went there for I have addressed all my letters there so far - C. is a very nice person to do things with. He is so nice & keen to do everything & see everything & is as pleased with everything as I am & such a nice competent sort of person, reliable in every way! The only tiresome part of the whole show are our fellow 2nd. class passengers - They really are appalling especially the Germans - The Post Office man who bosses them all is one of those aggresively agreable cheerful sort of people full of his own importance & always urging them all to "come on" - Goodness knows who they all are. Of course being "à deux" we needn't pay any attention & they probably think us very stand offish unless they see - which they probably do - that we are rather different to them. Of course we talk if ever there is occasion to do so & C. pulled in the tug of war when he was asked but I will not run in a potatoe race or hop, in the sports whatever they say! I wonder when you are going to Houghton & what sort of a life you are leading at present. Possibly you are still in Paris - so little do I know of your movements - Did you ever hear of such luck as we are having in the way of calm seas? The ship goes along without the smallest motion, except just the slightest sort of shuddering caused by the screw which we wd.n't feel at all if we were 1st. class - Of course it wd. be nicer there I've no doubt but what does it matter. DayNin were never fussers on those sort of matters & it makes a difference of £30 on each ticket so of course its better when one is travelling for pleasure & with the desire to see & do everything. It leaves all the more money to do things when on shore & of course the advantage of this line is seeing all these dozens of interesting places en route. I can now say I've been to Spain & Africa! Well dearie surely to goodness I'll get a letter tomorrow. Your 2nd. The 1st. will be forwarded when it reaches Algiers so that I will get it at Port Said where we will be exactly a week today. You don't know how I long to hear that you are getting along alright. I have a sort of feeling that you are quite happy at present or else some sort of telepathy wd. tell me otherwise & I sd. not be able to enjoy myself as much as I am for I am my child. Far better than I ever thought one cd. I felt sure that there were bound to be disagreeables of sorts but not one have I experienced & in spite of the tiny cabin we never dream of getting annoyed with each other & dearie, I know you love to hear it, I am as happy as I can possibly be & tomorrow shall know how the world goes with you. Bless you my own Twister yrs forever & a day.

D

Best love from the T.B.

S.S. Goben

22.10.08

My child, your letter to hand yesterday - A perfect ripper! I was so glad to get it. I do hope my diary will be one half as interesting for you. I must say I wish I c^d. write it to you alone but it is the best plan don't you think to do it so that anybody may read it? So many people are interested in me & want to know news & I c^dn't. possible write to them all separate tho' it does make it necessary (occasionally) to be less "intime" perhaps than I might be - I didn't get your letter in the morning when the majority of the letters came on board. People crowded round the chief steward in the saloon, myself the most excited of the lot! C. got one from his mother, but nothing for me. I was so disappointed I nearly cried. However after being on shore all day we came back to the boat in the evening & there it was!! I was pleased! In the morning I'd been in that rediculous mood (born of despair!) when one simply curses the other chap & says furiously that you'll "be blowed if you ever write to her again if she won't write to you" etc: etc: It is so childish but one does it for all that! I am not sending you the diary today as I shall keep it for Port Said - You will have got a good bit the day before yesterday (when you get this I mean) - There's hardly time to write up Genoa properly as we arrive at Naples tomorrow - I didn't think Genoa as nice as Algiers - Of course it is much more common & I felt as tho' I'd seen it all before, thanks to the millions of Italian snap-shots people take & show one by the book-load! but still it was very nice & I thoroughly enjoyed it. - as I do everything! (I wish I c^d. explain it as well as you did Paris - It was splendid my dear & I feel as tho' I'd been there. Indeed we will go there some day together). We have taken on heaps of new passengers at Genoa - 2 seem quite nice & are sitting beside us at this moment. I expect we shall soon get "into" conversation with them. Their name is Shaw - We went to the Opera last night "Thais" by Massenet. It was lovely. Beautiful music & excellent singing. I did enjoy it & so did C. We got a book of the words in Italian (all they had) & managed to follow in the most talented way & make out the story - I must say I do like to know what its all about especially with light music. The soprano was splendid - Carmen Melis by name - a good actress with excellent actions. It is the most tragic story & has some lovely airs - I'd give anything to see it again. I wonder what you saw in Paris. Poor Eleanor Chance - I am sorry for her. I really do think it hard on a girl after she has "kept house" for her father for some years for him to go & marry again but lets hope she doesn't mind. One of the most lively of the passengers is a lady's maid! Her lady is in the 1st. class & she comes over here & carries on with the young men & "queens" it over them all in fine style! It really is too amusing - Of course some people I suspect w^d. think it awful but it isn't a bit, tho' you needn't exactly rub it in to the likes of Mum & Father or At Alice! - you know.

23.10.08. It was quite rough last night! At least there was just a motion but I kept quite well I'm thankful to say tho' there were several empty spaces at dinner & 2 or 3 deemed it wiser to "leave the room Car, leave the room" quietly but swiftly. If it had got worse I've not the smallest doubt but what I w^d. have followed them. I have no confidence in myself whatever! - Our insides from child-hood were always of a bilious nature weren't they? When its calm I think "a life on the Ocean wave" is delightful especially in a ship like this where we stop & get ashore so often - I feel as tho' I'd made a mull of the Genoa pictures - I don't know that there are any really good ones there but we certainly didn't find them, tho' as we were walking back to the ship, I saw post-cards of what looked like some very nice Van Dycks in a gallery we didn't go to having been rather choked off by the one gallery we did go to - Never mind, perhaps they weren't very good after all - Its difficult in a town like that with a limited time at ones disposal to do & see everything & one almost invariably chooses out the wrong things - ha-ever - it was an extremely pleasant day - Its really very nice having meals in these nice clean hotels after this ship which tho' quite good is of course 2nd. class & we have the thickest of tumblers & cheap Servant's hall crockery etc: What does it matter - we dont care but it is rather nice to return to civilised life! I wonder what you're doing at Rosehill Cottage - From Port Said I suppose I'd better write to Comlongon as I dont expect you'll stay there very long - I do hope that there'll be no muddle with your letters at Port Said - Post them there before the given date sooner than let it occur again. Ha! Ha! Mr. Wetheral is tickling "Aunt Eva"! She is aunt to "Jimmy" who is the most awful little boy of about 2 years old you ever saw. He gurns without ceasing & nearly drives us mad in the mornings as their cabin is just opposite ours & we can hear all that goes on. Jimmy has a baby brother who is also extremely fractious at times. I am so sorry for the poor Mother & "At Eva" is so very little assistance & prefers to play about on deck (I don't blame her!)

I do hope that you'll go to Spookie soon & talk Paris - She is as mad on it as you appear to be. I must go there some day & with you too & we will revel in the Louvre. It must have been a real lark doing it all in such fine style - Do you suppose the Broadies always travel in that kind of way? I do hope you have got used a little bit to life as it now is - It really is maddening that I can't even get letters till ages after they're written - Must cease as the letters have to be in the box by 12 & its about that now. C. wishes to know how many hats you got for 10/- - I suppose with his frugal mind he hopes that you got 10!

October 21st. Wednesday - Arrived at Genoa about 8 o'clock this morning. The town doesn't look up to much from the docks & the harbour is small & not nearly so pretty as Algiers . Behind the town there are bare-looking hills with forts on them - The sorting of the letters was the first excitement & everybody crowded round the chief steward in the saloon in hopeful anticipation. We were only rewarded with 1 letter & a receipted bill! It was really cold & felt quite frosty in the morning with the most infuriating wind, which met us at all corners & filled our eyes with dust. We went on shore at once & scorning the assistance of guides - who offered us their services at almost every step - found our way to Cooks where we got a map of the town & for the rest of the day got about entirely by its aid! We spent most of the morning shopping & found that most of the shop-keepers c[d.] speak French while some of them were quite pleased to air their English, so we got on famously. The streets are very narrow & crowded with a great many "Plazzas": - in one there was a market going on & in another all the trams of the town seemed to be collected - There are some very fine buildings in the town - You look thro' a great arch-way to a sort of hall or court-yard with a magnificent staircase, all the decorations being most ornate. They used to be palaces of the nobility but they now seem to be used as Government buildings & such like - Some of them are picture galleries so we chose "Palazzo Rosso" but it was rather dissapointing. There were a good many pictures some Van Dykes, Veronese, Teniers etc: amongst the number but they weren't up to so much so we didn't go to any more! We had lunch & went & saw two churches - The town swarms with them & these were 2 very finest specimens - The first - the Church of the Annunciation - was most gorgeous, very highly decorated with a painted ceiling & gold in every direction - The other was the cathedral of S. Lorenzo & much finer, not so much decorated & better colour. A little coffin with the supposed remains of St. John the Baptist is there & some very old music of the 14th. century in the choir behind the altar - This choir is made of most beautiful inlaid walnut & we were pointed out - & I sat in! - the seat where Paganinni used to sit & play! The best thing in the church were the lamps. Lovely things, hanging from the ceiling & made of what looked like silver - By this time we felt we had done eno' trailing about the streets interesting tho' it was finding our way about, with frequent stoppages to study the map! so we went in a sort of electric railway to the top of the hill behind the town. It was fearfully windy up there but lovely air - All the hills round have forts on them which overlook the town & harbour. Unfortunately it was hazy so we didn't have a very good view tho' it must be lovely from up there on a clear day - It was quite nice to get a walk, tho' the road was perfectly disgraceful & made a hole in the sole of my shoe! We had dinner in the swagger hotel of the place & went to the Opera - "Thais" by Massenet - It was splendid, such nice music & the soprano - Carmen Melis - was really excellent. It is a big Opera house with no carpet or curtains of any kind so that it is excellent for sound - We got back to the Ship about 11.30 after a splendid day's "pleasuring"! We feel as tho' we had known Genoa all our lives & c[d.] find our way about anywhere. Nothing like struggling with a map to teach one! Tonights music was very unlike last nights when they had a concert in the saloon!! We attended the first part & it was distinctly painful - I'm afraid there is not much talent on board except in one of the sailors who plays the piano & the violin really awfully well - He is such a charming looking man too, looks exactly as if he had stepped out of a Gilbert & Sullivan opera when he is "dressed"!

October 22$^{nd.}$ Thursday - Didn't sail till 12 o'clock so had time to go on shore again but after we'd been to Cooks & bought a pipe cover & various other things there was only time to go & see the Jardin Publiques which were the greatest fraud! Just an open space as bare as your hand with a few scrubby little trees & bushes & not even the ghost of a flower - With dust fairly swirling round, it was not a beautiful spot so we left at once - in a tram! - Genoa is a very busy town & the streets are crowded, with people hurrying in every direction, - trams, busses & huge carts, with the biggest wheels I've ever seen, drawn by 3 or 4 horses or mules tandem - The cab-horses have pheasant's tail feathers on their bridles sticking straight up - a curious form of decoration! We took on a lot of fresh passengers here & what with fresh stores & piles of clean linen the deck was a sight to behold however they managed to get it all cleared up & we started punctually by 12 o'clock. It was still blowing & later on in the evening the waves were coming right over the fore deck! Mercifully it wasn't eno' to make much difference to the Göben tho' there were 3 or 4 empty places at dinner! I am proud to say it made "n' odds" to me! We passed a lot of little islands to our right, they looked most desolate - awful places to live. After dinner we passed what must have been Elba - It appeared to have a volcano in irruption on it but it was really only some sort of a blasting place - It looked very fine tho' all the same - They had what they called a "little meeting" in the saloon this evening in honour of the German Empress' birthday - They made a most deafening din singing & shouting which we got the full benefit of, our cabin being next door -

October 23rd Friday - Spent the whole morning writing & arrived at Naples about 1 o'clock - It is a lovely bay surrounded by hills with Vesuvius towering up behind the town. We were determined to see Pompeii so, as our time before it got dark was very limited we got on shore as soon as the boat stopped & threaded our way with some difficulty thro' the crowds of guides who persistently offered us their services & w[dnt.] be snubbed! A M[r.] & M[rs.] Shaw who joined at Genoa & whose acquaintance we have made joined us. (He is some sort of engineer & they live up at Tientsin & seem quite nice). We drove to the Circum Versuviana station in cabs. They are the most comic tiny little victorias drawn by ponies who have no bits in their mouths, only curbs & some sort of wierd arrangement on the noseband which I suppose answers the same purpose all right, anyhow we got to the station safely tho' it was the maddest drive I've ever had. The pony fairly scuttles along with the driver cracking his whip & shouting - The streets are absolutely dreadful with huge holes in them eno' to make a horse break its leg, let alone tear the wheels off the carriages! The smell & filth in the smaller streets was something awful - They may be very picturesque & all that but that cannot make (up) for the other horrors & it was a real relief to get out of them! The train was very dirty & smelly too but the country we passed thro ' most interesting - The first part like a large sort of market garden with patches of all kinds of vegetables & flat-roofed good-looking houses standing amongst them at intervals with the family washing adorning the country for miles, on strings amongst the vegetables! (N.B. Italian women must spend their whole lives washing, one sees it on lines across the streets, round the windows, in the gardens, <u>everywhere</u> & at any time!) Then we went thro' vineyards & woods having glorious views of the sea on the right & Vesuvius on the left until at last after an hour and a half we arrived at Pompeii - I feel absolutely incompetent to describe it - It is perfectly wonderful. We had a very nice English-speaking guide who showed us all it was possible to see in the 2 hours we were there - but what is 2 hours? one c$^{d.}$ spend days there & I s$^{d.}$ just <u>love</u> to some day. It was buried in 600 B.C. & was first built by the Oscans so its age is something enormous & to see it now just as it used to be then is simply extraordinary - The streets are paved with huge stones & as all the refuse etc was thrown into them there are stepping stones at intervals to let people get across clean. The houses are all built on the same plan with a courtyard out of which open the dining-rooms & pärlours, then a garden with pillars & a fountain & statues, then thru' are bedrooms, servants quarters, kitchen etc: & lastly most sumptuous bath-rooms, the baths made of marble. Hot steam baths they had in a separate little room with double walls, floor & ceiling where the steam came connected with the kitchen boiler by real lead pipes! The paintings on the walls of the houses were perfectly fascinating, especially the birds which they generally painted in a delicious loose style & the colour quite lovely - I c$^{d.}$ have stayed & studied them for hours - The theatre was extremely interesting too also the Forum & the temples & the Stock Exchange which surrounded the Public Laundry! We went to the top of one of the houses & the view of this wonderful dead city backed by the blue Appenines was <u>most</u> impressive & <u>quite</u> beyond my powers of description - They are still excavating but do it in such a feeble sort of way, about a dozen men & boys shovelling the stuff into baskets which they empty into two trucks drawn by ponies - I longed to seize a spade & help - It must be so interesting & yet they didn't appear to care 2$^{d.}$ or take the least interest - As the guide said if it had been English or American the whole thing w$^{d.}$ have been done in 10 years instead of about 200 & even now it isn't finished - Perhaps it was as well we only had 2 hours here or we s$^{d.}$ all have died of fatigue! As it was we were fairly well exhausted & very glad of the coffee which we just had time to get before we got the train back to Naples which we reached about 7 o'clock - We & the Shaws had dinner at the Hotel de Londres. Such a nice hotel & such a good clean dinner! Afterwards we went to the Opera. C. & I were awfully pleased to see, as soon as we got to Naples, that they were giving La Boheme but were greatly disappointed when it turned out to be Leoncavallo's & not Puccinni's! However Leoncavallo's version tho' totally different in story & everything else, is very nice with some delicious airs & the principals were all good so we enjoyed it very much. The chorus ladies were too dreadful for words - Never have I seen such a collection of awful old frumps! If they are specimens of Italian beauties then I don't think much of them. We had to leave before the end of the 3$^{rd.}$ act as the ship was timed to sail at mid-night (the opera didn't begin till 9.30) but we might have stayed till the end for, as a matter of fact she didn't start till about 2 o'clock in the morning - There were men singing with guitars & violins in true Italian fashion but as they clamoured loudly for money as soon as they had finished it rather took away the romance of the situation!

October 24th. Saturday - A tremendously strong wind blowing all day with occasional showers. We passed Stromboli about 11 o'clock, just a volcano stuck down in the middle of the sea. There is a town on it but how people can bear to live there goodness knows. We went thro' the Straits of Messina about 2 o'clock. There was a perfect hurricane blowing & with the driving rain & spray one cd. hardly see anything tho' before it got so very bad we saw Sicily - a most mountainous place covered with vine-yards & the town of Messina built right down to the shore ending in a narrow strip of sand with a lighthouse at the end of it - On the other side the coast of Italy looked much the same sort of country. The wind got worse & worse &the sea got up & finally I succumbed in company with most of the other passengers! C. is a perfect tower of strength. Nothing seems to affect him, which is a great mercy! If he was also bad I don't know what I sd. do. Its a pity I'm such a rotten sailor, as really, at the time it makes life not worth living!

October 25th. Sunday - A perfectly beastly day - Wind stronger than ever - I didn't get up till 12 o'clock - My only chance on these occasions is to lie perfectly still, any sort of movement causing me intense discomfort! however at last I managed to get on deck where I remained prone for the rest of the day - Nearly everybody else was in the same state. Bundles of miserable humanity spread out in chairs in every direction - a truely degrading spectacle. The wind tore on all day - not one moment's peace - The least said about this day the better I think - it was not a pleasant one!

October 26th. Monday - A real change this morning. The wind gone down & the sea quite calm - Such a relief & life has taken on quite a cheerful aspect again - Yesterday we were coming thro' the mouth of the Adriatic which was supposed to account for the vile behaviour of the elements. Spent the whole day reading & writing as really the decks are too full for walking - We visited the poor dear horse who is looking far from well. They have had to move his box as I suppose in the storm the waves were coming over him - He is now strung from the roof of the box & looks perfectly miserable - It seems too cruel for anything to keep him there all these weeks - I believe there was a carrier pigeon on deck today but we didn't see it. The wind got up again towards evening & I funked dinner! Cowardly no doubt but anything is better than a repetition of yesterday! The most glorious star-light night. We always go to bed very early but having dinner at 6 o'clock makes the evening otherwise so very long. We are generally pretty late for breakfast - which is supposed to be at 8 o'clock but it is so much nicer & cooler to have it when most of the people have gone. The ship is so full that when everybody is down in the saloon it makes a most awful crowd. The stewards are all such nice obliging men. The chief is a real friend & talks the most excellent English - Our cabin steward's is not quite so good & "Mister hive pas 7, shavin' wasser" with which he calls us every morning <u>means</u> $^1/_2$ past 7 tho' it might be 5 past! C. used to argue the point with him to find out which he meant but it didn't do any good as the man saw no difference & just repeated "hive pas"!

- S.S. Göben -

27.10.08

Chérie, we will be in to Port Said by 2 o'clock this afternoon so I must pen you a line to go "along" with the diary. Oh my dear such a foul time as we had the day before yesterday - I just <u>loathe</u> being sea-sick tho' now I can laugh over it - I wonder if I w$^{d.}$ have come if I'd known what a rotten sailor I am? I s$^{d.}$ doubt it, but am very glad I didn't know as the joys <u>quite</u> make up for the miseries tho' at the time one doesn't think so! I like the Shaws who we have made friends with. He, in looks, is rather like Paddy & has a nice voice - I don't know that they're anything extra exciting but they fairly <u>shine</u> in this company - as also does Mrs. Hong Kong (whose name by the way is Knott). Her husband was in the navy & she we like very much - Anything more wretched than she is when its rough I've never seen. She nearly dies of it poor woman & lies quite motionless, neither eating nor drinking with a newspaper placed firmly over her face! These 3 & ourselves are the only people with any pretensions. There are heaps of missionaries on board - 3 very youthful Englishmen who look as tho' they c$^{d.n't}$ possibly have any influence over anybody, let alone the Chinese, 2 Swedish women & hoards of priests - Italians I s$^{d.}$ think - The English ones have a service every morning & sing hymns in terrible raucous voices - until one feels they really ought to be shot, as if the Chinese will pay any attention to them. Your last letter from Paris was A1 & I just long to know if they missed the train! but s$^{h.n't}$ till Colombo - another fortnight nearly - I wish one c$^{d.}$ get letters everyday - or at any rate every week but that is just one of the disadvantages of travelling - I read your letter in the train going to Pompeii - My dear that is the most wonderful place in the world - Some day you <u>must</u> see it - The paintings on the walls are veritable chefs d'oeuvres, all painted de coup in a delicious sticky sort of way that makes ones mouth water & the colour quite exquisite. That is probably due to their emmence age - figurez vous! destroyed 600 B.C. so that it was probably flourishing 700 or 800 B.C. It is incredible. I do trust my brain won't cease to take in or lose all these impressions - So far everything is quite distinct but recollect we have only been away a fortnight! Bless you my child. What I long for more than anything is to know that you like my diary & don't think it very dull & discription-y. I think of you heaps & long for you to be here but Courage mon ami. Ta soeur qui t'aime, D.

Best love from the T.B. He is letting his moustache grow & twirls it up at the sides till I call him Kaiser Bill! It really makes him look rather lovely tho' I think I prefer the toothbrush! Milles des choses à la chienne. Bless its heart & face. Kiss it.

2

Suez - The Red Sea - Aden

S.S. Göben

28.10.08

My child, I must send you a line from Suez if possible, tho' we don't know yet whether it will be possible - I got your Algiers letter yesterday. Dearie, I am sorry about the diary but I really don't see how I can help it & trust you have got used to it now - You see the diary is to be a record for myself as well as for you in after life so that it makes no difference in the way I write it & I do hope that the letter to you I always send with it makes it alright. Its worrying me so frightfully to think that you perhaps dont care to have my diary under the present conditions of "showing it round" but I said from the beginning I was going to do it this way & its just a pity I didn't get your first letter sooner. But, as it is I think I must continue now I've begun. We are in the Sewage Channel! My dear, such an impressive place. Its beginning to get hot but nothing unbearable & I am still in Longtown tweed. We got up at 6 o'clock this morning to see it & anything more lovely at that hour of the morning I have never seen. We've never forgotten early mornings in Holland & this was even better - The canal is no wider than the big North Sea Canal in Holland - wh: surprised me somewhat - I thought it w$^{d.}$ be much bigger - & the colour & light of the whole place fairly made ones mouth water - Camels my dear being loaded with sand by glorious blue & white clad men with brown skins, browny green water & hazy blue sky - A sight for the gods - It was too far off to photograph but I've got it fixed firmly in my brain. Now we are in a kind of lake "The bitter lake" - Such a glorious spot - Calm blue water with a strip of golden sand all round. Indescribably beautiful. I now wish I had a painting box but after lunch am going to see if I can accomplish anything with a pencil. I bet I can't. Gib & this are the only 2 things that I have had the desire to paint so far. We are now tied up waiting for a ship to pass & as the bell is about to ring for lunch au revoir chérie - I am fearfully happy & its only occassionally that my heart is cut & sore pour toi & it won't be perhaps when I hear from you at Colombo in less than a fortnight now. I just loved your Paris letters - Loved them -

Best & bestest of love from us both

Forever & ever Amen D.

October 27$^{th.}$ Tuesday - A lovely day. The sun is getting powerful now tho' we are still quite happy in thick tweed clothes. Some of the other pasengers are now sporting white ducks & topis but it is quite unnecessary! The sea is a most glorious blue - As we passed Dannietta & were approaching Port Said the difference in colour was extraordinary - Miles out from the towns it is a dirty sort of yellow - A little girl excitedly asked her mother if we had got to the Yellow Sea! Port Said does not look very inviting from a distance, it is very flat - We got there about 2-30 - The entrance to the Canal is marked by the Statue of De Lesseps, the french engineer who made it - He stands sort of pointing up the Canal with an inviting gesture! We tied up a little way off the landing place - With shouting & wrangling & much - evident! - loosing of tempers, coal lighters came alongside & without a moment's delay began to coal - We went on shore at once & before we had got there - it only took 2 mins - they had started! A wonderful sight to see them filling their baskets, running up a plank into the ship with the basket on thier shoulders & then come running out again down another plank with the empty basket - A never-ending stream of coal black men, chanting a funny sort of little song all the time - It looked a horrid dirty job but they seemed to be so <u>keen</u> about it & quite happy - It was frightfully hot on shore so we didn't do much - there isn't much to be done at Port Said! - There seemed to be every nationality under the sun in the streets - The shops are small & poky & the men come dashing out of them to try & induce one to go in & buy which is rather a nuisance, we bought a $6^{d.}$ edition of "The Last Days of Pompeii" for 10^{d} so apparently they are expensive too! We went & had tea in a hotel in one of the principle streets & sat for some time looking out of the window watching all that went on. It was most interesting. Men go about slung with chains of beads & with scarves of all sorts & post cards & every sort of thing to sell & pester one at every step - A lot of fishing boats were in when we got back to the quay & the natives were arranging the fish most beautifully in flat round baskets & putting them on carts to sell. While we were watching them the P & O Macedonia came in & tied up just behind the Göben - Before you $c^{d.}$ say "Knife" the coalers were down upon her. There seems to be an exhaustless supply of them always waiting ready. It was now beginning to get dusk so we finished up by walking out on the break-water to the De Lesseps statue & then went on board again for dinner - By the time we got up on deck again they had finished coaling us but were still hard at work on the Macedonia by the light of great flaring torches - for it was now quite dark. It was a very fine sight to see those black bodies hurrying backwards & forwards in that weird sort of light & keeping up their chaunt all the time - A little further down the advertisement L I P T O N came & went in electric lights! A truly curious contrast - but Port Said is made up of these contrasts which is the attraction of the place to me - The worst part of it, is its dust which lies about 6 inches deep everywhere - it must be dreadful when there is a wind - We got letters here which had missed us at Algiers - We sailed at about 8-20 in the most beautiful star light but of course it was very disappointing not to be able to see the canal - It was lovely up on deck tho' until some ass spoilt the whole thing by playing selections on the gramophone! Really some people have no idea of the fitness of things. In disgust we went to bed - but not to sleep! First of all a girl sang Scotch songs in the real village concert style ("For its oh-h-h but I'm longing for my ain fouk" etc: etc:) until we nearly cried & then we had to tie up to let another ship by & that necessitated making the most dreadful noises with the capstan or something. Goodness knows what they were doing - It nearly drove us mad & seemed to go on for hours, tho' of course it didn't really. As a matter of fact we had to tie up 4 times during the night which of course delayed us very much.

October 28th Wednesday - This morning we got up at 6 o'clock & were well rewarded for our energy - I shan't forget my first sight of the desert with the sun just up. It was lovely - We had only done 34 miles in the night, owing to having to tie up so often but I was very pleased as I sd. have hated missing the canal. We sat all day on the upper deck right in the stern & drank in the beauty & strangeness & wonder of it all - The colour of it all is perfectly gorgeous especially early in the morning - The miles & miles of barren sand on each side with nothing but tiny little scrubby bushes that look more grey than green & very occasionally a few trees & rushes close to the canal where there will probably be some sort of Arab village, the houses being of the most fragile build - There were generally hens scratching about round them which was the only "homely" touch in the place! What I liked better than anything were the places where they were working at the banks of the canal, evidently widening it or something of that sort. Beautiful brown men with gorgeous blue (the best blue I've ever seen) & white garments with here & there orange & black ones ladening camels with sand & then leading them away in strings up the bank. My! but it was fine - The Arab boats or dhows are quite the best looking boats I've ever seen & we passed a good many of them being towed up to Port Said - the same way as they do in Holland - for the breeze was dead ahead for them - Every now & again there are signal stations on the canal kept by white men - They always have trees round them, palm trees, bananas etc: but I sd. think life in one of them must be very monotonous. Nothing but sand & sky & the canal month after month - After a bit the canal goes into the small Bitter Lake & then into the large Bitter Lake both of which are most carefully bouyed & then you get into the canal again till Suez - The lakes were lovely, glassy smooth fringed with a pale gold line of everlasting sand - We got to Suez as the Sun went down having taken 21 1/2 hours from Port Said - We had to tie up for 6 ships to pass during the day which of course delayed us but the longer we took the better, in my opinion & I enjoyed every minute of it! There are stakes driven into the banks all the way along to tie up to & every ship takes a little boat with Arabs in it slung to her side which is let down & the Arabs row out to the stakes with the ropes. At one place we had to wait nearly 3/4 of an hour while 3 ships went past us, a Glasgow, Italian & Swede! We only stayed 1 1/2 hours at Suez but right out so one cdn't. go ashore & then went on again about 7-20 into the Red Sea! Another glorious star light night & thank goodness no gramophone!

October 29th Thursday - In the Red Sea today & not a bit too hot yet - There is a lovely breeze which is making "white horses" all over the sea - Everybody says it is wonderful as it is generally glassy & boiling hot so we are being very lucky. They are having "sports" on board this afternoon which is causing an immence amount of excitement & much shouting & screaming. C. was woken up in the middle of a snooze to go & pull in a tug of war but otherwise we have taken no part or lot in them! Of course the tug of war ended in a row. They drew 2 Englishmen & 2 Germans for each team - C.'s one got into the final & it was then that the excite began for one side had pulled the other over altho' some said they hadn't - They were ever so long arguing & wrangling that the 2 Germans on C.'s side who I don't think knew in the least what was going on, disappeared so the final was postponed until tomorrow & a good thing too for they were all frightfully heated & the Germans drinking beer by the gallon - This didn't end the sports tho' for they went on for ages after with egg & spoon races & goodness knows what all with the most appalling energy accompanied by kitchen maid shrieks!

October 30th Friday - The heat last night was terrific & we began to feel the effects of our inside cabin - We had the fan going all night but in spite of that it felt like lying in an oven - "At Eva" (as we call one of the passengers) who appeared at breakfast with a scarlet face declared that nothing wd. induce her to endure it any longer, she cd. not & wd. not bear it! So silly, because she just must! After breakfast C. went down to the baggage room & brought up hot weather clothes which we were thankful to change into - It is grillingly hot today & the following breeze has practically gone except for occasional faint little puffs - which are better than nothing - If yesterday was exceptional then today is the rule for the Red Sea! - I must say I rather wish it was the other way about! We sat on the upper deck in the shade all day but in spite of that my face is burnt a fiery red & hurts like anything! - we have got a German species of Lanolin from the barber which ought to put it all right - It has been 96° in the shade today - This is the greatest heat I've ever experienced! The P & O Macedonia passed us today right away on the sky- line - We are evidently taking a course right down the middle of the sea for we cant see land on either side - There was a wasp on board today! Goodness knows where it came from. We often have birds paying us visits, very pretty little things but unluckily we don't know what they are.

October 31st Saturday - It was hotter than ever last night. Really the nights are worse than the days & one gets very little sleep in consequence. It is not so hot on deck today as the breeze is in front but it doesn't make much difference in the saloon & it is a real penance to go down there to meals - My face has more or less recovered itself & is not nearly so sore. It was extraordinary getting burnt like that in the shade. They had a dance this evening. How they cd. I can't think - We looked on for 2 dances & were then too hot to stay (even if we had wanted to!) -

S.S. Göben

31.10.08

Lord my child but its hot - to think of me writing to you from the Red Sea - The nights are the worst - Jamais de la vie! It feels as tho' your body will set the bed on fire such a heat does it get up & I, as you know, am not a "free sweater" which seems to make matters worse - But never mind, its an experience & I like to have it. Our cabin being an inside one makes it of course hotter but we have one of those electric whirligig fan things which we keep going all night & have the door open with only a curtain across & thus manage to keep alive - They say it will be cooler again after we've passed Aden which we get to some time tomorrow - Having no topi C. doesn't think I will be able to go ashore which will be an awful pity but its no use risking a sun-stroke & as a matter of fact I believe there is not much to see there.

Sunday. It was impossible to write more yesterday - The heat became intolerable. Today there is a lovely wind blowing which makes it perfectly delicious & such a change from the last 2 days. Services have been going on all morning which has caused me much thought. The Roman Catholics have had 2, the Germans 1 & the Scotch another to which we went. An American missionary preached such a good sermon & Miss Cook played the piano for all the world as tho' it was the harmonium in the Kirk. "My faith looks up to Thee". I thought of you & wondered whether you were at the kirk too - My dear there is something in it all & its wrong of one to persist in being indifferent to it all, but I wish there weren't so many different kinds - While we were finishing breakfast the Roman Catholics came & began to prepare their service - They had candlesticks, a crucifix & everything ready in a box & set it all out on a table like an altar, then one of the priests dressed himself exactly as if he was in a proper church & they began with the utmost solemnity & I thought well, thats all good & thorough & these preparations show a reverent spirit. But afterwards when we went to the Scotch & there they all were in their ordinary clothes with just the bare table & all praying & preaching direct from their hearts then I thought that seemed the best & simplest - so what is a poor beggar to do amongst them all except give it up? These are all missionaries so what the poor heathens must make of them all goodness knows. I am looking forward enormously to Ceylon - We are both of us getting a bit fed up with this old ship & longing for a nice clean hotel - When we do get off at Colombo - exactly a week today - we shall have been on her a month, all but 2 days! Thats a good long time you know but it has been very pleasant. If it had been a P. & O. I expect we s^d. have liked it better, the food at anyrate w^d. have been English but then of course we s^dn't. have called at all these different ports so we dont really regret it a bit. The 2nd. Class had a dance last night! How they c^d. goodness knows for the heat was something terrefic - We watched the first 2 dances & were much amused - Real servant hall style - a waltz & a 2 step! The costumes were too amusing, dress clothes with various styles of ties - One man was immaculate in tail coat white waistcoat, very high collar - but an ordinary blue tie with the ends tucked into his shirt! Some of the ladies were magnificent in low dresses *tho' most of them wore "dressy blouses"! I hope they didn't think us very stuck up not to join but really we c$^{dn't.}$ - Ones own Ladies Tea Parties are about the limit don't you think? Its horrid to think that there will be no letter at Aden, thats why I'm so looking forward to Colombo I think, but if they're not happy letters how miserable I shall be - but why conjecture thus? The children on the boat have the best time of it in the hot weather & go about in 1 garment, a curious sort of little combination arrangement buttoned up the back, girls & boys alike - It looks very cool & airy - One little cockney boy is a great favourite, Dudley is his name - We think it w$^{d.}$ be a mistake to take any notice of him in case he attached himself to us in the way children have besides he isn't a particularly attractive little boy & they're all rather grubby & inclined to be "germy" in this hot weather, poor little beggars - oh I <u>wish</u> you c$^{d.}$ see some of these people! There is every nationality under the sun! This is one of our days. "Rise" some time in about 8 o'clock, a bath is a lengthy proceeding & consists of soaping at the basin, sponging it off in the big bath in salt water & then standing by the basin throwing the fresh water over me to try & get the salt off for it is so sticky & beastly. This all takes time & by the time one is finished one is streaming with heat. We generally have the saloon all to ourselves for breakfast (wh: is what we like) & then we sit up on deck reading or writing till lunch at 12, then more reading or writing with a sleep till 3 when C. always has tea tho' I only have it sometimes. Then more reading till a little after 5 when we exercise up & down till 6 when we have dinner & then sit on deck again looking at stars & talking (we manage to fit in a good deal of this at other times too!) till between 8.30 & 9 we get so sleepy that we retire to bed. One s$^{d.}$ think time thus spent w$^{d.}$ drail, but it doesn't a bit tho' it is a cramped sort of existence & the want of exercise w$^{d.}$ soon tell on one - I <u>am</u> going ashore today. The chief steward is going to lend me his topi or if too big put a cabbage leaf in my own hat! A good job as I'd like to see & <u>do</u> <u>everything</u>. So long dearie. The T.B. sends you his best love - He writes regularly to his mother whenever we stop. Embrace the Pip an 100 fold from its twin.*

Toujours à Toi - thou whom thou knowest thine

D.

<u>November 1$^{st.}$ Sunday</u> - A lovely cool breeze this morning - It is such a relief to get up on deck after the stifling hot cabin - We got to Aden at about 3 o'clock. We had passed the island of Perica when we were in our baths so I, for one didn't see it at all tho' C. got a sight of it thro' the bath-room port hole. My first sight of land since leaving Suez was the most dreary tho' fine looking mass of black rocks & sand which towers out of the sea before you reach Aden - The only signs of life on them, to be seen thro' the glasses were about $^1/_2$ a doz camels stalking slowly across the sand - We anchored about 2 miles outside the harbour & almost before we'd stopped were beseiged by dozens of small boats filled with the most curious assortment of things to sell - They were no more curious than the men who were selling them! - The nicest had heads of fluffy light brown hair like mops, nice

bronze skins & the whitest of teeth. We were told we were only to be at Aden till 6.30 which meant that there $w^{d.}$ not be time to go up to the water tanks which are the only things worth seeing at Aden so we didn't land, but as a matter of fact there w^{d}. have been plenty of time as the Captain who has his wife & little boy on board went ashore & drove up to the tanks & wasn't back till 20 past 7. He never let on to the passengers that he was going to do this but sneaked off in the N.D.L. agents' little boat. We were <u>really</u> annoyed when 6.30 arrived & he had not come back. It really was a rotten thing for him to do, but all the same there was plenty of entertainment on board. They tried in vain for some time to keep the natives out of the ship but it was no good & in a very short time they were in possession - It was the funniest thing to see a whole lot of them swarming up the ladder, fighting & struggling to get up & being driven back with much violence by 2 burly German sailors while the chief officer, perfectly infuriated directed operations from the top! One Mohommedan in flowing white robes & a fez was knocked into the water & hung on for dear life to the side of a boat while his goods (feather boas!) floated out on the water behind him - Poor man, he looked so frightened, & everybody laughed! The deck was very soon like a bazaar! The chief things they had to sell were cigars, cigarettes, ostrich feathers, feather fans & boas, seed necklaces, fruit, sharks jaws & <u>of course</u> postcards! They seemed to do a roaring trade as they stayed there until sun down when they were turned out more or less by force & reluctantly rowed ashore - Aden itself looks the most dreary spot in the world & I'm thankful its not my lot to live there - Absolutely bare barren hills without one scrap of green of any kind - at least as far as we $c^{d.}$ see with the glasses. We didn't start till $^1/_4$ to 8, or $1^1/_2$ hours late, thanks to the Captain's wish to show his wife & boy the tanks! If he had only let us know <u>he</u> was going there of course there $w^{d.}$ have been time for us to go too! The most remarkable thing about natives is the noise they make. They seem to think it necessary to shout at the tops of their voices all the time - The gulls & hawks swooped in & out amongst them & added to the general excitement & restless <u>life</u> of the scene! It was rather a cloudy evening made hideous by the glee singing of Americans at one end of the deck while at the other a party of Germans deliberately tried to drown them by shouting German songs accompanied by a zither - The effect of course was dreadful so, in desperation we went to bed -

<u>November 2$^{nd.}$ Monday</u> - Much cooler so had a splendid night & today there is a lovely strong breeze - delightful after the heat. There was a very sudden & sharp shower of rain about $^1/_2$ past 9 just as we had got established on deck - It only lasted lasted 3 or 4 minutes & was considered very extraordinary for as a rule one never gets rain in these parts. One of the lady Missionaries - a Swede - enlivened things up in the evening by taking a header over the end of a deck chair, finally arriving in a sitting position at C's feet! It was the funniest thing I've ever seen - She smiled sweetly the whole time, her English is limited so she $c^{d.}$ make no ex-

planations except "I never see it" - Poor thing, I hope she didn't see us laughing - or hear us, after she'd picked herself up & moved on!

November 3rd. Tuesday - Another lovely cool day. We passed the Island of Socotra this morning. A big mountainous island which we were in sight of for some hours - This is the last land we shall see till we get to Columbo! We saw some flying fish this afternoon! They look exactly like some sort of fat little bird skimming along on the top of the water until they suddenly disapear into it - As soon as we got into the Indian Ocean there was a horrid & most unnecessary "ground swell"! I much prefer the motion of the Suez Canal (none at all!) - The poor dear horse is not at all well. I am sure they give him far too much to eat & of course he gets no exercise - He is getting so bored too - simply sick of life, but his troubles will soon be over now for he gets off at Columbo - The children on board also appear to be getting thoroughly bored & have constant rows, most amusing to watch!

November 4th. Wednesday - More ground swell this morning but thank goodness not eno' to make even Mrs. "Hong Kong" feel bad! - They had the Great International tug of war this morning! The English pulled the Dutch, & the Germans a team of 5 little missionaries & then there was great excitement when the English & Germans met in the final! The English won easily! They consisted of "Mr. Thomas", "Mr. Wagstaff", C. & "Mr. Reeves"! They were a fine burly lot, but the Germans looked just as big & strong but they didn't know how to pull & were full of beer so they were no use whatsoever - The stewards gave an Entertainment in the well deck this evening. It was most amusing - The "items" were nearly all comic & they appeared with their faces painted, dressed in the wierdest costumes & were really very funny tho' unfortunately being all in German we cdn't. understand a single word - Judging by the way the German portion of the audience laughed, they were being extraordinarily comic! The deck steward was the wit of the company backed up by one of our table stewards!

November 5th. Thursday - More of this everlasting swell today! We are both beginning to get bored with this old ship & looking forward to leaving her on Sunday - Absolutely nothing to say today as we have spent the whole time reading. We have got thro' all our books so it is lucky we are getting off so soon or I don't know what we sd. do. They have a small library on board but it is not up to much. A bird has been following us all day, we don't know what it is - It has the flight of a gull & the appearance of some sort of duck. A day or two ago we had a whole lot of swallows with us but they have all gone today.

November 6th. Friday - Nothing of any great excitement has occured today except that we ran into a shoal of porpoises - hundreds of them, jumping & splashing about in the maddest way - They look as tho' they were playing & chassing each other - In the afternoon we went right up into the bows & watched the flying fish.

There were any amount of them & they were most fascinating to watch - The ship appeared to disturb them & they were flying out of the way, sometimes in quite large flocks. They looked so pretty with the sun on them - I s^d. love to see one close - There is a lovely moon at nights just now & the phosphorus in the water tonight was most beautiful. It only showed on the top of the wave made by the ship & looked like great bars & streaks of the brightest silver -

November 7th. Saturday - Our last day on the Göben! & a most uneventful one. It is rather hotter than it was, tho' there is still a lovely cool head breeze - Anything more oily & glassy than the sea this morning I've never seen - We passed the coast of India this afternoon miles away in the distance - It looked very fine - Ranges of great high hills with a very rugged outline - I have seen India now even if I never set foot in it!

Göben

6.11.08

Petite, only tomorrow & then we will be at Colombo! Oh, how nice it will be - We are both sick to death of this old boat. A month, all but 2 days is a good long time & we are revelling in the thought of a nice clean hotel with plenty of room to move about in! These passengers too are beginning to pall. They're all so ugly & noisy especially the Dutch contingent! How I am looking forward to your letters - we thought of Cumberland a great deal on the 1st. Monday of Nov. & wondered whether you were out with the spotted dogs! We ourselves longed to be - a long sea voyage is a tedious thing - Its such a pity one must take it to get to these distant lands! I do hope your fears of getting fearfully tired when you hunt won't be realised - The first 2 or 3 times perhaps but I do trust not after that. Comment ça va-t-il chérie. I think of you many times & devoutly hope que ça va assez bien - I was reading over your first letters yesterday afternoon & they gave me a real "fillip" as regards you - I do trust the strength you speak of is growing a part of you now - it is sure to. Did I tell you The Oaks is off? Both C's father & mother wrote & said it was out of the question as it was too near Holm Hill!! Did you ever hear the like? What the devil do they mean - Is it likely we w^d. pester them with attentions? I can understand his father saying a thing like that but I didn't think his mother w^d. - ha-ever, it doesn't matter to us what they think but its a pity as The Oaks is a better house than Wreay Syke - Of course you won't mention this as the reason for us not going to The Oaks! We have read 4 large fat books of China & Japan which we bought at immence expence at The Times library before leaving London. What we s^d. have done without them goodness knows. One is "The War in the Far East" by The Times Correspondent - We intend to go & see all the battlefields so it was vastly interesting - & will be more so when we've seen them - "More Queer Things about Japan" by Douglas Sladen, also very interesting tho' rather too full of repetitions - "The Awakening of China" by some American missionary which I thought rather dry & lastly "Life & Sport in China", just an account of how Europeans live in China - C. is a perfect devil to read & fairly devours books. Luckily we brought our 2 Scilly Isle Thackerays *so the Virginians has been keeping him quiet for 2 or 3 days. He is now reduced to the advertisement sheet of the Carlisle Patriot for Oct: 16th.! Intensely interesting as we all know but it might with advantage be a little newer! There is <u>such</u> a cockney family on the boat - We call the man Putney Heath the wife Balham Common & the child the Tot from Tooting! Putney Heath "sorts" the Tot in fine style every now & then but she does nothing more than whine & seems used to it - There are a lot of Scotch people. We have a Scotchman who sits next to us - Such a nice intelligent engineer. We always call him Scotty & have long talks at meals - Some day I'll have to tell you all about them - I shall <u>never</u> forget them all! I feel as tho' I'd known them all my life! We had an opportunity of seeing the 1st. class passengers the other night at the steward's entertainment & pon me word they look precious little better than this crush - except that they were in society clothes! Of course we cd. change if we liked - but we don't like! Far too great a fag & the less we're in that old cabin the better - We'll have to pack tomorrow - That'll be pleasant except that we've unpacked so very little that it can't possibly take long.*

7. 11. 08. Talk about "oil upon the waters", you sd. sea the sea today, its as oily & glassy as it can be with sort of billows in it - Eno' to make one sick to <u>look</u> at it - No, I don't think I like the sea much, however this is the last day so "Courage he said & pointed t'ords the land" - There's no land to point to in the meantime but there soon will be & then we'll have a glorious fortnight until we have to embark once more - We're almost sure to come home by the Siberian railway - I think it will be perfectly ripping seeing Siberia & Russia not to mention the great advantage of no sea! One might get tired of the train for a fortnight but not worse than a ship for 6 weeks, & at any rate there'll be things to look at out of the windows & here in the Indian Ocean there's <u>nothing</u> to see. This sounds very "grousey" doesn't it? Its not meant to be for I really have enjoyed the ship until these last 3 or 4 days when one can't help getting sort of fed up -

I do wonder where you'll be when you get this - Houghton or Comlongon? I hope the former. My child, I think you needn't - & mustn't, mind leaving Bryde. Hang it all, it is just <u>her</u> cross in life - Poor devil, a bad eno' one in all conscience but you've got yours too & you must both lead your own lives in your own way & wrestle thro' with them. Remember when you <u>are</u> at home you hardly ever see her & its only at meals that you can be of any use . I wonder if you have been with Spookie - I do hope so & how is Muriel getting on? These questions will all be answered tomorrow when I get your letter so it seems silly to ask them but its difficult not to put down just what comes into ones head - C. thinks that most probably the mail for England will have gone by the time we get to Colombo & that there won't be another till Thursday in which case I'm afraid there will have been a long gap for you between Aden & next Thursday. Its simply diabolical for you my poor child but the posts & mails have always haunted us thro' life & been most disobliging so I suppose its all one can expect.

I'm afraid these letters of mine are very dull my child but so long as they aren't disappointing to you I'm afraid I can't make them any different. You see theres nothing to say in the meantime - The children on the boat romp round & afford us a certain amount of amusement -

Their mothers all seem to be incapable of controlling them in any way & never make the smallest efforts to entertain them or make them happy - I call it a beastly shame for the poor little beggars have the rottenest time - There are 3 dreadful German women on board who are going out to Shanghai or somewhere to marry missionaries - They have gone in answer to an advertisement - 3 missionaries wishing 3 wives. Did you ever hear the like? Oh the poor men, what a shock they'll have when they see them - In the meantime one of the women is having a high old time with a German parson (who is already engaged to somebody else!). Its perfectly disgraceful! I don't quite know how we learn all this. From Mrs. Hong Kong I think who being all alone poor thing makes friends with them all, not to mention the fact that shes probably a terrible old gossip at the best of times!

And now my child I must cease - Bless you forever & ever dearie & may you soon be a perfect Rock & not feel the effort of being so. Aurevoir chérie - Very best love from the T.B. & with mine

I am now & always Your own Twister

3
Ceylon

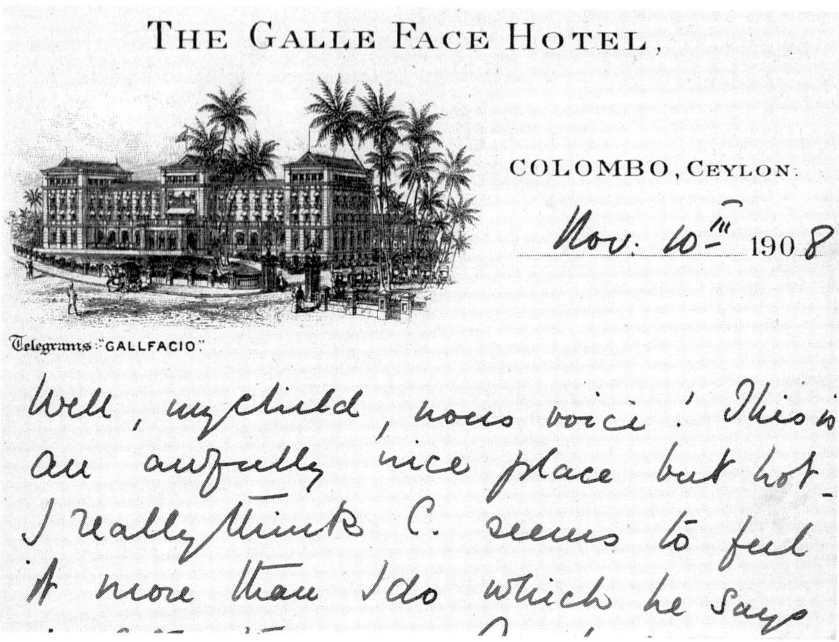
THE GALLE FACE HOTEL,

COLOMBO, CEYLON.

Nov: 10th 1908

Telegrams: "GALLFACIO."

Well, my child, nous voici! This is an awfully nice place but hot - I really think C. seems to feel it more than I do which he says

The Galle Face Hotel

Nov: 10th. 1908

Well, my child, nous voici! This is an awfully nice place but hot - I really think C. seems to feel it more than I do which he says is often the way - Any body who knows what a great heat is, like him, always feels coming back to it more than somebody who is experiencing it for the first time, like me - This hotel seems like a perfect paradise after that beastly old Göben! Such excellent food & every comfort, waited on by armies of these charming brown people. I'd like to live here (for a short time) & get to know the place & the people. Its impossible to walk much so we go about in rickshaws! They really are the greatest "lark" & remind me of childhood's days & the mail cart more than anything else! (The same old terror - tho' in a lesser degree- that the chap in the shafts will let go & the whole concern will tip over backwards! It used to be such a nightmare, dont you remember?) The Cingalese mode of hair- dressing is <u>too</u> amusing - All the men let their hair grow long & do it up at the back with a wee tousie for all the world like Betty & then stick a perfectly useless comb in it like a sort of crown. They are fascinating people.

This is a bullock cart! Look at that little wooden one of Sholtos in the 3 cornered cabinet on the stairs, they're like that - I think it seems too cruel for them to pull on their poor humps like that but they don't seem to mind - My child how bamboozled I get when I try to put all I've seen on paper. My diary at this place is perfectly rotten & doesn't half explain the place - I do wish I was gifted with a literary talent & c$^{d.}$ put things down with some sort of form & not this silly jumble - The mail with your letter didn't get in till yesterday. I *was* so pleased to get it. The first from Rosehill Cottage. Such a nice happy letter, you *good good* girl. Tomorrow we are going on to a place called Kandy & then to Newar Elya or some such name which is up in the mountains & quite cool which we are both looking forward to very much & where we will be able to exercise - Its like India here, one doesn't exercise unless one rides - My dear the Katamarans yesterday - I hardly thought it possible when Sholto made his that sane men really c$^{d.}$ use them, but there they were large as life & *sailing* if you please - I really did feel as tho I'd reached the limit of sight- seeing when I saw them first. The cocoa nut palms are very fascinating things, lovely thin stalks with a graceful sort of tuft at the end - Sunsets, as a general rule are gaudy things but really when it sets behind a graceful group of these trees it is pretty fine I can tell you tho' they really look best in the moonlight - This is a very swagger hotel & therefore expensive but that just can't be helped - We never buy anything in the way of curios. I never express a wish to as I'm sure its better to keep ones money & as far as I can see I s$^{d.}$ think the whole thing will probably be much more expensive than C. thought (things always are) also things will be more tempting in China & Japan *also* this is a very expensive place therefore its best to refrain - One hasn't the money to see *&* buy so its no use beginning - (My writing & spelling is going to pot - what matter) - The number of Göben people who have followed us here is fair *ridiculous* - Really yesterday evening when I heard that infernal German language I c$^{d.}$ have yelled! Tell Ollie I wear her black skirt & shirts nightly & bless her every time I put them on - just the ticket - I really *never* knew the joys of dressing till we got here, after the Göben - It is such a nice clean civilised sort of thing to do! We called on M$^{rs.}$ Dykes' friends this evening, walking carefully past the house first to make sure that there was no body there playing tennis or anything dreadful for C. said that a Colombo tennis party he w$^{d.}$ not go to! There didn't seem to be anybody so in we boldly plunged. "Out"! & with visibly risen spirits we came away! I really think introductions are a bore - We are quite happy fiddling about on our own. There really isn't very much to do here - I think we have seen all the "sights" - At the museum today we saw a specimen of "The rusty Spotted Cat" a native of Ceylon! The name fairly made me yell with delight tho' the puss itself was a perfect fright - eno' to frighten the french!

And now my childie I must just write up today's diary & "so to bed" for it is getting late - I do hope you have got used to letting people see it, but reading it aloud! No upon my honour that is too bad & makes me squirm to think of! Bless you, bless you chére petit chou chérie - Best love from the man - Yrs forever & beyond it D

<u>November 8th Sunday</u> - Got to Colombo at some unearthly hour in the morning but we didn't get up till ½ past 5 - We got up on deck just in time to see the sun rise. It was a lovely sight - It is a magnificent harbour with every kind of boat in it - from great big liners to catamarans! I was so excited when I saw the first one & instantly thought of the duck pond! The crows were very much in evidence - Delicious impudent people - as tame & cheeky as they're made! - We had breakfast at 6 & then got hold of Cook's man - a native with his hair done up in a "wee tousie" who took charge of our luggage & we walked up to the Galle Face Hotel where we are going to stay - It was quite nice walking at that hour tho' it was beginning to get hot - we got here about 8 o'clock - This is a charming place & the hotel is most comfortable. It stands close to the sea at the end of a long carriage drive (the sort of Rotten Row of Columbo) - It is a real Indian hotel, very bare & empty with polished floors & no carpets or curtains of any kind, shutters to the window's & cane lounge chairs in every direction - as different to an English hotel as can be. It <u>swarms</u> with servants. From a gorgeous head waiter with a comb the size of a tea plate stuck into his "towsie", (<u>forbye</u> the ordinary sircular comb which all Cingalese men wear!) to the most enchanting little brown boy in scarlet clothes & a fez - They make splendid servants & pad about with bare feet - the only native I've seen with boots on, so far, was a telegraph boy, in khaki on the regulation red bicycle! C. had to go down to the Customs House to get our luggage thro' & at about 11 o'clock it appeared - Armies of natives brought it up - (It always seems to take a dozen of them to do what one Englishman wd. do!) It took us till ½ past 1 to unpack, have baths & dress & by that time we were more than ready for lunch which we considered perfectly excellent after the horrid messes of the Göben! After lunch we sat on the verandah, which overlooks a sort of large green square. A most wonderful conjuror came & performed in front of us. He did the Mango tree trick & many others all equally marvellous - It was very hot in the afternoon so we waited till after tea & then went out - We walked to the Cinnamon Gardens, first past European bungalows - which look most delightful places to live in, standing in gardens, all looking beautifully fresh & green at present then thro' a native part. It was the same sort of thing as at Algiers & yet quite different - I was fascinated with it & love these nice brown Cingalese with their smiley faces! Everybody goes about in ginrickshaws here - Quite the most delightful form of locomotion! We came back in some from the Cinnamon Gardens, which are the sort of Hyde Park of Colombo apparently & it was ripping! They run so smoothly & the men tho' small seem to think nothing of the heaviest "fare" but run along with long easy strides - The bullock carts are very nice - The bullocks have humps on their necks on which the yoke rests & they pull & hold the weight entirely with the hump! I sd. think they must constantly be getting their poor humps very much galled - The carts are huge things covered in with matting - Sometimes the bullocks are harnessed to sort of governess cars & made to trot! Poor dears, they <u>don't</u>

look happy - It gets dark here almost immediately the sun has gone down so that our rickshaw drive back to the hotel was in the dark with all the lamps lit & the moon shining! All the rank & fashion seemed to be out driving at this hour. Certainly by far the nicest to be out especially along by the sea as there was a lovely cool breeze. Some of the private carriages are awfully smart with native servants in most becoming liveries - As we were having dinner we had our last look at the Göben - or rather her lights - as she steamed away on her voyage & were jolly glad we weren't in her!

November 9th Monday - We went down into the town after breakfast in rickshaws to Cook & Kodak & then to the station as we were going to have lunch at a place called Mount Lavinia - Something had gone wrong with the railway arrangements as the train was fearfully late to begin with & then took an hour to do the distance it was advertised to take 20 minutes! It was very tiresome as it was frightfully hot when the train was standing still. There seemed to be thousands of natives travelling & the 3rd. class carriages looked anything but inviting - The country we passed thro' was almost entirely cocoa-nut tree woods on one side with the owners (Cingalese) bungalows at intervals & on the other side the sea with fishermen's huts, curious little hovels, apparently made of rushes, built right down on the beach. Cocoa-nuts, a shrill-voiced youth in the train informed us, are most lucrative things to possess - The fishermen use catamarans with sort of oblong sails & most unsafe they look too! We got to Mount Lavinia about 1.30 & went to the hotel for lunch - It is beautifully situated looking right over the sea - All these hotels seem to have shops in them & one is never left in peace for 2 minutes, men come round & press one to buy things for all the world like a bazaar - After an excellent lunch we went out on to some rocks but didn't stay long as we found they were simply alive with green crabs, scuttling about in all directions - We strolled thro' a cocoa-nut tree wood up to the prettiest little native village - The wood was beautifully cool & shady & carpeted with some sort of little green weed which bullocks were feeding on - Some of the children in the village were too innocent for anything especially some little girls with long black hair & cheeky little faces! We went in to a Buddhist temple, a curious gaudily painted place with a huge image of Buddha in the middle - in front of him was a long table covered with flower's heads, offerings from the people - We were each given one which seemed rather a funny idea! The paintings all represented the life of Buddha & were most uncouth productions in brilliant yellow red & blue, not beautiful - We cdn't wait to hear the story which the man was most anxious to tell us as we had to catch our train back. (It was ½ an hour late so we might have stayed after all.) We got back to Colombo just in time for the King's birthday parade on the sort of parade ground place just outside this hotel - We watched it from an upstairs passage window - They fired a feu de joie & looked so nice in their khaki & white uniforms. There was 1 lot of

Native Infantry, & some Garrison artillery - The rest were volunteers - The crowd watching was almost the most interesting part - Such a motley collection - C. went down for our letters afterwards but I stayed up & did a little necessary sewing & washing! We gave our Göben washing out yesterday afternoon & it has come back this evening most beautifully washed - Pretty quick work that!

November 10th. Tuesday - We went down to Cooks this morning in rickshaws - it takes about 10 mins. (How cd. one ever get on without a Cook?) & then went to 2 magnificent shops, quite like London ones, & bought sundry trifles in the shape of tooth powder etc: - They are kept beautifully cool with fans & draughts in every direction & as it was very hot outside we found shopping there was quite the nicest way of spending the morning! In the afternoon it got much cooler, the sun went in & it looked as if it was going to rain, tho' it didn't so we went out to find Mrs. Dykes' friends, the Berwicks - They live in the Cinnamon Gardens - It was so nice that we walked all the way - They were not in so instead we went to the Museum which is close to their house & saw all sorts of most interesting things. What I liked the best were the specimens of animals, birds, insects, fish, snakes etc: all natives of Ceylon - Some of the birds are lovely, also the insects especially some butterflies & beetles - The leaf insects are too extraordinary for anything & look exactly like the leaves they live amongst - I hope we shall meet some of them when we are "up country" where we go tomorrow tho' I must confess that some of them wd. be simply terrifying! I wd. much rather not meet a certain centipede about 6 inches long like a great fat worm with millions of legs - We were shown round by a dear old Cingalese whose English was decidedly quaint - There was one small monkey about which he said "By day he sleep, at night walking"! Unluckily it got dark while we were there so we had to leave as we cd. see no more & came home in rickshaws. We came past the "Garden Club" a sort of sports place where they play tennis etc: It looked rather nice & must be a perfect boon to the residents - There were simply rows of rickshaws standing outside, smart private ones & others for hire while some of the very swagger people had motors waiting for them - It does look too funny to see the mixture of things in these places, a motor for example driven by a regular chauffeur does look so out of place scorching past a bullock cart being goaded along by a Cingalese - They have the most excellent lime squashes at this hotel - Quite the most delicious drink I've ever tasted - Our waiter is a perfect dear & gives us information about the country & people - He seems very proud of Ceylon & I must say I don't wonder!

November 11th. Wednesday - Spent nearly the whole morning packing, a loathsome & hot job & started off at about ½ past 1 for the station in rickshaws, our luggage going in a bullock cart - We have brought as little as possible leaving the rest at Cooks so as to travel as "light" as we can - The train was very full, they put on so few 1st. class carriages, so we had to go in the dining car, but it was quite comfortable & cool & I enjoyed the journey enormously. We passed thro' quite the most beautiful scenery I've ever seen - We bought a splendid book on Ceylon at the Station which explained all the country as we went along which of course made it doubly interesting, also there was a very nice European man in the train, evidently a resident, who gave us much useful information - The first part was thro' rice fields, in every stage from being ploughed by teams of oxen, onwards, cocoa-nut woods which are most beautiful, native villages, little native huts made of the dried cocoa-nut leaves sprinkled about thro' the woods, herds of oxen wading about & even lying down in the swamped paddy fields (at one stage they swamp the fields many inches deep in water) rivers very dirty & brown owing to the rains thay have had lately, with generally a company of natives enjoying a bathe, (the natives appear to love washing tho' its a pity the water they use sometimes is anything but clean!) In the distance we c^d. see the hills which were our destination & as we got nearer to them the views were quite lovely - paddy fields & swamps with here & there great clumps of some sort of rush or bush (goodness knows what they were!) backed by cocoa-nut woods & with the hills appearing behind them, "Adam's Peak" the highest of them - The nearer we got to the hills the more beautiful did the vegetation become until it really passes my prowess to attempt to describe it even! Hills & valleys simply one mass of trees & creepers. Palms, bananas, arecanuts, bread fruit trees, rubber & tea plantations, cocoa & hundreds of others that we didn't know. There is a wild sun-flower which grows everywhere like a weed, one mass of yellow but they say it is being superseded by another weed a white climbing thing which grows over everything even the tallest trees like a sort of shroud - In every available corner of this vast forest there are paddy fields most wonderfully arranged in terraces with little mud ledges round them to keep the water in. In places the train climbed up regular mountains or went round clinging on to a perfect precipice - We got to Kandy about 6 o'clock as the sun went down - For the last part of the journey the sun was of course low so that the light was beautiful & we couldn't have seen the country under a better advantage - We are staying at The Firs Hotel, quite a small almost private hotel on the shores of the lake - It is most beautifully cool here, such a change from Colombo - We were quite glad of a blanket at night - Insects kept up an incessant hum & chirping all night otherwise it was perfectly still & silent as we sat on the varandah after dinner - There were only 5 other people at dinner besides ourselves -

<u>November 12th. Thursday</u> - Started off about ½ past 10 to see the sights of Kandy - It was a perfectly lovely morning, about the temperature of a really nice summer's day at home so we were able to walk the whole time in spite of rickshaws following close behind in the hopes that we w^d. use them! We went first to the Temple of the Tooth - It is lovely outside with a wall all round it pierced with holes for putting lamps on feast days - There was a sort of moat inside the wall simply "hotching" with small sacred fish & turtles - We were simply pestered with beg-

gars whining & persistent - There is nothing very much to see, only some curious old frescoes & many images of Buddha. Wherever we went they wanted backsheesh which was most tiresome especially as it is written up in English that it is quite unnecessary to give any. After seeing everything there was to see at the Temple (it is called "of the Tooth" because one of Buddha's teeth is there in a sort of shrine carefully kept behind iron bars) we went for a most glorious walk right up in the forest. It was called "Lady Horton's Walk" - The trees, creepers & undergrowth were lovely, there weren't a great many flowers - We heard birds in every direction but cdn't. see them tho' we gazed up into the trees till our necks ached. The foliage is so thick its impossible to see them. Some of them make the queerest noises, one like a blacksmith's hammer & anvil & another like a curling stone on ice! The views of the mountains were magnificent - This is the first real walk we have had since leaving England & I feel quite stiff this evening! In the afternoon we went to the most beautiful Botanical Gardens at a place called Peradiniya - We drove there in a rattly sort of little victoria drawn by quite a good swift horse - there seem to be no horses here except those used in the towns for cabs & carriages, everything else is done by bullocks - The road to the Gardens (4 miles) passed thro' an almost continuous native village & was shaded by tall trees all the way. The gardens were most interesting. We were there over an hour & a half, in fact till it got too dark to see any more & the gates were shut! It is a great big place most beautifully kept & arranged & one cd. spend a life-time there learning all the different trees & flowers - We had a very nice English speaking guide to begin with & when he went we explored by ourselves. They are all tropical trees & plants & one became perfectly bewildered trying to grasp even a few of them - What with the sights & the lovely smells & the birds singing & the low sun casting long shadows over the grass we had a most enjoyable 2 hours & were quite sorry to leave but it was practically dark - at 6 o'clock - so we sdn't. have been able to see any more. Our "Machine" was waiting for us so we got in & drove back in the dark. The native villages looked most squalid & wretched at night - The most of the houses had a candle burning in them so that one cd. see in - They looked so uncomfortable & the sort of places we wdn't. put a dog, but they don't seem to mind - When we got back to Kandy & were going along by the lake there were any amount of fireflys in the grass flitting about like little stars got loose! I never saw anything so pretty. Fewer people than ever at the hotel tonight - I can't help feeling sorry for the manager but hope it isn't always the same! There are more waiters than people at dinner so the attention we receive is quite embarrassing! The whole lot stand round quite close watching every mouthful, offering things & anticipating ones wants - With English servants it wd. be unbearable but one doesn't mind it from a bare-footed Sinhalese (I've always spelt this wrong up to date!) They all wear a sort of petticoat reaching to their ankles bound tightly round them & ordinary European cut coats - or the lower castes none at all -

The Firs, Kandy

13.11.08

Oh the glories of this place Tu n'as pas d'idée! I just can't describe it. It is too gorgeous for words & what adds to its charm is that it is so delightfully cool - In ordinary thin summer clothes & topis (I got one in Colombo) we walk for hours every day & see the most lovely sights & enjoy ourselves to the full. Pon me word its a paradise of a place & the nicest we've struck so far. I hope Newara Eliya where we go tomorrow will be as nice. Dear, dear but life is full at present - Will I burst, or will I get used to it? I somehow never took much account of coming to Colombo, which was perfectly silly for its heavenly quite heavenly - My child, some day some day I do hope you'll come here too - Photographs give no idea, words less, one must see -

I wonder if you're hunting today. I hope so & that you're having a good day - On Irish I hope for when all's said & done she is the mare of mares I think, (tho' one c$^{d.n't}$ say it at Houghton in case of its getting to the old mare's ears!) I know you like to hear of me having such a good time, the same way as I love to get your cheerful letters - To think that I've only had 4 from you since leaving England but no matter I'll get one when we go back to Colombo - This must be a scrubby little letter I'm afraid but its better to send it by this mail than to wait for another week don't you think? C. is splendid at mails & ports & always knows when to post! Something so talented about it I can't help thinking! We are going down to the town to post these so I mustn't write more. This hotel is a little way out which makes it most beautifully quiet. There are so few people tho' that meals are carried on in a sort of whisper! There are more waiters than people - We buy books of views & post cards at the various places which will be very interesting to us afterwards & how I will love showing them to you! You just shall look at them whether you're bored or not!! Heavens how often one has done it with other peoples! This afternoon we are going to see elephants bathing in a river so in my next letter you will hear about them. I think I'll like that entertainment. The birds are the most irritating things. We cannot see them tho' we hear them all round & quite close. They are as bad as cuckoos -

Et maintenant dors ma petite. In other words ta ta for the present. I wish oh I wish I wrote decent letters tho' probably you like better this kind of rigmarole - Its me anyhow, which the other w$^{dn't.}$ be -

Best love from the T.B. He is enjoying himself here very much & likes the exercise. He loved the Botanical Gardens & wanted to learn everything! tho' he is even worse than I am at retaining names & doesn't even always recognize the trees when he sees them again! I must say I generally do that (I wonder, do I? Not always!)

Comment va la chienne? Bless its heart, I wonder if its with you. If so kiss the face of it from the other twin. Yesterday I sore a dog! Yes, it was a dog tho' you might have thought it was just a yellow spotted face! C. thought it dreadful, I didn't!

Mes amours chère coeur Ta soeur qui t'aime D -

Nuwara Eliya
Nov: 17th. 1908

Chérie, I got your 2nd. letter written from Rosehill Cottage the day before yesterday & have revelled in it ever since. Its the best I've had yet, chiefly because in it you assure me that you really do like my diary & letters. I was so frightened that perhaps they weren't very satisfying & it was sort of worrying until you told me they were all right, since when I have been perfectly happy - My word, but this is a lovely country - I enjoy every minute of it - tho' when writing about it I may appear to gush, I really mean every word - I don't think I put anything in the diary to make one blush if read by the likes of Sholto as I? That wd. be dreadful! Such a day as we had yesterday - It reminded me of you'n me going up the Kirkstone pass tho' the scenery was very different tho' pon me word in parts way up here there is a distinct resemblance to the highlands or lake district especially with gorse bushes, blackberries & bracken - Isn't it peculiar that one sd. find them here? Not really I suppose but somehow one never thought to meet them! Our excitement when we first saw the gorse was intense & our minds instantly flew to Palmer's Whins, foxes & spotted dogs! We walked for nearly 3 hours yesterday up this pass, climbing gently all the way up - Hard work, but "seeing round the next corner" was always a weakness of mine so on I plodded (C. of course as fresh as paint dash him!) & coming down was mere child's play - Kandy I think was really the nicest place, certainly the best looking but we cd.n't have walked there for 3 hours without expiring - All the same by the way we did do it one day at the Perediniya Gardens, but that was so intensely interesting I just cd.n't have stopped the "tour" of them mapped out by the guide book & dash it all a good night's rest is all one wants to put one on one's legs again! I eat enormously here but am not getting fat so I'm dashed if I care - Why not have a sausage as well as an egg at breakfast if you want it for bye a couple of bananas at the end! N.B. these latter are perfectly excellent in this country & grow like blackberries -

I think you seem to have really enjoyed Rosehill Cottage - D. & M. are such rippers - I wonder where you all are now - my child we gave you the list of dates & where we wd. be on them at the back of the paper in case anybody wanted to telegraph, but here they are again - Leave Colombo Nov: 22nd.; at Penang Nov:26th.; at Singapore Nov:28th; at Hong Kong Dec:3rd; Shanghai Dec:7th. - where we leave the Bülow & stay in China making our way up to Pekin where we will probably be for Xmas (figurez vous!) - From China we will go to Japan, then back to China to do the battlefields after the winter "thence" home via Siberia - but of course I'll be able to give you further information for this latter part later on - In the meantime I am revelling in Ceylon & am loth to leave it especially as it means that bally old sea again - Talk about loosing ones nerve - I cd. scream with fright at the thought of being on it again, I do so dislike being sea-sick & I just <u>know</u> I shall be. A truce child to this idle folly - you must either face the sea or stay here the rest of your life so choose between them & no more nonsense - I don't know what people mean about not reading on a ship. We read by the hour, & cd.n't have got on without books. George Saul has secured

Wreay Sike for us - There was a little bother at the end, the new adjutant wanting it at once etc: but it will be all right now - Do try & go & see it again & remind us of what its like - That half hour we had there was really not long eno' to take things in. We both get so excited when we think about it & quite long for May so as to get into it! My dear it will be exciting won't it? C. is now writing reams to George Saul about it - We have taken this morning for real solid work & are getting thro' all sorts of letters & things - The afternoon shall be devoted to pleasure! Another walk I think - Its far nicer to walk while one can - The time cometh when no man shall walk (except up & down the deck of the old Bülow!) We went to Church when we got here. I don't know why I didn't put it in the diary - I just somehow couldn't knowing the number of people who w^d. read it - C. likes going to church you know & I think I do too (with him) tho' I get precious little out of it still - I don't quite know what he gets - Some day I must make him tell me but I somehow don't feel as tho' he knew himself - Well so long dearie - I'm sorry to say that the Bülow will more than likely sail before the mail with your next letter gets in to Colombo so that I shan't hear from you again till Shanghai on Dec: 7th. - nearly a month - too dreadfull. You are much better off for letters than I am but that of course is only fair -

Well my child I must cease - Best love from the T.B.

Thine forever D -

November 13th. Friday - We got up at 7 o'clock this morning & went for the most glorious walk right up one of the hills thro' dense woods - There are always good roads leading all thro' the woods, also paths & one can wander about all over the place - We finally came out at a bungalow standing in a cocoa plantation - We c^d. have gone on miles further for at that early hour of the morning right up there one c^d. walk forever but 9 o'clock was fast approaching & we were beginning to long for breakfast so we had to turn back. A charming native in the bungalow most kindly volunteered to put us on a short cut down to Kandy thro' the plantation so we went that way & weren't so very late for breakfast after all. These woods are really marvelous & quite beautiful - With the help of guide books & the Peradiniya Gardens we are beginning to learn a few of them but it is most confusing & difficult to remember the names - This afternoon we went for a drive (in the same cab as we had yesterday oddly eno'!) to a place called Katugastota where we saw 4 most charming elephants who belong to a native chief bathing in the river - (Mahawali Gauga) They were such rippers! The mahouts called to them & they came out at once like dogs & went thro' some innocent little tricks for our benefit, standing on 2 & 3 legs, salaaming etc: for which we gave them bananas & sugar cane supplied by troops of little native children who accompanied us down to the river to see them & came pattering along after us until we got into the carriage again, jabbering together in their curious gibberish - The wild elephants in Ceylon live in the north of the country & aren't found round about here - These originally came from the north I suppose but they're tame eno' now in all conscience! One of the boys who had attached himself to us spoke excellent English & offered to show us a flowering Talipot palm & as these only flowered once in 40 years & shortly after die we wanted to see it so went with him - Talipot palms are the biggest of the palms (there seems to be 100's of different sorts which is so bewildering!) & are most magnificent things & this one with its huge white flower growing out of the top of the tree like a sort of shower bouquet was a most beautiful sight - We drove back another & longer way thro' the woods - The road was very steep so the horse walked all the way up - rather nice as we c^d. take in all we were passing - & simply rattled down! At the top there was the most glorious view of the valleys & distant mountains - Birds, beasts, insects or goodness knows what were making the most curious noise like a reaping machine - very loud & whatever it was must have been quite close to us but search as we w^d. we c^d. not see them - so tantalising - We got back just before dark about 6 o'clock - It has been a lovely day, a little cloudy in the afternoon but thats rather nice - There is a very large & stout French woman staying at the hotel, who evidently felt the heat for we overheard her saying to a friend as she got back from a walk - "Sun is hot - Much flesh"!

November 14th. Saturday - Got up at 7 o'clock again this morning & went for another walk. This time we walked all round the lake - We made efforts to find a way up to the top of the hill on the opposite side but every road we tried only led to a bungalow so we gave it up in despair but it was very nice down by the lake - The water is a sort of dull green, a lovely colour but very dirty & full of small fish & turtles. All around it there are some very fine trees, they seem to grow to such an enormous size here - There is one in flower at present, quite a common one, a beautifully shaped tree one mass of scarlet flowers with dark green leaves. Amongst all the other trees it looks perfectly gorgeous. At the top of the lake there are about ½ doz of them - Before lunch we paid a visit to the Kandy Art Association, a Government concern where there is a collection of various kinds of Kandian works of art in brass, copper & silver both on show & for sale - Some of it is really lovely but unfortunately so fearfully heavy that it w^d. take a small fortune to either send them home or take them with one - We got 2 specimens tho' in a sort of mixture of brass, silver & copper - One old industry, still kept up & most effective - The afternoon we spent at the Peradiniya Gardens again - We went by train this time armed with a most splendid guide book which we found at the hotel - We really "did" the Gardens thoroughly - The guide book was invaluable & told us exactly where to go to find all the specially interesting things so that we weren't wandering about in an aimless sort of way. Its impossible to write about all that we saw there but I enjoyed it thoroughly & now feel as tho' I know something - tho' a very little - about tropical trees & plants! Half way thro' we were forced to seek rest & refreshment outside the Gardens, in the shape of tea at a "Rest House"! It put new life into us & we went back as lions refreshed returning to the entrance

5 minutes before closing time our brains whirling, worn out but mad keen to the bitter end! Our train back was of course late (nobody seems to mind much when they start!) but at last we got back & drove up here in rickshaws in the dark -

November 15th Sunday - Got up early this morning to pack & were ready in heaps of time to catch the 10-35 train to Newara Eliya where we now are, staying at the Grand Hotel - We had a carriage all to ourselves so we were able to look out at either side as we liked - The wonderful book which we bought at Colombo tells one just exactly what to look out for & when & which side so it is really invaluable! This is the highest part of Ceylon - It is a tremendous pull up - 6240 ft above the sea - Kandy is 1602 so we came 4638 ft in 6 hours a distance of 50 or 60 miles - Nearly the whole way up there was nothing but the plantations - These are not exactly beautiful seen close as they consist of endless rows of tea bushes planted in straight lines about 4 ft apart & with trees at frequent intervals to give shade. Every available spot seems to be planted up & there is no end to it, in the valleys, on the hills, everywhere. Tea doesn't seem to mind where it grows! Some of it had been picked, leaving the bushes quite bare, other parts were being prepared for planting which made the ground look as if it had been skinned - just as bare as it cd. be - & all of it looked most flourishing - The higher we got the better did the view become until when we were nearing the top it was simply grand for one cd. see for miles & miles, ranges of hills getting fainter & fainter in the distance. The railway twists & turns in a truly wonderful way & pounds bravely on with 2 engines - Looking down, one can sometimes see the line miles below - One wonders how it is possible to get up at all! We had luncheon on the train - quite good - changing into the dining-car & then back to our own carriage - The train stopped at every station but they are so teeming with natives hurrying about (there are always crowds of them travelling - that it is very amusing & not a bit boring as it wd. be at home. There seem to be no villages up amongst the tea estates - only bungalows for the owners with tea factories & sort of settlements generally made of corrugated iron for the coolies - Any of these who were travelling in our train looked a dirty rough lot muffled up in ragged coats & blankets for they hate anything like cold - We didn't think it a bit cold - in fact just right - but I suppose at this time of year they think it dreadful. We saw a few of the planters themselves walking about on their estates - It must be a dreadful life I think miles away up there with nothing but tea, tea, tea in every direction - One wd. think it impossible that such a large quantity is required! At a place called Nanu-oya we had to change & went the last 5 miles in (*left blank*) minutes climbing 1000 feet! The train was the most innocent little affair I've ever been in & was like being in a toy! It is only a 2 ft gauge & the engine the pluckiest little beggar I've ever seen - It puffed along gallantly - very slow of course - being fed with wood. The line twists in & out here like a serpent - a wonderful piece of engineering We passed thro' real old forest here which has never been touched - a regular jungle & quite unlike the tropical vegetation lower down - Arum lilies grow about in the ditches & places here like primroses do at home! This hotel is very comfortable, about a mile from the station & with a golf links - said in the guide book to be the best "out of Scotland" - & I must say it does look excellent - at its very door! There are very few people here, apparently this is not the time of year for visitors - It began to rain soon after our arrival but didn't last long - It was quite refreshing after the heat of Colombo & Kandy. Its extraordinary the difference between these 3 places. One day last week it was 88° max. & 68 min: in Colombo, 81.3 & 62.5 at Kanday & 69.7 & 41.5 here! This is certainly the most agreeable for the likes of us, used to the Borders!

November 16th Monday - It simply poured last night & woke me up clattering on the corrugated iron roof outside our window - It was quite fine in the morning tho' &, when the sun was out really quite hot, for of course there is a tremendous heat in it - We went out after breakfast & had a splendid walk - We went up a mountain pass, going thro' the town en route, rather a dirty smelly place - much more so than Kandy - The road after leaving the town winds up one side of the valley, twisting & turning to avoid dips & chasms on the side of the hill - The first part is entirely tea but in places & right at the top of the pass the hand of the white man has not yet been so that the forest still holds it own - It is very wild & tangled with entirely new sorts of trees to those at Kandy so we feel more hopelessly at sea than ever! Rhodedendrons grow here like trees - great thick knarled trunks - Unfortunately they are not in flower just now - I sd. love to see them when they are - They are red & pink ones & must look perfectly lovely mixed as they are with other extremely ancient-looking trees festooned with creepers - We were both surprised & pleased to see bracken & blackberries growing here also masses of gorse in flower! Somehow one doesn't expect to meet them so far from home especially when they are mixed up with lovely tall tree ferns, arum lilies, (as common as weeds here & in full flower) & all sorts of other flowers which I'm sure I've seen in Gardens & greenhouses but can't "put a name to"! The colour of these jungles is the best part of them, a sort of dull greeny-grey with some almost black trees amongst them - They are really very fine - The guide book says they abound with monkeys, elephants, leopards & all sorts of wild beasts but we haven't seen any yet! We kept meeting & passing coolies all the way up & down - They all wear a filthy dirty- looking sort of blamket made like a hood worn over their heads & look a very poor low-class lot. It began to pour with rain soon after lunch, a tremendous thick mist coming down the valley. It seemed quite funny to hear rain again! We went out after tea in spite of it & walked a little bit by the side of the lake - It looked very nice & grey in the rain with the tops of the hills towering black over the mist & the frogs in the rushes at the edge simply croaking themselves hoarse! There is an awfully pretty little race-course which we came across encircled with gorse bushes in full bloom while there were more in great clumps in the circle inside mixed with these tree rhodedendrons - The natives look most wretched & out of place in the rain, splashing along with their bare feet amongst the puddles, their poor flimsy petticoats getting so wet & umbrellas over their heads! Somehow one only associates them with sunshine & heat, but up here I believe they have any amount of rain so they know all about it! This is a very nice hotel, only one story high with a big porch simply one mass of white creeper - There is a tree which grows here with a yellow flower just like Shimosa - Some of them are in full bloom & look quite lovely - Grass grows here! It doesn't at Kandy so it is quite nice to see it again - There its place is taken by some sort of coarse weed & in the Peradiniya Gardens the place was carpeted with sensitive plant - growing like grass! Lawns of it kept mown, under the trees & everywhere. The Kandy weed had tiny little prickly things which stuck on ones clothes like burrs & even now we sometimes find we have not finished plucking our selves!

November 17th Tuesday - Today we spent nearly the whole morning writing letters & then went for a short stroll in what they call the Park - It is not a very beautiful place as apparently it has only just been laid out so it is rather bare & new with the exception of the rhodedendrons which look as tho' they might be thousands of years old & aren't bushes at all but real tall trees (growing 70 ft. high) with thick trunks! We found one with one flower on it, that lovely crimson - They all look as tho' they were just going to flower which seems strange at this time of the year - I do wish they were all out now for they must be lovely - After lunch we set out to walk to "The Moon Plains" but by taking what we thought a very clever short cut we missed the road altogether & never found it out until we had gone miles & miles in another direction! We asked several natives we met if we were going right but they cdnt. inderstand us but at last we asked at a little native hut by the roadside - thinking it wd. be absolutely no use - & what was our surprise when the woman answered in the most excellent English & conversed away, perfectly at home with the language! She told us we had come 5 miles & must return the same way - She was such a nice woman, old with white hair & one tooth & had such a nice manner & way of speaking - It didn't really matter having gone wrong as we had had a lovely walk, first of all beside the lake & then right down a most glorious valley almost to the foot of one of the highest mountains - At first there were great open spaces amongst the forest which rather reminded us of Greystoke Park except that there were no rabbit holes! (Rabbits dont live in Ceylon) but further on it was nothing but the densest forest with a burn running down far below the road - It was all very well going down but we had to toil up again which was quite another affair! On the way up a motor passed us - grinding slowly along! - It did look so out of place in that primeval forest tho' doubtless it is a splendid way of seeing the country - There seems to be a rush of new visitors at the hotel this evening - A good many "golfing guests" I think to judge from scraps of overheard conversation - Co. & Mrs. Webster (Mrs. Dykes' Colombo friends father & mother!)

called on us this afternoon but of course we were out. It is a horrid bore as we shall have to return the call when there are such heaps of other nicer things to do & only about 4 more days to do them in!

November 18th. Wednesday - Wrote letters again this morning & C. had his hair cut in the hotel! We then went up "One Tree Hill" - The Manager said it was a 10 mins: walk but it took us well over an hour & I'd like to see him doing it in 10 mins:! The path leads up thro' tea all the way, in fact the whole hill is covered with it. There were some coolies at work picking it which was most interesting - They only pick the new & tender green leaves & having gathered a handful at lightning speed throw it over their shoulder into a large deep basket which they all wear strapped to their backs for the purpose - The view from the top was lovely, the town lying in the valley with the lake - which is artificial, tho' it doesn't look like it, being of an excellent shape - After lunch we set forth once more for the Moon Plains carefully studying the map before starting - but we never got there! Took a wrong turning again! There seems to be some fate against our getting there anyhow we're not going to try again! We saw what we thought must be them, large open spaces of coarse grass with rhodedendrons scattered about - On getting back to Newara Eliya we went to call on the Websters having some difficulty in finding their house - We found her in & sat & made conversation - She never gave us any tea which we had been rather hoping for! Another woman, the wife of some general or other came in but they were neither of them vastly exciting - We heard from Cook this morning that our ship gets in to Colombo on Saturday so we shall have to leave here that day to catch her - Only 2 more days which is very sad -

November 19th. Thursday - Started this morning at 20 mins: to 11 & went to the top of Pidurntallagalla - It is the highest mountain in Ceylon being 8280 ft above sea level so we had a climb of 2000 ft - We took an hour & ¾ with 2 rests of a few minutes each - There is an excellent path all the way which zig- zags up so it doesn't seem so very steep - It leads thro' dense jungle all the way - The trees are small with very twisted knarled trunks covered with a growth of moss which hangs down in festoons & a lovely grey lichen - The path is so shut in that one can only see just what is on each side of one except where gaps have been cut & seats put where the view over the valley as one gets higher & higher is lovely. There is a cairn at the top - The view from it is absolutely the most beautiful one cd. ever see - Being so very high one can see for miles & miles in every direction - It was simply glorious - There was a ring of white cloud like a sort of frame round it all. We sat for half an hour drinking it all in - The sun was shining, with a lovely cool breeze - most refreshing after the toil of getting there - not that it was much of a toil for the air as one got higher & higher was so fine one cd. have walked for- ever - Before coming down we cut S 1908 in the flag staff on the cairn & hope to find it there the next time we come! (The flag staff is decidedly ancient so unless we hurry up they'll replace it with a new one!) The carving is on the west side about

5ft. 8in. from the bottom of the flag staff which is let into the rocky cairn - A few of the rhodedendrons were in flower, or rather a few flowers on them were out, that lovely bright crimson - Mixed up with the purple trees, black with age & hung with grey lichen they looked quite lovely - We came down in 1 hr. 10 mins (its about $2^{1/2}$ miles) - It seemed far steeper going down & I felt like a groggy old cab-horse by the time we reached the bottom! We started at 20 to 11 & got back at 2.19 quite ready for lunch - We didn't feel very energetic in the afternoon but very sleepy - after the mountain air I suppose so didn't go out again till just before dark when we had a stroll round to take away the stiffness - This really is an ideal place - Lovely bright sun & yet not a bit too hot - In ordinary thin summer clothes one is just right & feel as fit as possible - It was rather colder after dinner this evening & there was a fire in the drawing- room but as smoking is not allowed there we sat in the hall with our coats on & kept quite warm tho' without them we were quite chilly -

Nuwara Eliya Hotel

Nov: 20th. 1908

My child, This will probably be a bit of a surprise for you getting another letter so soon - I can just imagine how excited you will be - One's heart does beat doesn't it when one sees t'other chap's writing? This has to be posted at 1 & its 12 now & simply millions of other things to do so you mustn't mind rather a scrappy letter. This is our last day & we are overcome with sadness at the thought - Ugh! to think of that d-d old German ship after this paradise of a place - I'd give my boots to come back to Ceylon some day - going up that mountain yesterday (see the diary) was the best thing we've done yet. Jamais jamais jamais de la vie - C'etait vraiement superbe - No that doesn't half describe it - There are no words in any language to convey to you what that panorama was like - When we emerged from the jungle on to the top & cd. see what appeared to be the whole of Ceylon spread out all round I fairly gasped - It was a sight for the gods & I shan't forget it in a hurry - C. has just paused in his writing to light a pipe & broken a long silence by saying "Give the old Ninty Pinty a kiss from me" - He is such an absolutely adorable person - but then we always knew that didn't we? To think that the next time I write it will be "with best Xmas wishes"! & heres us sitting in summer garb in the hall of this hotel, bright sun shining & a gentle zephyr coming in at the open door whilst you doubtless will read this in the Houghton dining-room, possibly by yourself, H & M not down yet, having lately shut the open window to keep out the cold, sitting on the fire side of the table without "the screen" - Perhaps its a hunting morning! If so well well can I see you with your hair looking rather as if you were going to the bath, without a billy-cock on - I hope you haven't had trouble with your tie! & that you're wearing my breeks if you want them - Up to date I have not wanted Sissy's. I must say I felt rather a cad taking them but in Manchuria they'll come in handy I've no doubt. I do trust they're not going to have any fuss in China to prevent us going there. News here is of the scantiest - Nothing but the telegrams in the Ceylon papers, the rest of the paper taken up with local news about tea & rubber plantations etc:! not very entertaining -

Well, so long my Nin - I hope Life is going well with you at present & that "standing alone" is getting to be quite an easy pleasant habit - It must get to be both those or it wont be right - Dec: 7th. till I hear from you again! Days & days however it just cant be helped. Speak about the nip in your next letter -

Yr forever & beyond it D -

November 20th. Friday - Our last day at Newara Eliya - Very sad - We spent the morning doing all sorts of odd jobs before going on board, writing letters, buying cake & biscuits at the big English shop to supplement the food on the Bülow, which if it is anything like the Göben will need it! washing hair-brushes, darning stockings etc: (Needless to say I did these 2 latter!) & in the afternoon we went for a last walk on a road which took us right up to the top of a hill from where we had a lovely view over Newara Eliya & by going a little further saw right down the next valley - It was very cloudy & looked like rain - which however did not come - The hills looked very fine under this new aspect - Great banks of black cloud hanging over them with thick white mist drifting about. We had to come back the same way as there didn't appear to be any other! We might have taken to the tea plantations & found our own way amongst the innumerable paths with which they are intersected but thought it better not! On the way home we met a man - an army doctor - & his wife who C. knew in India! He is quartered up here & of course was much surprised to see C. as C. was to see him!

November 21st. Saturday - Got up about 6 o'clock this morning, packed, had breakfast & started soon after 8. We were really sorry to leave - Newara Eliya is the most charming place & we had a most delightful week there - The hotel is one of the best we have "struck" - Excellent food & very comfortable in every way - It wasn't so very hot in the train even nearing Colombo as it was a cloudy sort of day with even some rain. It was most interesting travelling thro' the same country we had passed before, recognising it all as we went - The chief excitement being a talipot palm in flower which we had noticed on the way up & wanted to see again - Even coming down we had to go very slowly owing to the many curves & had to have 2 engines to steady the train. One trembles to think of what wd. happen if it "got away"! The precipices in parts are absolutely sheer down, 100's of feet! We had tea & high mountains to look at first, gradually getting into the tropical forests & rice fields until at last we were on the level again & were able to rattle into Colombo where there were violent showers of rain which cooled the air - otherwise we sd. have felt it very hot coming straight down from the hills - I enjoyed the journey enormously, it was so interesting seeing all the country again. We got in at 5.40 to learn that the Bülow had not yet been sighted but was expected any hour - She didn't get in till about 9 o'clock, very annoying as we had meant to go on board at once - Instead we had to go to the Grand Oriental Hotel for the night - It is quite close to the harbour & is supposed to be the swagger hotel of Columbo but it isn't half so good as the Galle Face - During the evening it simply poured with rain - I've never seen anything like it - In 2 minutes the streets were swimming & the poor rickshaw men with their one thin garment drenched & looking perfectly miserable - Got the Field, The Overland Mail & Carlisle Patriot this afternoon so devoured them all evening!

November 22nd. Sunday - The luggage had to go at 8 so we had to be up "betimes" to have it ready - The Bülow was due to sail at 10 so we just had time for breakfast & to visit Cooks for letters etc: before we went on board, going off in the Company's tender - We have got a rather bigger cabin, an outside one which is a great advantage but on the lowest deck so it is quite an expedition to get there! We cd. see the coast of Ceylon until about 6 o'clock - The first part we passed quite close & cd. distinguish the Galle Face Hotel & Mount Lavinia - The hills towering up behind looked lovely tho' there were clouds over the highest so we cd.n't recognise Pidurntalagala - which was very sad! I wd. like to have seen him again - This boat seems to be better than the Göben, cleaner & better food - We sit next to the purser who talks English fluently but is rather difficult to understand -

4
Singapore - Shanghai

November 23rd. Monday - It seems very funny to be back on the sea once more & its extraordinary how different one feels at once. Not at all a nice feeling especially after our splendid time in Ceylon! No, I do not like the sea tho' I daresay I shall get used to it again in a day or two - Its such a lazy loafing sort of life - This boat is sister ship to the Göben so is exactly like her - The passengers are much the same tho' quieter & don't seem to go in for sports, or gaieties of that sort - not even sweepstakes, which they had every day on the Göben & which we never won! We quite miss our friend - Mrs. "Hong Kong" - who always used to sit in the same place - There seems to be nobody on this boat to speak to - not even a horse! Only 2 pointers & a setter in kennels right up in the 3rd. class who we discovered in our walk yesterday & a tiny dackshund puppy in a box - We always go for a walk soon after 5 & pace up & down till dinner at 6 - Its an awful wrench to get up & do it but one certainly feels all the better for it. We went thro' another large shoal of porpoises this evening, also saw some more flying fish - Otherwise the day passed off without any excitements - There was a good breeze blowing which made it very nice on deck but it is still frightfully hot below & the fans work continuously - This is a much better cleaner boat than the Göben - The food is really quite good, tho' of course still very "German- y" - There are any amount of children on board & a dreadful fat German baby with a voice like a bull - & it knows how to use it too!

November 24th. Tuesday - Began to write letters for Xmas to be posted at Singapore - With this, reading & our usual afternoon sleep from after lunch till 3 o'clock & "exercise" from about 5 till 6 got thro' the day quite successfully! The 1st. class had a fancy dress dance & went thro' the ship in procession - They did look such asses! Even the captain was dressed up - Most undignified! There was a good head breeze all day & several little showers of rain so it was quite nice & cool. The people on this boat aren't nearly so entertaining as those on the Göben & we haven't even got names for them! A lot of them seem to be getting off at Penang so we shall soon have more room - There are 95 2nd. class passengers on board whereas the Göben had 110 - 15 doesn't seem to make much difference tho' -

November 25th. Wednesday - Got up this morning to see land out of the port hole! Most exciting - It was Sumatra. We cd.n't see it very distinctly but it appeared to be just like Ceylon - High & very jagged hills with a most luxuriant growth of trees covering them from the shore up to the very top. We had dinner at 5.30 this evening! It was what the chief steward called a "gala dinner" & was in honour of all the dutch who get off tomorrow at Penang - It seemed to us quite an ordinary dinner except that the stewards had decorated the saloon with green paper garlands & hung flags about & that the ice cream came in in the dark with a beautiful little tower on top lighted up with a candle inside! The "table-piece" a magnificent erection of macaroon stuck all over with flags & crackers was ruthlessly destroyed to eat with the ice! The dutch didn't seem much moved by the honour done them except to eat a hearty meal & then they all stuck cracker caps on their heads!

November 26th Thursday Got to Penang this morning about 6 o'clock. We were on deck almost as soon as she stopped - Three huge lighters came alongside at once & began to load with cargoe from the Bülow - Boxes & boxes of Swiss milk, small barrels & sacks of something or other - "Made in Germany" I suppose! We went ashore in the N.D.L. tender. There were heaps of little Chinese boats or sampans who wd. have liked to have taken us but they were bobbing about in such a truely nasty manner in the "choppy" little harbour that we preferred the steadier steamer! Penang swarms with life - as all these Eastern towns seem to do & in the streets one sees Chinese, Malays & Singalese - Of course we were instantly besieged by rickshaws! They are bigger than the Ceylon ones & have the most beautiful designs of birds & branches painted on their backs & are drawn by Chinese with thin pigtails tied up in a knot behind & wearing enormous great straw hats made without any distinction between the brim & crown - It is a very smelly town & frightfully hot. We soon got tired of walking about so, on the advice of an English shop-keeper who we found & consulted in Whiteaway Laidlaw's - a big firm in the East who have shops at all these places - we took rickshaws & drove to the Gardens. It took about 1/2 an hour & was a most delightful drive - First thro' streets with shops, the names being written up in Chinese characters. Any Chinese writing is lovely & these, generally in a sort of dull gold were beautiful & I thought quite "made" the place. After a bit we got out more into the country & went on lovely shady roads thro' cocoa- nut plantations & past charming looking Chinese bungalows each standing in its own garden - The most of them had such lovely gate-ways - Beautifully designed stone ones with a most charming beast of sorts sitting on the top painted in really good colours - The gardens are lovely - We stayed there about an hour wandering about & looking at all the different things - They are all labelled like at Perideniya so it makes it most interesting - We recognised quite a lot of old friends we knew in Ceylon & were quite pleased with ourselves but there were dozens of new ones we'd never heard of before which filled us with dismay! Its hopeless to try & learn them all, unless one was staying in the country for months - These are particularly pretty gardens I think - Beautifully laid out & kept, lying in a valley with a very good waterfall crashing down the hill just above & a burn winding thro' them with little bridges & glorious sort of iris' - red & yellow growing on the banks. We had a rest on a seat under the shade of a mango tree for it was very hot walking inspite of quite a good breeze which was blowing & ought to have made it cooler & then drove back. Chinese rickshaw coolies are much bigger & look much stronger than Singalese ones therefore one feels rather more humane! Ours ran all the way there & all the way back - They got frightfully hot poor dears but otherwise didn't seem to mind - Both going & coming we passed endless streams of traffic, very much the same sort of things as in Ceylon & yet quite different - They vary from bullock carts to motor cars. A drive thro' these places is the best thing one can do I think. One can see so much more of the life & the people & everything that way. We had lunch at the Railway Hotel (recommended by the man at Whiteaway Laidlaw, & very good it was too!) The odd part was there didn't appear to be a railway within miles & it was not an hotel - only a restaurant! It wasn't quite 12 & yet having had breakfast before 7 we were quite hungry & "made" an excellent lunch - Afterwards we sauntered slowly down to the quay, followed by a procession of rickshaws - they seem to think it impossible for white people to walk a step! - & went off to the ship in a little British tender. A sister & clergyman who are on board were being taken off in her by a friend who most kindly offered to take us too - We were just in time to see the lighters being towed away to the shore by a little steam tug loaded with cargoe from the Bülow & dozens of jabbering & apparently irritated Malays. Natives always sound as tho' they were exasperated beyond words when for ought one knows they are having the most amicable conversation! Penang is a very pretty little harbour - One can see hills almost all round, up behind the town which is on an island, on the mainland & on Sumatra - Some lovely sampans came sailing in while we were waiting to start - It was a very hot evening & at night there was a tremendous storm of rain & lightning that seemed to come straight in at the porthole & lit up the whole cabin - Thank goodness it made no difference to the sea which remained quite calm!

November 27th Friday - Wrote dozens of letters & post cards to post at Singapore to arrive home by Xmas. It has been fearfully hot all day, not a breath of wind - Of course we are very close to the Equator now which accounts for the heat. Dreadful fuss on deck all day with people who are going to get off tying up & labelling their chairs & making themselves thoroughly uncomfortable long before they need! We have been in sight of land all day, either the coast, most mountainous (one exactly the shape of Criffel but round the wrong way as tho' in a looking glass!) & thickly wooded islands. Are now in sight of Singapore! 3.30.

S.S. Bülow

27.11.08

Well my child & so here am I writing what is called a Xmas letter - Oh my dear I do hope it won't be a very trying time & yet no I can't think it is extra beastly now-a-days as it used to be - I expect you'll get this a day or two after, we're going to post letters at Singapore where we get this evening. It has been very hot since leaving Penang & will be until we get round Singapore & begin going north. Fancy I haven't written to you since Newara Eliya & we've now been more than 5 days on this bally old boat. I whisper it to you but no one else - & have not mentioned it in my diary - but I didn't go down for lunch the first day! I wasn't sick but felt a tiny bit queer having spent a good deal of time unpacking in our cabin & got very hot & had to come up on deck somewhat hastily & sit down in the air when I speedily recovered - The first day or two I think one does feel pretty rocky - I can't imagine anybody enjoying a voyage - of course I did myself at first but then that was only because it was all so new. This is a far better boat than the Goeben & really the food is quite eatable if only it wasn't at such queer hours - Lunch at 12 & dinner at 6 really is un peu trop fort! The only thing is we can go to bed about 9 or even before! One seems to want a lot of sleep on the sea, anyhow we're always quite ready for it! The people on this boat aren't the least amusing, only quite impossible - Theres not one that one w^d.n't^ much rather not talk to except the purser who we sit beside & converse with - The 1st. class people look almost as bad so I don't think we miss much by not being there. Penang was an awfully nice place & a sort of "first view" of China - Everything reminded me so of San Toy! I think China is going to be a fascinating place - I am so looking forward to getting there - Which we will in 10 days, thank goodness! Just fancy being quit of this old ship & go on shore for quite a long time! Remember we'll be in Pekin for Xmas so you can think of me there but goodness knows what it will be like, that I can't tell you till I've been there. I am yearning for your letters at Shanghai - with accounts of hunting I hope & no more thoughts of being too tired to enjoy it. We bought a lot of p.c's in Penang which we are sending round as Xmas cards. The one I have sent to "the girls" gives one quite a good idea but photographs aren't much good - I've taken very few myself, somehow the camera is never there just when one wants it & is much too heavy to lug about with one always, in these hot climes which we have been frequenting - It will be different in China where "they" say it will be fearfully cold - I hope so anyhow - it will be a "nice change" - We have brought far too many clothes - One doesnt do eno' to get really dirty - I have only worn one of the old "piquers" - & most suitable it was too & the green that White made me - It certainly is a bit grubby now but whats the good of being spotlessly clean on a boat & it is such a fag getting anything out as there isn't room in a cabin to unpack properly. Before getting off at Shanghai we have got to have a real old "sort" of all our clothes, getting out nothing but thick things - & as little as possible, sending all the rest on to Yokohama to pick up when we get there - Well my childie so long in the meantime - I'm so hot I can write no more, also I think there's no more to say

Bless you forever & ever my child

Toujours à toi

D

And had I forgotten the dog. No I had not - I was thinking of it repeatedly & wishing it well. Kiss its face most warmly from its other twin. It was such a lillikins pop & this twin thinks of it many times & knows it is being a real comfort to the other -

The Season's Greetings again my child with all my heart. I am sure we shall be going to church in Pekin so you go too & we'll both do our best to really pray -

Hong Kong Hotel
Dec: 4th. 1908

Chérie I must write you one line from here to let you know I'm still alive. There is no diary to send you this time for lately I've not been able to write it! Oh my dear after we left Singapore!! We were in the N.E. Monsoon & misery simply wasn't in it. I never in my life was so miserable. It lasted 4 days without ceasing & seemed to get worse & worse. The first 2 days I struggled on deck being literally dressed by my good good C. who mercifully wasn't the least sick himself, but the two last days I stayed in bed & just existed! Take my advice & never go to sea. It is the most foul invention - I haven't seen the funny side of it yet (perhaps there isn't one) & still think of it quite gravely. Oh how glad I was to get on shore yesterday but for hours after everything rocked & swayed just like the boat. I tell you a monsoon is just the divil - One wd. think the boat must break in half. The worst of it is, this afternoon we've got to begin again - they say it will be just as bad going to Shanghai but thank the Lord not so long - Oh heavens how pleased I shall be when we are quit of these d-d ships! Our latest plan is to go from Shanghai to Ichang up the Yangzte (another boat by the way but a river not the sea!) where we can get a house boat & get some shooting - (I think this part will be ripping) Then we go back to Shanghai & get another German ship & go to Yokohama, stay in Japan 6 or 8 weeks, then across to Tientsin to Pekin & the battlefields & thence home via Siberia. We spent hours with Cook yesterday & this new plan was the up-shot of it - The man said Pekin wd. be so unbearably cold just now that we ought to leave it till the end & go to Japan now having first had our little trip up the Yangzte. Its an awful pity that our letters have of course gone to Pekin however it only means we'll get them forwarded a day or two later. We like this place very much. Its so nice to be back into warm clothes again & see fires. It was too hot for words at Singapore & in the monsoon for we had to keep our port-hole shut in the end & nearly died. It was open & a wave came bang in - "Gosh" was all C. said with much emphasis as he sprang to his feet to shut it! He hated it all as much as I did poor dear, even tho' he wasn't sick. Hour after hour did he sit there - Impossible to read or write or do anything - walking of course out of the question. He & the purser & one rock of a woman were the only people as a rule at our table & there are generally 17! We went to Jardine Matheson's this morning to see if we cd. find John Johnstone but he is still at home - Huge grubby looking offices. C. has now gone to see a General Broadwood up at Government House who he was with in South Africa & who has lately "done" the battlefields & may be able to put us up to some tips - I am writing in this big hotel - where we had excellent lunch & dinner yesterday, then we are going to have lunch here & go on board again sailing at 2! Isn't it a perfect mercy that things do come to an end? Really if I thought I s^d. always have to toss about in the old Buelow I w^d. shoot myself - I w^d. I swear I w^d. & am not being like Arthur Broadhurst! I wonder if you w^d. be sick too? Yes, I'm certain you w^d. I really don't know why or how people aren't! They must have insides like leather! This letter is full of sea-sickness I'm afraid but its the thing uppermost in my mind & I cannot get it out!!

Yesterday afternoon we went to see our friend M^rs. "Hong Kong" from the Goeben! It was so nice seeing her again & we met as the greatest of friends! I told you her husband was in the navy didn't I? She used to know Eustace Leatham years ago. I believe his ship was at Singapore just before or after us - It w^d. be nice if we were to fall in with him somewhere also Albert. I have told the latter to write to me in case we s^d. be anywhere about but China is such a very huge place I s^d. think the chance is remote. I long to hear about Xmas & oh to hear how you are getting on petite - Never mind I'll get a letter on Monday at Shanghai. This is Friday so thats not so very long now - The number of things I thought of lying sick & motionless those 4 days! The pleasantest & the one I forced to come when I felt more than ordinarily as tho' I was going to die was hunting, Houghton & Irish Mail's face looking thro' her bridle at me! It comforted me greatly! In Hong Kong there is no such thing as horse traffic - Isn't it funny? The only bit of horse-flesh I've seen was a roan pony evidently a racing one being led along in a rug! We went to "The Country Girl" last night! done by amateurs! It was quite good. If you please Desmond Maxwell R.N. was in the caste! I c^d.n't recognize him tho' Really the smallness of the world! Well, bless you & the dog forever & ever Amen

Yrs forever

D -

November 27th. *(continued from previous instalment)* - The entrance to Singapore is intersected with islands of all sizes, thickly wooded - We had to thread our way amongst them, sometimes seeming perilously close - We were taken in by a pilot - The harbour is a very big one & enclosed by all these islands is a very pretty one - There was any amount of shipping lying there. We got alongside the wharf about 5 o'clock & went ashore as soon as they got out the gangway. As the ship steamed slowly in - to the music of the brass band as usual! They always play the same old thing very loud & brassy, we know it so well & are sick of it! - a regular flotilla of small canoes bore down upon us each with a Malay boy in it, paddling along for dear life, jabbering & shouting, asking for money to be thrown for them to dive for - as soon as the money was thrown, they dived as quick as lightning & always returned with the coin between their teeth & struck out for the canoe, which in the meantime had been left to itself, scrambled in & were clammering for more - They were most amusing to watch - The town is 2¼ miles from the wharf where the Bülow was. We started to walk but even at that hour of the evening it was very hot & tiring so we were glad to get into a tram which came up behind us - it went thro' streets that oddly eno' reminded us of Genoa, the houses are painted in rather the same way & have outside shutters, but there the resemblance ends! We went to the Post Office where we posted 15 letters & 25 post cards! our Xmas correspondence! By the time we had finished sticking on all the stamps it was quite dark so we went to the Hotel de l'Europe & read the Singapore paper & some ancient - tho' latest - English illustrated papers till 7-30 when we had dinner - It was very hot reading but the dining room was nice & cool. The waiters were all Chinese. Ours was quite a little boy with the most innocent face I've ever seen! We went back to the ship about 9-30 & found perfect pandemonium going on - They were coaling & unloading cargoe! Anything like the noise I've never heard - Every man seemed to be shouting at the top of his voice added to the deafening din of the capstan working the crane & every now & then a most almighty crash as they dropped an enormous sheet of cast iron on to the top of a pile they were making of it - there was a long corrugated iron shed alongside which echoed & resounded with the whole thing which made matters worse! I didn't think it was possible for human beings to make such a dreadful noise!

November 28th Saturday - We had an awful night! The heat was appalling & the noise continued without ceasing all night - in fact until we sailed! The pile of cast iron was conveniently placed just outside our port-hole, which we had to have open or we wd. have suffocated, so we got the full benefit of that & what with all the other noises & horrors we had a most dreadful time & not much sleep - We were by way of sailing at 11 so there wasn't much time to do more than take the same tram back to the town where we walked about looking at the sights - The cabs (or gharrys) are the same here as at Penang, funny sort of little things with windows all round & no box for the driver - I think he sits on the shaft, & drawn by ponies about 12 hands high - Some of them are real rippers & trot along at a tremendous pace with their little heads tucked in in spite of the load which sometimes looks a lot for a small pony - Singapore is a very busy & prosperous town & has its streets watered by a motor water cart! We felt as tho' we were back in London again except for the rickshaws & the scores of Chinamen who might have stepped straight out of San Toy! We didn't sail till about 1 which was most annoying as we might have had plenty of time to see the sights, however there was lots to see on the wharf & we sat & watched it all - They were selling boat loads of shells & corals besides hundreds of other things - We threaded our way out to sea amongst all the islands again - It was fearfully hot until suddenly it began to blow & it got much cooler when we got round the point -

<u>November 29th Sunday</u> - }
<u>November 30th Monday</u> - } In the N.E. Monsoon -
<u>December 1st Tuesday</u> - } = <u>MISERY</u> =
<u>December 2nd Wednesday</u>- }

<u>December 3rd Thursday</u> - Far less motion this morning when we woke up for we were nearing Hong Kong. (Oh! how we have longed & prayed for this day!) We got in about 11-30 & went on shore at once. The N.D.L. wharf is at Kow-loon which is on the mainland - Hong Kong being an island we had to go across the harbour to get there - It was good to be on dry land again but one seemed to feel the motion of the sea for ages which was most trying - We had lunch at the Hong Kong hotel & then had a long talk with Cook about our future plans & got them all fixed up. After this we went to see our Göben friend Mrs. "Hong Kong" (her real name is Knott!) She was staying at the Peak hotel. The hotel is on the top of a steep hill which towers up behind the town called the Peak. To get there we went up a perfectly perpendicular tram- way! It was a very dull day so we cd.n't see very far but the view over the harbour was lovely - Any amount of Ships were lying there with Chinese Sampans & Junks by the 100. After leaving the tram we walked to the top of the Peak to see the view - It was beautifully cool, & a great contrast to the last place we were ashore at - It rained a little part of the time which made us feel quite at home - It wd. have been a delightful walk if my legs had not felt so shakey! Coming down was a work of pain & danger! We found Mrs. Hong Kong at home & she gave us tea & we had a long talk - When we left her we went down in the tram again & walked about looking at the shops a little until it was time for dinner which we had at the same hotel - A great peculiarity of the streets here is that there is absolutely no horse traffic! Everything is done by coolies instead - They carry things at each end of a long bamboo pole over their shoulders & most uncomfortable & painful it looks too when the load is a heavy one - The men & women all dress alike in baggy trousers & coats - The women work with very often a baby strapped to their backs who don't seem to mind in the least tho' it looks dreadfully uncomfortable! Rickshaws & sort of chairs slung between 2 poles & carried on the shoulders of a couple of coolies take the place of cabs - There are some very fine buildings in Hong Kong & seemed any amount of others in course of construction - scaffolding in every direction - The streets are very full & busy & it seems a most lively place - In the evening we went to a performance of The Country Girl at the theatre by an American Company - They really did it very well & it was most amusing - It didn't begin till 9 o'clock & went on for hours & hours so that even tho' we didn't stay to the end we just caught the 12.30 ferry back to Kow-loon & the old Bülow!

December 4th Friday - Had a splendid peaceful night, inspite of the fact that they were unloading cargo - It was such a blessing not to have that everlasting pitching & tossing! We went back to the town again soon after beakfast going across the harbour on the ferry - There are 4 of our battle ships there also 2 Germans - The latter are painted dazzling white with yellow funnels & don't look nearly so business-like as the British grey - The whole harbour swarms with Chinese junks which luxuriously make their way in & out amongst the other ships with 2 men or in many cases women standing up to each oar with another oar behind to steer by - Outside the harbour they sail & look lovely with their brown or dirty white & much patched sails. Whole families live on board, the junks being their only home - They look so dirty & uncomfortable & bob about in the most dreadful way but I suppose the people are quite used to it & wd. probably miss the motion! Theres no accounting for tastes! C. went to try & find a friend of his - General Broadwood - who is here but having tracked him over half the town unfortunately found he was out - In the meantime I stayed at the hotel & wrote letters - We had already been to Jardine Mathison's office to try & find John Johnstone but he is still at home - The Office is a huge dingy place on the quay - We had rather a hasty lunch & caught the 1-30 ferry back to the ship - She hooted in the most alarming way just as we got out of the ferry - We thought she was off so tore along amongst the trucks & cranes & coolies & other "impedimenta" of the wharf - where it is not easy to hurry - However it was a false alarm as she didn't sail for another 20 mins or so. We went out the opposite way to which we had come in sailing between the Island of Hong Kong & the mainland - It is quite a narrow channel so we cd. see both sides - It looked a bleak rocky sort of coast & reminded us of Cornwall! When we got outside there was a strong wind blowing & it got quite cold but thank goodness quite a nice calm sea still!

December 5th Saturday - A lovely day with a bright sun but necessary to have coats on when sitting on deck as it is beginning to get quite cold. We slept with blankets & no fan going the first time for many a long day - We got thro' the dreaded Formosa Channel in splendid weather - We were by way of having another monsoon here & everybody made their preparations according before starting expecting as bad or worse than we had getting to Hong Kong - But thank goodness it was perfectly all right! We passed any amount of junks out at sea fishing & nets on bamboo poles apparently floating about by themselves!

December 6th Sunday - Another splendid calm day so that we shall be at Shanghai early tomorrow morning & all our troubles at an end! (in the meantime!) All yesterday & today we kept getting glimpses of China but too far off to distinguish anything except that it appeared very mountainous - We came thro' perfect fleets of fishing junks sometimes passing so close that we cd. see everybody on board & the family washing hung up to dry! They are really lovely boats but preserve me from having to live in one! They had a service on board this morning. The Bishop of Mid-China preached - All the passengers on this boat seem to be missionaries - We have made several friends & some of them are very nice especially a Miss Brooks. She was one of the very few who remained quite well in the monsoon & seemed to look after all the other wretched sea-sick people in the most noble manner - two of the men missionaries wear Chinese clothes with their heads shaved in front & long pigtails just like Chinese men - It does look so funny - They are most interesting to talk to & all seem so keen & interested in their work. Its extraordinary to think that this is our last day on the Bülow - If it hadn't been for her behaviour in the monsoon I s[d.] feel quite sorry to leave her - far more so than the Göben - The Bülow is certainly a far nicer boat, better stewards & 50 times cleaner - We got to the mouth of the Yang-tze Kiang at 10 o'clock tonight - We steamed slowly up the river till past 1 when we anchored -

December 7[th.] Monday - Got up at 7 this morning & had breakfast as the tender to take us to Shanghai was expected any moment - The big boats have to stop right outside & it takes about 2 hours up the Whampoo in a small steamer to get to Shanghai. It was a perfect sight to see the mails being put on the tender as soon as she came alongside - There were 400 bags stacked high on the well-deck of the Bülow - It was extraordinary the way the sailors & Chinamen from the tender hurled them into the smaller boat, at a tremendous pace & until they were streaming heat in spite of the fact that there was quite a cold wind blowing & a real frosty feeling in the air. All the passengers went in the tender, the luggage following in 2 huge lighters which were towed up by a fussy little tug apparently laden with blue-clad coolies - Where they were going to put the luggage I don't know but it did all come eventually, 2 or 3 hours after we did - It was most interesting coming along up the river - The country is very flat & was looking most autumnal - It somehow reminded one of bits round about Houghton! The river was crowded with junks & as it was a lovely fine morning with the sun shining it all looked lovely & made a splendid introduction to Shanghai! We got to the landing place about 10.30. The last part of the way was past busy wharfs & ware-houses with all sorts of boats & steamers waiting beside them - One might almost have been on the Thames! We are staying at the Astor House Hotel - We walked here on landing & took our room - The streets are rather dirty but good wide ones & very busy - The coolie class all seem to wear butcher blue clothes & pile them on one on top of the other, very ragged & dirty looking. I suppose its to try & keep warm but they all look miserably cold inspite of it - We had to go to the N.D.L. Office to get our luggage - when it came, & see about booking places to go home that way so that with lunch in between there wasn't time for much more - C. has got a bad cold in his head so we didn't go out again after unpacking. This seems a very nice comfortable hotel - They are building on to it in front so it is not looking its best. While working the coolies chant the weirdest sort of little song - We stood & listened to them for some time but c[d.n't] catch the tune - One c[d.] imagine a Tchaichouski Suite written on it!

The food is excellent here & we are waited on by nice Chinese boys. "Boy" is the name given to any servant. He may be as old as the hills & yet he is still "boy" - This was the same in Ceylon - They don't make quite such quick attentive waiters as the Singalese but they're very good all the same - We bade the purser of the Bülow quite a touching farewell this morning! with many promises not to forget the Bülow (I'm not likely to in a hurry!) & hopes of meeting again! (Five minutes later we <u>did</u> meet again in the Office which somewhat marred the effect!)

Astor House Hotel, Shanghai

7 - 12 - 08

My dear, your last 2 letters! How can I describe how I loved them nay adored them, fairly revelled in them!! They arrived when we were in bed! We got to the mouth of the Yang- tse about 10 o'clock when the pilot came on board & brought the letters with him - We were not aware of this fact so were peacefully sleeping - or nearly so when there came a knock at the door & here if you please were bundles of letters! It was thrillingly exciting & we stayed up for ages reading them & then didn't get to sleep for hours with the excitement! I hunted hard till I did go to sleep as you can imagine & thought "horse thoughts" till I thought I s^d. never stop. I had your 2 letters one from Mum & one from Mog - If you write either of them thank them muchly from me & tell them how I loved their letters - Dearest I perfectly lived with you whilst perusing those letters & have read & re-read them many times - We're not going to stay here very long but are going up the Yang-tze to shoot - It will be such a lark! Its nice & cold here. Its much nicer than heat, theres no doubt. I wore knickerbockers & black petticoat with thankfulness. Poor dear C. has got a bad cold in his head, started it on the boat for some reason or another & is very stuffed up today & pretty miserable I'm afraid but lets hope it will soon pass off. Fancy you going to Ireland & me been "picturing" you at Houghton all this time! I <u>do</u> hope you weren't sick going over & that you enjoyed it & that it was worth giving up those 2 meets. This by the way is a New Year letter I suppose - My darling girl, as you know you have <u>more</u> than my <u>good</u> wishes for it - It will be a real happy time for you when I come home anyway, that simply goes without saying - Sometimes just <u>long</u> for the time to come, do you know - I so look forward to it! As to C. he positively <u>yearns</u> for Wreay Sike at times! You like me to tell you that I simply adore him don't you? You see I c^d.n't tell anybody else in the same way & I love to tell you things from my inmost heart. He is such a darling & never changes in the least tho' he is a fussy packer, theres no doubt of that but its wonderful how I bear with him! (Plenty of practise with Mog has perhaps made it easier!) I am going to wash my head tomorrow! Ships & the Colombo railways have made it simply filthy. My brush in spite of repeated washings is black so its high time I did it. We have almost booked seats in the Trans-Siberian railway in April which will bring us to Victoria on Tuesday April 27th. at 7 in the evening! I hope it doesn't seem very far off to you. C. will be out with the Yeomanry the first fortnight in May so DayNin *will have a good time together & talk till they're silly, just won't they? And now I die of fatigue & must to bed & finish in the morning -*

Bonsoir petite -

C. has got the deuce of a heavy cold in his head poor dear. Last night he had a boiling hot bath & a whisky toddy & got boiling hot so I think he's better this morning. A heavy cold is such a beastly thing & apparently he gets very heavy ones - We have a bath-room attached to our room which is very nice. The sanitary arrangements in these hotels is of the sketchiest order! C. says it is the same in India. Its a wonder it isn't unhealthy but apparently it isn't. Well, dearie you'll hear from me again very soon I think. We are going to find out for sure at the post office but C. thinks you ought to be able to get plenty of letters from this place via Siberia -

Well, so long my child - Very best love from the T.B. (poor old sniffly thing)

Yrs forever & beyond it

D -

5
Shanghai - The Yangtse Gorges

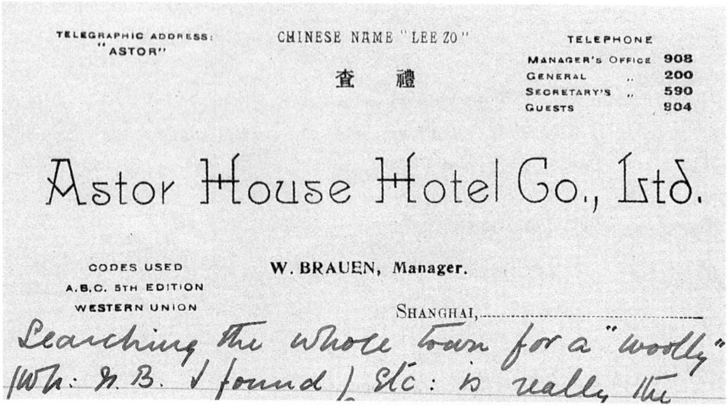

TELEGRAPHIC ADDRESS: "ASTOR"

CHINESE NAME "LEE ZO"

查 禮

TELEPHONE
MANAGER'S OFFICE 908
GENERAL ,, 200
SECRETARY'S ,, 590
GUESTS 904

Astor House Hotel Co., Ltd.

CODES USED
A.B.C. 5TH EDITION
WESTERN UNION

W. BRAUEN, Manager.

SHANGHAI, ...

Searching the whole town for a "woolly" (Wh: N.B. I found) Etc: is really the

Astor House Hotel, Shanghai

10. 12. 08

Well, doubtless you'll be quite pleased to get another letter so soon! I shall get one this evening! The one following on from Colombo. You can't think how I'm looking forward to it! Shanghai is a most interesting place in which to study Chinese life for the streets simply teem with it & in a few minutes walk you see eno' strange sights to fill a book - London streets have always fascinated us so you can imagine how interesting this is when it is all so new - Otherwise there is not much to do here - No regular "sights" - at least we haven't discovered any - Tomorrow night we start on our expedition up the Yangtze - This I am looking forward to immensely - We go in a Jardine Matheson steamer & when we were in there having some difficulty seeing about it all with nobody but a Chinese clerk we asked what Dumfriesshire people were in the office & were told Mr. Landale! Of course I knew of him tho' I didn't know if he'd remember me however I thought I might trade on coming from Dumfie & sort of half knowing his wife - "Winnie Fortune" - so we asked to see him - We were taken to his office - of course he didn't know the name but we sort of half recognized each other - I murmured something about having met before, Johnstone Douglas & he knew at once - He was most helpful, in fact it wd. have been very difficult to do anything without his assistance - You must get a map & see where we are going - The first part to Hankow we do in a steamer taking 4 days (Dec: 20th.) - At Ichang we hire a house boat, a thing with 2 little rooms. They provide us with food & an English speaking servant & we shall be quite independent & "on our own" which I think will be ripping. C. is taking a gun & hopes to have heaps of shooting which of course is all free & consists of pheasants, snipe, duck etc: in abundance so they say but of course that remains to be seen! If it is good & we are having a rattling good time & not too cold we will probably stay there but in the meantime the plan is to catch another of the N.D.L. steamers here on Jan: 4th. & go to Yokohama - You see our N.D.L. tickets take us as far as Yokohama for no extra charge so why not use them? They only go every fortnight so we must either go by the o ne on the 4th. which means leaving Ichang on the 28th. & wd. only give us 8 days on the house boat or wait for the next but we can't decide which to do till we see how we get on. Mrs. Landale was in the office when we were there so he went off to get her & she expressed great pleasure & surprise to see me, said she'd seen about our wedding & promptly asked us to dinner! We are going tonight & thoroughly bored at the prospect I am too tho' I daresay it will be perfectly alright - I think those Fortunes all seem nice - He seems a shy little man & may perhaps be hard work but no matter! They are sending their carriage for us which is very kind but the horror of it is how are we going to get away? We can't very well order our host's carriage when we want it. What is the correct thing to do under the circumstance? We have been shopping all morning - Trailing about in that most dreadfully tiring way so that I feel quite tired this afternoon & have let C. go off to see about leaving some of our luggage etc: by himself & am writing to you up in our room in a very comfortable chair with my feet on another feeling an awful slacker at not going out but I am tired. I suppose its silly not to own it whether there's a reason for it or not - wh: there isn't - except that shopping - searching the whole town for a "wooly" (wh: N.B. I found) etc: is really the deuce isn't it? C. always gets into a long conversation with the shopman! & a terrible lot of information he gets out of them too. A man in the bank told us all about the money, an american in the Kodak shop gave us a vast amount of information about the sale of magazines & the art of advertising while the man in the cartridge place gave us the account of his shooting experiences in the places we are going to! He was a Scotchman too whats more & such a nice man! I have bought such a nice blue tammy. Exactly like the red ones we used to wear - I had to have a cap of sorts & this was all I cd. find. I feel like 15 when I put it on! C.'s cold is quite alright again - At least he still blows his nose & snuffles (not to mention snoring of course eno' to waken the dead!) but the misery of it & the aches & pains have quite left him & thank goodness I have not caught it. It does vex me so to think that we have not been able to keep to our original plans & that therefore we shan't get letters as early as we ought but we will get them eventually of course forwarded from Pekin & it just can't be helped - Pekin wd. have been too cold for pleasure at this time of year - Instead of being at Pekin for Xmas we shall be in our house-boat! Well dearie so long in the meantime - I'm not sure that this hasn't to be posted tonight, if not until tomorrow I will be able to add to it & tell you about our dinner party. I put on my black dress for the first time! Poor thing, it will be pleased. Its not getting much improved by constant packing! Fondest remembrances to the Pip - The pips here all wear muzzles - such a shame.

Well, now I must stop - Ten thousand blessings down on you fall -

Best love from the T.B. - Toujours à toi

11. 12. 08

We were terrible lothe to dine out yesterday but were rewarded by really enjoying ourselves very much, such is often the way! "Winnie" & I discussed Dumfriesshire people & entertained each other vastly! She remembered us going over to Blackwood that time & the fancy dress party at Newton & seemed so interested in recalling it all! A real nice creature - They sent a carriage with a swiftly trotting little white China pony - We are to go this afternoon to see their ponies. Apparently they keep a lot for racing so it will be very nice. The post is just going so if you want to get this I must stop -

Yrs

D -

December 8th Tuesday - In spite of boiling hot bath & whiskey toddy C's cold was very bad today - We went out for a short time this morning but there was a very cold wind which made him worse so he stayed in the rest of the day & we had a fire in our room to see if that wd. do any good. The reading room of the hotel is a most cheerless place & the draughts in the passages & on the stairs are something dreadful - I had a walk in the afternoon to return some papers to the Trans-Siberian railway office - It was really very nice out & reminded me of an autumn day in London, just the same sort of grey look & cold atmosphere - Well to do Chinamen have their clothes padded or lined with fur & seem to keep more or less warm but the poorer ones look wretched - They don't seem to have warm clothes but heap on veritable rags of cotton instead until they look like walking rag bags with drawn faces & hands "muffled" in their sleeves - The women's feet are simply too dreadful for anything - They are not like feet at all & make me feel quite ill. The poor things can't walk, they just totter along in the most top-heavy painful way - They all wear trousers! The wheel-barrows they use here are rather nice - They have one large wheel in the middle with a sort of little platform on each side of it on which they put the load & I sd. think have to balance it pretty well or they'd be sure to upset - Sometimes you'll see one man wheeling 3 or 4 others when he doesn't happen to have anything else! The loads some of them take are something enormous, staggering & straining under the weight - If a horse was so over-loaded in England, the driver wd. be had up for cruelty to animals pretty quick! Horses are only used for cabs & carriages here & they aren't really horses, only ponies - Some quite nice ones but others most awful old crocks poor dears - Shanghai is divided up into different concessions leased from China to the various powers. This hotel is in the American part.

December 9th Wednesday - C's cold very much better this morning so we went out soon after breakfast to arrange about the trip we are going to take up to the Yang-tze gorges. The steamers belong to Jardine Matheson so when at the office we asked what Dumfriesshire people belonging to the company were at Shanghai. The clerk told us Mr. Landale was here so, as I knew him we asked to see him & were ushered into his private office - He said he knew me at once for a Johnstone Douglas & he was most kind & helpful & took no end of trouble & had arranged everything for us when we went back in the afternoon - After our interview we went & got his wife who happened to be in the place & she & I met as old friends! I don't believe I've spoken to her since the days of tennis parties at Gribton in the year 1 when she was "Winnie Fortune" but that didn't matter! They asked us to dinner tomorrow night & were most friendly! We spent the afternoon in the Bond Street of Shanghai looking at the Shops! There are a lot of European ones but lower down they become entirely Chinese & are most picturesque. Every sign is a work of art, gilt with black lettering & there are just dozens of them - In some of the narrow side streets they jut out over the pavement & almost meet in the middle of the street! Very often the outside of the building is most gorgeously decorated & painted & has the quaintest roof - The colours are always good & not a bit gaudy - The people themselves never seem to wear bright colours but nearly always dress in black or blue of different shades. The children are most awfully innocent looking people with their ugly little flattened faces! C. ordered a suit from a Chinese tailor, to be copied from a flannel one of his own - The tailor was a most charming person & talked pidgin English which is most fascinating but difficult to understand - The clothes are to be ready in 2 days which seems extraordinarily quick! It has been a cold raw sort of day & felt like snow. All the offices & bank that we have been into are tremendously heated up so one feels the cold all the more coming out of them -

<u>December 10th. Thursday</u> - The tailor arrived before breakfast ready to try on! He had to wait till C. was ready for him! The clothes seem to fit beautifully & are going to be a great success - We spent the whole morning shopping, getting things for our trip up the Yang-tze - It is very difficult to find exactly what one wants & they are very expensive - It was not nearly so cold today & the sun was shining in the morning - We dined with the Landales - We had an excellent dinner & enjoyed ourselves very much!

<u>December 11th. Friday</u> - Spent a most busy morning packing & preparing for our Yang-tze expedition - We have taken as little luggage as possible, only C's portmanteau, the big canvas bag with rugs, coats, cushions, etc: & gun case. The rest we are leaving at the hotel to pick up on our return - It was a horrid day, raining the whole time & the streets in a perfectly dreadful state - I never saw such mud, inches thick splashing in every direction - The coolies looked more wretched than ever under these circumstances, plastered with mud from head to foot but they make an attempt at keeping dry by holding up real Chinese umbrellas (like people put in their fire-places during the summer at home!) A whole lot of them were dragging a great big roller, mending the road straining & struggling with it & yet each carefully holding his umbrella over his head! It did look so ridiculous! We

had lunch very late & then went to Jardine Matheson's office where M$^{r.}$ Landale was ready to take us to see the racing ponies which they all keep by the dozen - He took us in his motor & whirled us along thro' the mud & the China-men, who are as bad as Carlisle loafers at getting out of the way! There were just dozens of ponies being walked round & round in a string by Chinese "mafoos", as they call the stable boys. The ponies are China ponies & come from Mongolia - They come down in large droves in very poor condition & ragged as bears - Even in good condition they are not much to look at coarse & ugly looking but for all that rather rippers - Some of them are not much more than 13 hands, the biggest ones being perhaps a little over 14 - M$^{r.}$ Landale told us their weight carrying prowess are enormous & that the best of them are very fast, tho' they certainly don't look it! The most usual colour is grey but the one that had won the biggest race was spotted, like a plum pudding dog! A truely innocent beast! They have a spring & an autumn meeting when the whole of Shanghai goes racing mad for 3 days - The offices & shops are all shut & the whole town takes a holiday - Mr. Landale also took us to their club, a great big comfortable building standing in quite a large garden. After this we went to their house & had tea when they insisted on sending us back in their carriage - It was pouring with rain & a perfectly horrible night so it was really most kind of them - We came on board the "Kutwo" at about 6.30 - We have a splendid cabin - a perfect palace in comparison with the Göben or Bülow! The other passengers did not come on board till much later but we were given an excellent dinner to ourselves - we went to bed about 10 o'clock - The boat was not due to start till 12 so there was much running about & excitement with luggage till a late hour -

<u>December 12$^{th.}$ Saturday</u> - It has been cold & grey all today with a good deal of rain at intervals - The first part was dull as the river was so broad we c$^{d.n't}$ see the banks but gradually it got narrower until at the end of the day we c$^{d.}$ see the banks on both sides - The water is brown & muddy with a very strong current - Junks going down simply fly past us while we seem to make slow progress against it - The country on both sides is very flat with any amount of trees - The colour today is quite lovely - Brown & grey & when a big junk in full sail comes along it is really beautiful - Unfortunately it was too cold to sit out so we had to spend a certain amount of time in the saloon - There is only one & as the boat is pretty full it is rather tiresome - All the people seem to be missionaries & dont look very promising - There are also 3 small children so the saloon is nursery as well as dining-room & drawing-room! It is really a very comfortable little boat if only there was somewhere to smoke. C. has to go outside or to our own cabin when he wants to which is rather a bore - The boat is long eno' to get quite a good walk & we tramped up & down, getting far more exercise than we ever c$^{d.}$ on either of the N.D.L. boats. We saw clouds of birds flying over the water, duck I s$^{d.}$ think but we were too far off to see - This is far the best boat I've ever been in! There is no

motion at all & one has to look at the bank to see if she is moving or not! We stopped 2 or 3 times in mid-stream opposite Chinese villages to allow a sort of lighter to come alongside & take off some of the Chinese passengers who have a deck of their own below ours The captain & officers dont wear any sort of uniform but go about in ordinary clothes which is not smart - The crew consists of Chinamen ragged & dirty looking but the boat itself is spotlessly clean & quite luxurious with bathrooms & even arm chairs in the saloon - tho' unfortunately a limited number!

December 13th. Sunday - There was thick fog in the night so we had to tie up most of the time & had not got very far by the time we got up in the morning - Last night we stopped at a place called Cehn-Kiang-fu at about 10 o'clock. It was a lovely moonlight night but of course we cd.n't see much of the town tho' we noticed large & powerful electric lights in some of the streets! It has been a lovely day with a warm bright sun so that with coats & rugs we were able to sit on deck - The morning was very misty which added to the beauty. It was a grand sight to see a great junk come sailing down out of the mist - At about 11 o'clock we got to Nan-King - It is the ancient capital & has a city wall of 32 miles! We only stayed about half an hour so it wasn't worth while going on shore but we just went on to the landing place - which was an old P & O. boat! - & saw what we cd. of the town from there - I must say it didn't look very inviting, nothing but brown mud & very dirty. Whenever we come alongside a wharf the rush of natives on to the boat is something extraordinary - Before the boat has stopped they jump & scramble on board jostling one another & all talking & yelling at the tops of their voices - This morning one of them missed his footing & fell over board - The commotion which this caused was terrific! They threw him a rope which he clung to with a face of agony & then all gave directions & made suggestions - or seemed to! making the most deafening din! In the meantime some of them had hauled the poor wretch out, one of them assisting by winding the man's pig-tail round & round his hand as if it had been a rope, & then tugging for all he was worth, which can't have added much to the poor thing's comfort! At this place there were several Chinese gun boats with wire-less telegraphy & all the latest improvements. This is an extraordinary country - the height of civilization side by side with the very reverse! The country before getting to Nan-King appeared to be flat with enormous rushes growing right down to the river's edge which they cut & use for thatch - We saw a lovely old Chinese bridge in the distance, a very high single arch with a tall & narrow watch tower in the middle - Later on in the day we came thro' a much more mountainous country - flat in the fore-ground with high hills in the distance - in part cultivated & making a most welcome patch of green amongst all the brown - So far our experience of China is nothing but brown - Brown hills, brown valleys, brown rushes, brown fields, brown water, brown junks in fact brown everything - Very lovely especially when half shrouded in grey mist with the sun shining - There are any amount of farms & villages on the banks, all made of mud with rush roofs (brown of course!) They all have trees round them but otherwise there aren't many trees. The leaves are falling just now - The river is tremendously wide - 5 miles from bank to bank in places but of course it is gradually getting narrower - At about 5-30 we stopped at a place called Wu-hu but here again it was too dark to see much. It has been a most interesting day - With weather like today it is lovely sitting watching the banks & all the junks which go by by the dozen. We saw simply millions of duck on the water - I agreed with the American who was standing by us when we came to the first lot & who said in an awed voice "My, thats grea-at"! At one place there was a huge flock of mag-pies amongst the rushes - I'd no idea they ever lived in flocks - just like crows - There were a good many buffaloes working in the fields but this was all the animal life we saw -

December 14th Monday - Another lovely day today. Some parts of the country very like what we came thro' yesterday but others very much more mountainous, at least on the left bank - Away in the distance there were ranges of enormously high mountains - It is most fascinating gliding along like this watching the banks - We pass an endless succession of Chinese houses, villages, brick factories, (made from the mud on the banks & most primitive looking) people fishing with curious sort of nets which they let down into the river - at the edge - by means of a rope, the net itself being on a sort of frame -, others cutting the rushes & carting them away either on the backs of buffaloes or in clumsy looking carts drawn by buffaloes or else loading junks with them - In fact there is no end to the sights to be seen! The people all wear blue - It seems to start life by being a regular butcher blue but apparently washes badly for one sees it at all stages of fading until it becomes almost white - It is the material & dye of the country & evidently they can get no other - At about 5.30 we stopped at Kin-ling for about 3/4 of an hour so we went ashore & had a walk on the Bund, a most swagger place with very good houses & trees planted down it - like a boulevard! The native part of the town as seen from the river (we hadn't time to visit it) looked the very reverse, very dirty & squalid tho' at the same time most picturesque - We saw part of the city wall, a magnificent construction apparently as old as the hills, very high & over-grown with moss & greenery - There was a lovely old grey pagoda outside the wall & standing by itself on a high rock - This is the place where they make a lot of china & the usual crowd who boarded the steamer as soon as we stopped brought a whole lot of it on board to sell - A man first asked 4 dollars for a pair of lovely vases that look extremely ancient even if they aren't but eventually & with the assistance of a missionary who spoke the language we got them for 1 dollar! The dreadful question now arises - where are we going to pack them! However - sufficient unto the day! We are still seeing millions of duck also a lot of shell drake & dozens of cormorants sitting on an enormous pile of rock which we passed in the middle of the river. The cormorants & a Buddhist temple seemed to be all that was on it - This is the only rocky part we've come to as yet -

S.S. Kiang-Wo, Hankow, China

15. 12. 08

Well, here we are after 4 days of the river Yang-tse Kiang! I have enjoyed it all so much - Don't you remember the sort of fascination there was in Holland gliding along between banks idly watching everything as they went by & this is much more so being so much bigger & altogether different to anything else one has ever seen. Its difficult to describe it all my dear as you can imagine but its lovely. All brown & gray - regular "monotone" & oh! the junks! Thames barges & Dutch tehalks simply aren't in it & I rave over them! What impresses me is the size of the place - Its perfectly immence & so fearfully interesting - The Kut-Wo was a most comfortable boat & we are hoping this will be the same but have only just got on board so can't tell yet - They are both Jardine Matheson - Mr. Landale gave us a letter of introduction to their man here, such a funny little cove who has been most attentive & kind all day - Gave us lunch & then sent us for a drive in his carriage to see the race-course. His wife was the same style as himself & laid herself open to be so pleasant - It was a comic luncheon party altogether & lasted hours! Soup, fish, omelette, duck, beef, tartlets, cheese, fruit, coffee not to mention hors d'oeurves & sherry in the drawing-room beforehand! Something like that lunch we once had at the Manse, do you remember? Everybody gives us a different account of the shooting we are going to find beyond Ichang - Some say it is a perfect paradise while others say the very reverse. Some seem to think life in a house boat absolute bliss & others think we'll never stick it more than a few days! I hate these kind of wet blanket people - Its so annoying to be solemnly warned that you won't enjoy yourself! Of course if it is horrid we'll just come back as quickly as possible - The river is falling so we stand a jolly good chance of sticking in the mud which wd. be the devil of a nuisance - The dinner bell so I must cease for the moment & continue afterwards -

Well, have had a good dinner but really the company on this boat - & on the other - is the limit! Such dreadful missionaries! Weedy looking men & hard voiced agressively pleasant women - Heaven knows whether they do the Chinese any good. I sd. think it was very doubtful but they all seem keen eno' & jolly pleased with themselves - We don't have much to do with them but have spoken to some - Yesterday we were talking to one of them (he was one of the ones that wear Chinese costume) & he suddenly began to sermonize, for all the world like Johnstone of Ladyhall! It was most embarassing & so difficult to stop him. I'm sure I don't know whether he was trying to convert us but it seemed rather like it - But not us! I wd.n't be a Chinese missionary, no not for anything - This man & his wife were going absolutely to the back of beyond - 4 months solid travelling from home & wd.n't dream of going back for at least 8 years! They live at this place with one other European & his wife - Can you imagine any more dreadful life? There are just millions & millions of Chinese - Its the most thickly populated country in the world - as no doubt you know - & one realizes it being in the country, & seeing how they fairly swarm - Petite, petite, I wish you cd. see all these places & see the sights which I have seen - I shall never be able to convey it all to you & besides one doesn't take in things from hearing about them, one must see. I hope you've got some sort of map & are following us round also my child, the stamps on my letters w^d. make a most valueable collection so do stick to them! We've been to so many different countries now. As to C. what with S. Africa & India he feels as tho' he had now seen the most of the world! I haven't got over yet that its ME ME thats doing all this & as we swagger along down the bund (esplanade sort of place my dear!) of some such place as Kin-ling it will suddenly come over me & make me sort of gasp - Whoever has ever heard (of) Kin-ling may I ask? & yet there it is, as busy & full of life as possible & there it has been & will be & I I, if you please have seen it! Its simply "movie" & every place we go to I think the same! My own belovéd girl I do hope you are having a good time - This is Tuesday - You were hunting yesterday - Oh my how I wish I c^d. hear all about it - In all these towns there are foreign concessions - I'm horribly vague about Chinese government but apparently the different nations lease a part of the town from the Chinese & that part becomes British, French, Russian or whatever it may be. The consequence is one finds English shops everywhere & can buy almost anything - To-day amongst other things we got books, 3 Dickens & Pendennis in that nice limp leather edition the same as we have got 4 of Dickens in! A Chinaman sold them to us. One must have books when travelling - Its all very well to say that we want to see the scenery but its too dreadfully tiring for words to do nothing but look at scenery - You wait till you try! I know I did it the whole day without a break in the Suez Canal & was "fair din" at the end! I've been pretty bad on the Yang-tze too but have a "go" at the Virginians every now & then just to keep myself going - Of course what w^d. be nice w^d. be books of the places one passes thro' but they apparently are impossible to get, besides I think perhaps it w^d. be better to read about them afterwards, anyhow we can't get any here so its just as well to think that! I'm sure I've read heaps of books about China in my day but not one ounce of good have they done me & its my belief I'm incapable of learning anything thro' books! I wonder if you think the diary is getting drier? You've no idea how difficult it sometimes is to select out of the whole day for it w^d. be a physical impossibility to put down everything & sometimes in the evenings I feel positively bamboozled with the day's work & don't know where to begin! Its cold here but not too cold & with knickerbockers & my black petticoat & my big blue coat which is absolutely the joy of my heart I keep quite warm - I loved seeing the racing ponies at Shanghai - Such innocent looking creatures but we c^d.n't touch them as they hate all Europeans & won't let them do anything to them - until they're on their backs of course. I'm afraid you won't get my today's diary but it will come with the next opportunity - which will be at Ichang I suppose on Sunday - We thought we were going to be here till Thursday & go on in the Tungling as I told you in my last letter but M^r. Dunne (the Jardine Matheson man here) has sent us on in this as being the best boat - Well, dearie adio in the meantime. How I wish you c^d. walk into this chilly, vilely lighted little saloon - let me have a sight of your familiar face - (Sometimes I look so like you in the glass - more especially one day when I was sea-sick!! - that I get quite a shock! or C. will suddenly say "oh you look so like the other one"! I wonder if you ever look like me - I believe I'm more like you than you are like me & now I mustn't ramble on any more. C. has got to take the letters ashore & it is late & dark - I w^d.n't go ashore alone at night amongst all these rough dirty coolies, not for nothing - He is writing the envelope so don't get a shock when you don't see my writing! Best of love my child from us both Yr D.

December 15th Tuesday - We got to HanKow about 10-30 - Two boat loads of coolies came out to meet us. As they were swept past by the current at a tremendous pace the men simply hurled themselves on to the steamer - It looked quite the most dangerous game I've ever seen for either they wd. miss the whole show or slip off when they got there or else the boat iself wd. be dashed against the steamer & wrecked if they miscalculated the distance! However there were no accidents I'm glad to say - The first thing we did was go to Jardine Matheson's office taking a letter of introduction from Mr. Landale to the manager - Mr. Dunne - He was a most pleasant little man & ready to do anything for us - We have to go on board the Kiang Wo this evening - She sails tomorrow morning at daylight - She is also a Jardine Matheson boat. The river is low just now he says & there have been many steamers stuck on the way up to Schang but the Kiang Wo is a good boat & we have the best chance of getting up in her than any other - The landing place at HanKow is quite the crankiest I've ever seen & then you go up a flight of the dirtiest steps - We had to thread our way amongst hundreds of coolies taking cargo from the boat - the dirtiest most ragged men I've ever seen - They all grunt or chant a curious sort of song as they work. I suppose it is a kind of encouragement to each other but when hundreds of them do it all at the same time the noise is deafening & not particularly musical either! It was a horrid morning, raining & drizzling so we didn't see HanKow to advantage but it seemed quite a respectable clean sort of town - at least anywhere where we went. It has a pop: of 300 Europeans & 2000000 Chinese! Mr. Dunne had asked us to lunch - or "tiffen" as they always call it - so we went back there at 1 o'clock & were right royally entertained by him & his wife! They were both most affable & eager to make themselves pleasant but it was a mighty long luncheon & we didn't "rise" from the table till 3 o'clock! We now had to go to the bank & do a few other jobs before returning to the Dunne's house at 4 o'clock to go for a drive - They had most kndly lent us their carriage - It was an innocent rattly little concern drawn by a China pony. The "Mafoo" was told to take us to the race-course so away we went down the Bund past all the big buildings the mafoo jagging & slashing at the pony who bustled along in fine style - They have such a nice little race course with quite a good club - They say the ponies don't quite come up to the standard of the Hong Kong & Shanghai ones which we cd. quite believe as we saw some of them quite the most "racers" that ever were! After our drive we had to pack & get our luggage taken on to the Kiang Wo - Our fellow passengers were all on the Kut Wo - are all missionaries - We have long talks with some of them & find them most interesting in telling us all about the country & people. They will talk by the hour & the only difficulty is to stop them!

<u>December 16th Wednesday</u> - We started early this morning so were well on the way by the time we got up - Our cabin opens into the saloon which is somewhat awkward but it is quite a nice big one with a certain amount of room to move about in - This boat is smaller than the Kut Wo with not so much space for walking. She only draws 5 ft 8 in - Anything bigger than this can't get up any further than HangKow at low water - It has been a dull & cloudy day & the banks in places so high that we can't see over them which is very dull - The water buffaloe are sent out to graze with small boys to look after them & keep them off the crops - They sit on the back of the beast with a great straw cape over their shoulders & look most comic! We had to anchor at dark for the night - These steamers always do for the night as it is impossible to find their way down the channel in the dark - It is difficult eno' even in the light, for the channel constantly changes - they are forever "heaving the lead" as we go along - We got Patience cards in Hankow & have gone mad on "Steps"! C. did it this evening! The missionaries played "Quit" & seemed to enjoy themselves very much!

<u>December 17th Thursday</u> - A most horrible day - Very cold & windy & raining - There is quite a "sea" in the river - They say such a thing has been known as passengers getting sea-sick in the Yang-tze!! It was far too cold to sit on deck & not even very nice walking there so we had to spend most of the day reading & playing patience in the saloon - We are 10 passengers altogether & a fat little boy of about 2 years old belonging to one of the missionaries exactly like what Bill Broadhurst used to be! The captain, 1st & 2nd officers & chief engineer feed with us - We are a most friendly company & have many long conversations! The misssionaries were very gay & frivolous in the evening & played "Up Jenkins"! The saloon gets very cold & the stove needs constant stoking - The chairs are just ordinary dining room ones & very uncomfortable after one has been sitting for some time - Its worse of course on a nasty day like this when one can't be out much - We pass an endless succession of little houses & villages on both banks - we anchored again in the evening as soon as it got dark -

<u>December 18th Friday</u> - A much nicer day to day. Still too cold to sit out but quite nice for walking - Just like a winters day at home - We have made great friends with the chief engineer - He is a Scotchman & comes from Stirling. He knows Blair Drummond - He has also been to Lockerbie - One of his friends is a son of McLure at the Bank (he is a captain on a Jardine Matheson boat). He also knew Betty's nephew who was drowned - It was like meeting somebody from home talking to him - He didn't know the name of Johnstone Douglas but then he has only visited in Lockerbie. In the afternoon we passed Sunday Island. This is the most difficult part of the river to navigate as the channel is continually changing & is very shallow even in the best parts - we went very slow & they were sounding both sides of the boat calling out the depth in sing-song, <u>most</u> unmusical voices. We only draw 5 ft 8 in & yet we touched once, however we got thro' safely after all. It wd. have

been a great bore if we had stuck as sometimes these boats get hung up for days waiting for the river to rise a little so that they can get thro' - Of course this only happens at this time of year - In the summer it is very much the reverse, the river rising to an enormous height with a tremendously strong current. This boat is now doing 6 knots an hour - They say that coming down when the river is big she has been known to do over 20!

<u>December 19th. Saturday</u> - Another bright sunny day tho' cold - We stopped at Sha-Shi this morning - from where we saw it it looked a fascinating place with real Chinese gateways & roofs ornamental with curves & carvings but I daresay at close quarters it wd. be as dirty as all the rest of them! In the afternoon the scenery altered & instead of the high banks & flat country we have been passing thro' lately, there were brown hills covered with some sort of little bush & huge high hills towering in the distance - We didn't anchor tonight but went steadily on in the dark until we finally arrived at Ichang at 9 o'clock - we bumped every now & again & collided with a junk but there was no harm done! It is pitch dark & nothing to be seen but a few feeble lights in the town & on junks. A missionary of sorts came on board at once & bustling into the saloon asked if <u>we</u> were the China Mission party! We being the only ones on the boat who aren't! He soon found who he wanted & they are all fussing round now in a tremendous state of flap. We of course shall not go on shore till the morning. We made the terrible discovery this morning that C's glasses have gone - The captain had great hopes that after he'd said a few words to the Chinamen that they wd. come back but I'm afraid its too late now to hope for that. They say Chinamen have a perfect mania for glasses watches & clocks & will steal them if ever they get a chance. C's must have been taken either by a passenger or one of the sailors, reaching in thro' the window - They were with him all thro' S. Africa so it is very sad -

S.S. Kiang-Wo

In the Yang-tse - not far from Ichang

19. 12. 08

Dearest child, we are by way of getting to Ichang tomorrow morning so I must write this afternoon to be ready for the post. I shall be very glad to get to Ichang - I'm getting rather fed up with these little boats, more especially with the passengers! These missionaries have plenty of most interesting things to tell one but once they start there's no stopping them & they're rather an awful class. <u>So</u> English, with dreadful voices, goodness knows what they'd be at home - At least I know what <u>one</u> of them wd. be & that is a teacher at a High School! She's just the very moral of those Graham St. women we used to know! Its apt to make one curl up a little - inwardly - not that I show it I hope - Their men folk are worse of course *but we don't need to have much to do with them. There are 2 tables & we sit with the Captain & 3 other officers & 2 of the missionary women who, as a rule monopolize the conversation - I love when we can sit on deck in comfortable chairs but the last 2 or 3 days its been too cold so when we have had eno' tramping up & down on deck we have to come down into the saloon, seat ourselves on the chairs round the table & read or play patience. The nice Scotch chief engineer solemnly advises us not to be long in a house-boat! He says they are very dirty & uncomfortable & he is sure that we won't like it! We shall have to wait till we see but if it (is) beastly we can always get back quickly. What takes days perhaps to get, being towed by as many as 100 men sometimes will take only a few days coming down.*

Until we get to Ichang & test the house boat we can't tell what we shall do or where we shall be for Xmas. I'm afraid you fondly imagined that we were at Pekin. It does seem funny that there is only a week to Xmas. I wonder if you are still at Houghton at this minute - We often & often think of you all & imagine what you're doing - If you ever want to imagine us you must remember that we are 8 hours ahead now & calculate according! - It is very cold now - & I use my hot water bottle with joy - For life on a ship I think heat is really the nicest, one can sit in the air anyhow but this of course wd. be ripping if we cd. be on Shore - The silly boat is shakeing & shivering so I can hardly write - Something so irritating about it! They now want to lay the table so I must stop in the meantime -

I'm afraid this letter & diary are dull - but thats because the last 2 or 3 days have not been very entertaining so you must excuse me - Your letters are never dull so write every little scrap you can think of, it will all be more than welcome! Isn't it funny about the chief engineer having been to Lockerbie & knowing that nephew of Betty's. One wd. have thought China was big eno' in all conscience & yet the first thing we do is to knock up against somebody who knew this poor boy! If Betty had asked me to look out for friends of his one wd. have smiled in a superior sort of way & thought it the most improbable thing in the world to find any of them - Ha-ever, such is the way of the world - I wonder if you are working yet & if so what at & how you're getting on. I had the desire to paint strong on the 2nd. day in this river, it was so paintable, but I must honestly confess that with the exception of that & the day in the Red Sea I haven't had the smallest desire to paint. I have had out a sketch book I've got with me once or twice & tried to do things from memory but dear me they were so dreadful they only served to make me squirm. You never mention the dog, you are so cad a girl, & the other twin just dying to know what its doing with its little self. I beleive we are quite close to Ichang - We are going on in the dark tonight so as to get in - we keep touching the bottom with that sickening kind of jerk which we know so well from Ariel experience but so far we haven't stuck altogether - It wd. be a bore if we did as of course here its not a case of only waiting for the tide - Sometimes when these boats are stuck they can't get off for days!

Well, my belovéd girl aurevoir for the present. Best of love from the T.B.

Thou whom thou knowest thine D.

By the way I refer in the diary to the difficulties of our cabin leading into the saloon - There is another door in it which leads into the ladies bath room & apartment so we get on better than one w^d. think unless the last "lady" has left the door locked between us & the bath-room which is very awkward especially when they're all at breakfast (We don't think it necessary to be in extra good time for this meal!) C. has to slip on his clothes, go thro' the soloon, march boldly thro' the door labelled "Ladies' W.C." & unlock it! so as to let me thro'! Well dearie once more à toi - This is a silly letter & no mistake. I am so sorry -

21. 12. 08

Ichang, China -

Chérie I must write to you to let you know of our latest plans. We got to Ichang (as you know from the diary) the night before last & now about to proceed up the river in a house boat on a 13 days expedition! We were on our boat this morning & it is really not bad! I do hope we shall enjoy ourselves. We had only meant it to be a 3 days expedition but they were all so keen here that we s^d go right up that we decided to do it - I am writing this in the house of M^r. Ross, the Jardine Matheson agent. He & his wife are such kindly hospitable Scotch as can be folk! He comes from Stranraer. His father was D^r. there & knew Balgreggan & Aunt Matilda - He himself left to go to sea at 15 so doesn't know much about it latterly but no doubt At Mill will remember D^r. Ross! His wife comes from Perthshire, the village of Almondbank near Crieff - I think her father must be a farmer - She knows Millearne & talked of Lord Mansfield as "Alan Murray" & told me she'd once spoken to him ! Of course they are quite "people" out here & really are extremely nice & know how to do things too which is the extraordinary thing! There is a man staying with them for a few days who has just come down from a year's travelling & shooting in China who used to be in James Johnston Stewart's regiment & knew him well. Such a nice man - a Capt. M^c.Neil. He has a place next door to Craig near Oban, is 1st. cousin to Jack Kennedy of Dunure, knows the Vans Agnews & the Walkers of Crawfardton & altogther its too silly the way we keep picking up acquaintances! Pon me word it is! Yesterday C. called on the gunboat which is lying here with M^c.Neil & M^r. Ross & they promptly asked us to lunch. The commander was lunching out so I don't know what he was like (C. said he was an awful bounder) but the other 2 officers & the D^r. who I did see really were rather terrors & the rest of the party - 2 couples) - were also of the bounder class so lunch was rather painful. I w^d. far rather be with these nice simple Scotch folk & of course Capt. M^c.Neil is a "real person" - Yesterday afternoon the Ross' took us into the Chinese city. It was extremely interesting to see it but I don't think I ever want to go again. My dear you simply cannot conceive of the filth - it was quite unspeakable - & the smells - Good lord! - & the sights - Heavens! Oh my! but it was awful & yet at the same time I w^d.n't have missed it simply because it is China, pure & unadulterated. We were there quite a long time wandering about guided by one of the Chinese boys out of the office going in & out of some of the shops, they don't seem to mind where one goes or what one does tho' all the time we had a perfectly friendly crowd following us. C. smoked till his throat burnt & I had to endure it with no smoke & was quite glad to get out! We then had dinner with the Ross' - An excellent meal & pleasant talk - It rather reminded me of those meals we used to have in the farm houses when we were at Holland that time except that it was a real dinner & Mrs. Ross caught my eye in the most approved style & we rose & went to the drawing-room leaving "you gentlemen" as she called them to smoke! We went off to the steamer for the night tho' they were full of apologies that having Capt. Mc.Neil there they had no room to put us up. So awfully kind. And now my childie, I must cease. I have been left to myself so far in the little drawing-room but Mrs. Ross has now returned & it is practically time for lunch so I must stop - It may be a fortnight or more before you hear again I am sorry to say - So long my dearest love

Ever & ever thine D -

December 20th. Sunday - We got up early this morning by the light of a candle so as to pack & be ready to start for the Gorges at any time - After breakfast we went ashore & called on Mr. Ross the Jardine Matheson agent to whom Mr. Landale had given us a letter of introduction. We found he & his wife the kindest & most hospitable Scotch people - They took us into their house at once & we began to discuss what was the best way of seeing the Gorges - A Captain Mc.Niel who was in the Argyle & Sutherland Highlanders & knew James Johnstone Stewart - & who is also a cousin of Jack Kennedy of Dunure! - was staying with them on his way down the river after a 9 months shooting expedition in the country & was most useful in giving us advice as he had just come from where we want to go - After much talk it was decided that we are to take a house-boat or "Kwadza" or go up thro' the Gorges a distance of about 180 miles, the whole trip to take 13 days - Mr. Ross undertook to get the boat for us with crew, provisions & everything else that we wd. require as the boats have nothing in them & have to be fitted up by the passengers themselves - We can't start till tomorrow evening so there is plenty of time to see Ichang! C. went with Mr. Ross & Capt. Mc.Neil to call on the British gunboat the "Kinsha" that is stationed here while Mrs. Ross & I sat & conversed! C. came back with an invitation for us to go to lunch on the "Kinsha" - but we didn't stay long as Mr. & Mrs. Ross had promised to take us thro' the Chinese city. Never never have I seen so much filth or smelt such smells! It was indescribable & unspeakable! All the same I was very glad to go just to see what it is like - The streets are very narrow & simply packed with people - The houses are low & seem to almost meet overhead, blocking out the sky - We had one of the Chinamen from the office to act as guide & interpreter if we wanted to go into any shops - He led us thro' a perfect maze of streets - The officials have quite big houses with large court-yards & great Chinese gates leading into them - In the court-yard of one were some wretched men with large squares of wood fastened round their necks so that they can't lie down & worse still, can't reach to scratch their heads! We went back walking on the city wall - This about 4 yds. wide & is built of stone with parapets & loop holes - Looking down on the city it appeared one mass of roofs all carved & ornamented in the way Chinese roofs always are - It was getting quite dark when we got back to the Ross' house which is in the British concession & faces the river - We stayed to dinner with the Ross' going back in a sampan to the Kiang-Wo to sleep - Captain Mc.Niel was there too - He is such a nice man. His house is quite near Craig where he has a museum of all the beasts he has shot - we have a cordial invitation to go & see him next time we are there! Mr. Ross is a Stranraer man. His father was Dr. there & he knows Balgreggan! Mrs. Ross is a Perthshire lassie coming from Almond bank, knows Milliame & had once spoken to Lord Mansfield! so we all feel like old friends!

December 21st. Monday - Today we have spent entirely in making preparations for our trip - C. called on the consul & arranged that we sd. have what they call a "Red Boat" to take with us - They are Chinese life boats & can only be got thro' an official so that it will give us a mark of distinction & be most useful to go ashore in if we want to - The Chinese compradore thro' whom we got the boat supplies us with all provisions & an English speaking cook boy - Mr. Landale provided us with camp beds & bedding & the Ross' have lent us wicker chairs (out of their own drawing-room) curtains to hang up & keep off the draughts, towels & table cloths, not to mention a large basket of additional eatables, a bit of ham, cakes & shortbread of her own making & a "plum pudding" to be "'otted up" & eaten on Xmas day! And also, by the way a bit of mistletoe for Xmas decoration which hangs in the middle of the "dining room" ceiling & gets very much in the way of C's head for the cabins are not high! The kwadza consists of our 2 rooms the living room first - 7ft. high 9ft. wide 10ft. long - It has a table, the 2 wicker chairs, the portmanteau, gun case, a pile of books & writing things on 2 Chinese chairs which are really just like small tables or stools & a little stove rigged up for our benefit - With this furniture & us in it, it is quite full eno'! The inner room is rather smaller - Our camp beds just fit in on each side & we have a basin on a minute table & another Chinese chair to put our clothes on besides a few very cranky nails in various parts of the wall - (we wanted some more but the only one the boy cd. produce was so crooked & blunt & rusty that it wdn't hammer in!) Beyond this room is the kitchen, very small & with a large useful looking stove in it. Then there comes a small open space & at the very end the Captain's quarters (a sort of "fore-peak" - at the back!). Our "dining-room" doors open on to the deck which has a small well in it where the cooking for the crew is done. Here they also sleep roofing it in for the night with matting - The windows are all painted with little vases of flowers & fruit etc: Very quaint innocent productions - We started about 5-30 - The Ross' & Captain Mc.Neil came a short bit of the way with us - The crew consists of a captain & 15 men, at least one is a mere boy - The captain is supposed to supply 15 men but makes up the number with a boy who he can get for next to nothing as his "squeeze" as Mr. Ross put it! We only went a mile & a half the first evening tying up amongst a lot of other junks that were ready to start in the morning - The boy gave us a most excellent dinner & waited on us in a spotlessly clean long cotton coat, like servants always wear.

December 22nd. Tuesday - As soon as it was light this morning the start began! First tho' they fired a perfect cannonade of crackers to bring good luck & ward off evil spirits - China men apparently can't work unless to an accompaniment of shouts & singing so the noise goes on without ceasing all day! Progress is made by a curious sort of rowing in little short jerks with 2 huge oars & towing or tracking, the same as they used to do in Holland - today there was a lovely breeze so we were able to sail sometimes too. The scenery is perfectly lovely - We were in the Ichang gorge - the river winds in & out of enormously high rocky hills - It was a lovely day with the sun shining - Words of mine can't describe how wide & beautiful it was. There was quite a lot of vegetation on the ledges of rock & some lovely little valleys with burns coming down in waterfalls - The rocks are grey & are so curiously rugged & broken up that they look like great ruined castles towering up above. We went ashore in our Red boat & walked alongside the boat. The going was all thro' enormous rocks & deep pinky grey sand so we cd.n't get on very fast - The trackers hadn't such very hard work today as the sail was up all the time helping them - We were out of the gorge in the afternoon where the river widens (In the Gorge it was sometimes not more than 1/4 of a mile across). Here the hills were not so high, & brown instead of grey. We got out again & had another walk after tea - There are heaps of junks going up river with us & at night we all tied up together near a small village - Chinese people seem to have heaps to say to each other & even after a hard day's work jabber far into the night. We had a fire in the stove this evening - It gave some trouble to begin with (as what stove does not?) & smoked the whole place out but when we had given it up as hopeless it suddenly began to burn of itself so we had to cease abusing it! Our boy is a real trump! He cooks as well as a £50 cook & gives us the most excellent meals - We might almost be in a London restaurant! The crew have a cook of their own, a most lugubrious man who seems to be cooking rice all day in an enormous pot. He adds some sort of vegetable & little bits of meat of sorts which he first of all beats with a bit of stick on the deck - They seem to think the mixture delicious judging by the way they shovel it down with chop sticks out of small bowls held close to their mouths. They are not pretty eaters! Our first day on the Yang-tse has been a great success. It is all so big & grand, one gets quite exhausted looking & admiring so ceaselessly!

December 23rd. Wednesday - Another lovely day - The river ran today thro' totally different scenery. A broad sandy valley strewn with the most enormous boulders, low hills on either side with a few scraggy trees & great high distant mountains 3000 or 4000ft high shutting it in on all sides - The colour of the whole thing was magnificent, grey rocks & pinky grey sand & water, hazy blue distance, the junks standing out brown against it - altogether perfectly fine but what <u>is</u> the good of trying to explain it? There was no breeze so we had to track & row ("wriggle" $w^{d.}$ be a much better word & more expressive!) all day - The men are splendid & work like galley slaves & so cheerfully - When tracking 2 are employed freeing the rope from the rock when it catches & very hard work it looks too for they have to run like hares or the rope $w^{d.}$ break & even dash into the river, for which purpose they throw off all their clothes in the space of 2 seconds & hurl themselves into the water! It must be very cold too inspite of the sun! We had a very nice walk this morning far outstripping the boat for the current runs strong here so that progress is very slow, in fact the boat hardly seems to move - At about 2-30 we came to the bottom of the Padunzai rapid, the first of any importance that we have come to yet - We had to tie up with a lot of other boats & wait our turn - We went on shore & watched the trackers & most interesting & exciting it was too! Dozens of them get on to a rope 2 or 300 yds. long & pull on it for all they're worth, sometimes almost on all fours so great is the strain - Considering that they are pulling like this amongst enormous boulders its perfectly marvellous that they can keep their feet - of course they have bare feet or they $w^{d.}$ never get on at all - Four or five men have to be employed to keep the rope from catching - In places the ropes have worn great deep furrows in the rocks from constant friction, in a way which seems almost incredible - The men left on board have hard work too, keeping the boat off the rocks with long bamboo boat-hooks while one keeps up an incessant "tom tom" on a drum! The movement is scarcely perceptible & with all this enormous expenditure of labour the boat only gets up by inches, however it <u>does</u> get up eventually & this is the way the Chinese have managed for centuries & centuries! Its wonderful! At last it came to our turn & by 5.30 we were "up"! There is a small village at the top which supplies extra trackers for of course one's own men $w^{d.}$ not be nearly eno' at a rapid. They all crowded round us & <u>stared</u> very friendly & talkative but unfortunately we $c^{d.n't}$ understand each other! One man when we were taking a photograph this morning was frightfully interested & laughed with delight when he saw the boat in the finder! We were so sorry we $c^{d.n't}$ converse with him. After the rapid we tracked on for about another hour & then tied up for the night - The men are jabbering away together, not at all as tho' they'd had a hard day's work - "The Squeeze" as we call the boy is the most cheerful of the lot but then he really doesn't do <u>very</u> much work tho' he makes up for it by singing! Always the same weird song in a harsh penetrating little voice which we $w^{d.}$ gladly dispence with at times!

<u>December $24^{th.}$ Thursday</u> - We have been all day coming thro' the Tung Ling Gorge. The grandest place imaginable. Huge high hills sometimes absolutely precipitous on all sides, the voices of the trackers echoing thro' it, the junks looking like toy

boats in comparison - We couldn't get out to walk as the going was too rough - its a marvel to see how the trackers get along at all - Today they were scrambling over rocks & scaling great hills of soft sand, in which it is most difficult to get a footing & in one place going single file on a narrow little path cut in the face of the rock with a precipice sheer down into the water! - All day they were tracking or "yuloe-ing" (as we have found out their curious kind of rowing is called) without ceasing first on one side of the river & then on the other - It is much nicer for us when they track for yuloeing is accompanied by such stamping & singing & grunting that we can hardly hear ourselves speak - We stopped for a short time at a village & we went on shore & got to the top of a rock that juts out into the gorge & had a most glorious view up & down it but this was all the walk we c^d. get today until we came to the foot of the Shin-Tan rapid which is at the end of the Gorge - Our Red boat captain sent one of his men to walk with us (why, I don't know!) with one of the official red coats with black velvet lettering on - We walked to the top of the rapid & watched some of the junks getting hauled up. They appear to have more men for this rapid that the other - It is a bigger one with a very strong current - As it was getting dark our captain only had our boat towed by our own men a very short way up into a little bay where we are tied up for the night, ready to get up in the morning - There is a village here but we didn't go into it. Chinese villages are so <u>much</u> nicer as seen from a distance!

<u>December 25th. Friday</u> - Christmas day! The noise & commotion this morning was frantic for we were getting up the Shin-Tan rapid which was at last accomplished about 9-30 - The last part was a veritable waterfall which of course meant a case of getting up by inches - It was a curious feeling being in the boat while this was going on - She rocked & swayed about, creaking & groaning with the strain while the water rushed by with a roaring sound - After the rapid comes the Shin-Tan Gorge, a beautiful one with perhaps the highest hills round it of any that we have seen yet. It has been a grey day, quite fine but no sun & consequently colder - In spite of this scenery looked as grand as ever - This morning we were able to get out & have 2 walks, pounding thro' deep sand & scrambling over rocks the same as usual. At lunch time we tied up at the foot of the Ho-load-se rapid & before we'd finished our lunch they began to haul us up - It was a <u>very</u> strong one with 2 wrecks lying in it - Poor forlorn things, been dashed on the rocks in the downstream passage - We rocked madly in this rapid scarcely making any progress at all while the men on board screamed & roared with excitement keeping us off the rocks at the side with all their strength with the bamboo poles - One w^d. have thought that the rope <u>must</u> break with the strain but they must be very strong - curious looking things made of bamboo - for it only creaked & eventually we got to the smooth water at the top & all concerned must have heaved a sigh of relief - all afternoon we were tracking & yuloeing by turns up a wider valley with several smaller rapids - It was frightfully rough walking so we sat in the cabin & read & played

patience - At 5 o'clock we came to Kwei-Choo. There is a rapid here so we only tacked up a short way to a good place to tie up - We went ashore & had a lovely walk on a tracker's path cut into the face of the rock - The hills here are very steep & covered with vegetation which at present is very wintry & brown - We didn't get back to the boat till it was getting quite dark & found that the men had already got up their roof of matting & were gobbling down their "chow"! (About the only Chinese word I know & which means "food"!) - Our Xmas dinner was excellent.

Kwadze 2623! Kwei - Choo, China -

25. 12. 08

Well, my Ninnie V, here's Xmas day & here's me in a house boat moored to the banks of the Yang-tse - It seems incredible! It is $^1/_4$ past 9 in the evening which means that it is about $^1/_2$ past 1 with you. What are you doing my child? Having lunch I suppose at Comlongon. I just suddenly felt as tho' I must write to you tho' it won't get posted till we are once more in civilised lands, but the desire coming on me so strong I herewith take up my pen - Of course its silly to think of "Xmas" as anything different but this has been a curious one & we've remarked on it many a time! It has been spent in getting up rapids & scrambling along in sand & rocks with intervals of reading "Sketches by Boz" & playing patience! This is the most delightful expedition - I thought I s$^{d.}$ like it. It reminds me very much of the Ariel except that we are so much grander! Our boy is a real "nailer" of a cook & "serves" us the most excellent meals - For dinner tonight he had arranged our napkins in lovely little fans in our wine-glasses to begin with - While we were having an extra wash (we washed our feet, but don't tell anybody!! It sounds so dreadful & yet on these sort of expeditions with no proper bath-room, only one tiny basin with water from a kettle who'd be so silly as to do this every day? Not me anyway - nor you either so don't pretend you w$^{d.}$ & anyway we've only been 4 days as yet!!!) Dinner consisted of soup, clear with green peas, add a little Worcester sauce & it was excellent - Sausage & potatoes - delicious! Roast pheasant with roast potatoes & peas - Mrs. Ross' plum-pudding - ripping & so kind of the woman, cheese, oranges & walnuts & a bottle of claret in which to drink your healths ("Ninty" had a special gulp to herself!) Now don't you think that an A1 dinner? All our meals are as good as that. These gorges are really beyond words - I try vainly to describe them in the diary but its simply beyond me - All I can say is that they are just grand & I can't say how glad I am we came - I w$^{d.n't}$ have missed it for anything - It sort of leaves one gasping & trying to realize the vastness of the whole thing & the valiant tho' primitive efforts of the people as they struggle against the waters - They look such flies but such plucky ones & they always win - unless the boat is wrecked - It gives one plenty of food for reflection I can tell you - I like Chinese people, they are splendid - if only they were cleaner in themselves & their habits - Brussels people simply aren't in it so you can draw your own conclusions! I am doing my hair in a cart-horse's tail tied with my brown tie, having no ribbon & a tie with a shirt being an unnecessary luxury on the Yang-tse - C. says I look *about 17! He is not shaving & has already got a fine black growth on his chin - he wears a sweater & a scarf round his neck & with corduroy breeches looks a regular ruffian! He'll be worse before the end of the 13 days too! Lord, how this lamp smells! Its too appalling for words. Why do lamps in cabins always smell? This leaks whats more & all over my diary too so that if it nearly knocks you down when you read it you'll know the reason why. It scarcely gives any light either & has to be supplemented with candles - Of course we ought to be energetic & get up in the mornings early but I'm afraid we don't! "After" 9 is our breakfast hour which is really disgraceful. Its such a pity C. is not a good "getter up", it w^d. be so good for me - The men make the most fiendish noises as soon as it gets light but it makes "n'odds" to us - Its such an effort getting up & so nice & warm in bed. (All these little failings I know you will sympathise with to the full - Getting up to see the sun rise is no doubt charming in theory but not in practise!) And now my belovéd child I must stop for tonight. C. says I'm to wish you a merry Xmas from him & a sincere hope that you have not over eaten yourself! If Robinson has made another of her lovely Xmas cakes I s^d. think you & Shosh probably have! Goodnight my own twinnie - I wish I c^d. see you now - Bless you a thousand times*

Yrs forever & a day

D.

December 26th. Saturday - Got up in the morning to find that we had scarcely moved from where we were last night tho' judging from the noise & shouting that had been going on since daybreak I thought at least we w^d. have got up the rapid. The fact was a large junk in front was giving a lot of trouble & we c^d.n't get up until she has been hauled to a place of safety. It has been a very grey day today & not quite so "good-looking" as it has been - There was quite a strong breeze so we have been doing a good deal of sailing which the trackers must be thankful for. At lunch time we got up the Yeh-Tan rapid & just before tying up this evening were hauled up another - The Niu-Kou - There are so many of them now that one gets quite callous! We have also learnt not to pay much attention to the hysterical yells & screams of the crew which they always indulge in at a rapid, hurling themselves about in a perfect frenzy as tho' they thought the end of the world was coming - or at anyrate that we were going to be wrecked! They only do it to encourage each other to make further exertions & it really means nothing - tho' at first it was most alarming! Thank goodness "The Squeeze" has lost his voice! he has yelled himself so hoarse that all he can produce is the most pitiful little croak & he can't even speak properly! He still tries to sing so lets hope that by tomorrow he won't be able to make a sound!

December 27th. Sunday - Not nearly such a nice day today - It must have rained a little in the night & has done so on & off all day. It makes the rocks slippery & therefore impossible to track so we have been yu-loeing nearly all day - There is a particular song which they sing when doing this, at least one man & the Squeeze do the singing (the latter's voice has returned - worse luck!!) while the others make a curious noise in time, a cross between a pig & a duck! As it goes on incessantly its apt to become a bit monotonous! the scenery this morning was very like yesterday, low brown hills with villages at intervals. We were able to get out for a walk & found the sand a good deal easier to walk in when wet - We had 2 small rapids to get up this morning - The boy did tell us their names but we c[d.n't] catch them - Some of these Chinese names are dreadful! After lunch we entered the Wu shan Gorge - It is 20 miles long & not more than 350 to 500 ft wide - It is very deep & the hills rise out of it almost perpendicularly in places - Here & there little glens run up at right angles to the river with a burn trickling down over the rocks & glimpses of enormously high mountains behind with patches of snow on them. We had another walk this evening when it became possible, for a great part of the way there doesn't appear to be any path - it was drizzling & there were banks of mist on the highest tops the hills showing out black & most impressive-looking - We have had a series of mishaps today! To begin with "Old Ugly" - as we call one of the trackers - (he is so ugly poor dear!) fell into the river while scrambling back into the boat after tracking - he got soaked thro' poor wretch & was simply beside himself with passion, as evidently it had been somebody else's fault. He had no clothes of his own to change to so some of the others nobly divested themselves of some of theirs & rigged him out while his own rags dried - His frantic efforts to get into a coat kindly lent by a smaller man made us all roar with laughter tho' he himself was not yet in a fit state to join in! Secondly I upset my tea & flooded the table cloth, then C. had a violent choke with his tea going the wrong way - A little while after I knocked the ink on the floor & C. trod on it! (Luckily it wasn't broken) & to crown all when we were walking I slipped when stepping over a tiny little stream about 6 inches wide & went in up to the knee & got a great mouthful of sand. Extremely unpleasant & unnecessary!

December 28th Monday - We have been in the Wu-Shan Gorge all day - It has been a lovely sunny day, which is delightful, for a change - We have "negotiated" two rapids but they were quite small & comparatively easy ones - This morning's walk was most perilous! We went along a path which must have been about 200 ft above the level of the water - In places a slip w[d.] have landed one in the river! These sort of little facts certainly add to the excitement. The hill both above & below us - & those on the other side too - were a mass of vegetation, I don't know how the things manage to grow on such precipices. There is one lovely little bush which grows everywhere & which at present has turned a most beautiful crimson & makes a fine splash of colour amongst all the grey - We found a mangy little Michaelmas daisy clinging on to the face of the rock! The captain of the Red boat evidently got anxious as to how we were getting on, on this path for he sent 3 of his men to meet us! I must say the last part was rather beastly, so steep & narrow & rough - The men were most attentive & 2 of them insisted upon assisting me down & I must own I was quite glad of their aid tho' it was rather dreadful having them so close! They are nice men but oh! so smelly! At lunch time we tied up at the bottom of the Pei-Shih rapid - There was a village on the right bank built on ledges on the face of the hill & a lovely little glen which forms the boundary of the 2 provinces of Szechuen & Hapeh with a bridge across it & up which one c^d. see ranges & ranges of mountains with snow on them. This certainly is a beautiful gorge - The best thing is to get up somewhere high so as to look both up & down it, tho' one realizes the height of the hills better from down below & feels such a flea!

December 29th. Tuesday - A perfectly glorious day - The best we've had as yet which is saying a good deal. We were still in the Wu-Shan gorge until shortly after luncheon time - The gorge ends in a pretty bad rapid & has the town of Wushan-hsien at the end of it built on the slope of the hill, the other side of the river from which we were on - it looked quite an important town with a city wall & a lovely pagoda overlooking the river - In the morning we found a most excellent path to walk on above the rocks & sands - These latter must be more or less covered in the summer when the river rises - Of course progress is much harder in summer - It sometimes takes days to get up some of these rapids & the coming down is a great deal too quick & frequently ends in disaster so I am thankful we came here in the winter! This afternoon we were walking thro' highly cultivated land! Its a wonder how the things grow in this sandy soil - There is some sort of vetch which they literally plant in the sand, also some young green stuff that looks like wheat & some very measly looking turnips - The banks of the Yang-tse certainly don't lend themselves to much cultivation but the Chinaman makes the most of every opportunity. There are any amount of rose bushes trailing about over the rocks - It is such a pity they are not out, I s^d. like to know what kind they are. The coal has given out so we now burn char-coal in the stove - the boy uses it in his - & it gives out a splendid heat. The rest of the things are lasting out well, tho' we have to be canny with the candles - The lamp was such a brute & leaked & smelt to such an extent - forbye giving practically no light - that we have dispensed altogether with its services! Ended the day by getting up a rapid about 7 o'clock in the dark - There was a lovely crescent moon shining so the effect was most beautiful & impressive but I s^d. have thought it was rather dangerous work in the dark, however we managed it safely -

December 30th. Wednesday - A most disturbed early morning! They seemed to be taking us up an endless succession of rapids with even more than the customary noise & shouts! As a matter of fact I think it was just rather a strong current but being half asleep it was not easy to judge! It wasn't nearly such a nice day today - No sun & cloudy. We were in a wide valley all day & progress was very slow as there were many small rapids. We ought to have got to our destination - Kwei-choo-fu some time today but have tied up for the night about 8 miles off - The Lauban (captain) walked on there this evening for some reason or other leaving us to the tender mercies of the crew.

December 31st Thursday - We didn't get to Kwei-fu this morning till 12 o'clock - We had to come thro' "The Bellows" Gorge - The town is just the other side. The gorge is the rockiest we have seen yet, immensely high & absolutely perpendicular rocks so that tracking was impossible but luckily there was quite a nice following breeze so we were able to sail sometimes & not have that dreadful yuloeing the whole time! At the end of the gorge there are enormous rocks sticking up in the middle of the river which are extremely dangerous going down when the river is high - The town of Kwei-choo-fu is quite big & seems most flourishing. There is a sword factory & a brick factory & altogether the place appears most wide awake. The town is built on a slope above high water level but during the winter months when the river is low - as at present - there is a large track of sand & stones which is covered with a 2nd. town composed of rush houses which, when the river gets big again the people have to take "up top sides" out of its reach - It is not a very attractive place - Very dirty & squalid with quantities of black pigs wandering about everywhere - The mast was down (the masts always come down for the downward journey) & we had taken in a cargo of coal - for the Lauban's use at Ichang! - & we were all ready to start at 3 when the Lauban came - with our boy as interpreter - & said we couldn't go till tomorrow morning as there was too much wind, or some such bosh - There's hardly any wind - The truth is he wants to have a night ashore, but it was no use trying to argue so having impressed upon him - or tried to! that we must be in Ichang on Sunday to catch a particular steamer we had to resign ourselves to wait. It is apparently impossible to hustle a Chinaman! We took the Red boat & went to the other side of the river where it was far nicer to have a walk, away from the people, their houses & smells - not to mention the dreadful fact that they killed a pig just opposite our boat - The last day of 1908! We are not going to see the New Year in! Candles are too scarce!

Kwadza No. 262

1.1.09 Friday

The first time I've written '09! A Happy New Year to you my child & many of them. It was my first wish when I woke this morning & I bet it was yours too, for me - wasn't it? We turned this morning at 1/2 past 7 & have started on our downward trip & will be at Ichang on Sunday when if we don't get some letters I shall be vexed, but we will, of course we will & then more at Yokohama! I have been re-reading all your old ones this morning & getting a vast amount of pleasure out of them - I'm afraid you'll have been a long time without any too & have doubtless been reading my old ones. You & I were always glut-

tons for old letters! This has been a thoroughly nice trip & no mistake - The worst of it is going down we can't walk or of course we s^d. get left behind - As a matter of fact we managed to get a walk this afternoon as one of the yuloes broke & while they were mending it we got out & walked for about 1 ½ hrs till they were ready - They're very slow over that kind of thing & we were warned that it is no use trying to hustle them for they dont understand hurrying - Time to a Chinaman means nothing - C. has enjoyed this as much as I have & we are most cheerful & comfortable in our little house - Its the nearest approach to a "home" that we have had since we were married! Up to date we have lived in hotels or other people's houses. You don't know how much we are looking forward to Wreay Syke - I wonder if there is anybody in it just now. If you know mention it in your next letter - It w^d. be interesting to know. We have stopped for the night tied up to the bank - The men are having their food & oh the smell which is coming in thro' the cracks in the door - I wish to goodness I hadn't such a keen nose for it really spoils the pleasure of an otherwise enjoyable evening which we spend reading, writing & playing the Monte Carlo patience - This latter we do by the hour having the fever on us badly! My hair is coming out in handfuls my dear - I shall soon have none left & shall have to apply to the Brussels mauve confetti bag! I really believe I will! Isn't it a bore? I long to hear of your Irish visit - also further hunting news - I do hope you've been having some good days & that the wire is no worse & that "Christopher" is showing good sport - in short that everything is going smoothly without too much "gurning" & fault finding on the part of the field which is always so very annoying - not to say depressing! You must give my love to all the Houghton folk, the Erringtons, Pulleyns, old Nicholson etc: & tell them I was "asking" for them - I sent Mrs. Errington & the Pulleyns Xmas cards - or rather p.c's - feeling very shy but that it really w^d. give pleasure! I wonder if you gave the usual Xmas presents! How's the money hanging out dearie & I wonder if you are getting an allowance. Upon my word I think you might now save yourself that endless fuss & worry of not getting things that you really want - Darning away (or not, as the case may be!) at ancient stockings & forcing them to "do" another week is weary work & quite unnecessary now-a-days - so I hope you are receiving the vast sum of £25 now instead of Muriel - After all thats all it amounts to.

2. 1. 09 - Another rather nasty day today & we are fugging away in the cabin with the stove lit, me in great danger of burning my shoes - ("Sparks" with spats). We deliberately stayed in bed this morning till ½ past 9! Disgraceful of course but after all theres nothing to get up for so what does it matter? It was different going up as we used to get out & walk. The Captain says he'll get us to Ichang on Sunday but I bet he won't - It will be a blow if he doesn't as we shall miss the "Kiang Wo" to go back to Hankow in & perhaps have to go in some inferior steamer & they say that some of them are shocking bad - If we have any time to wait at Ichang we have a cordial invitation to go & stay with the Ross' - Really I don't know how we s^d. have got on if it hadn't been for them & all their kindness - It will be a new experience staying with those kind of people - As long as M^rs. Ross doesn't think it her duty to make conversation the whole time it will be alright! They are the kind of people who show one photographs, "Thats a cousin o' mine", "This is m'aunt, his mother" - You reply "Oh yes" & look at them with searching interest but its next to impossible to make any further remark unless you murmer "She's got a nice face" or some such drivel - I thought of you yesterday getting your "New Year" with Betty - I hope you told her about my hearing of her nephew - By the way my dear if you are at Houghton (which I sincerely hope you are) look up Black & White for Nov: 7th. or 9th. - some date like that - & you'll see the very elephants that we saw in Ceylon at Kutugastota! I've always meant to tell you to look them up. We saw them when we were at Shanghai. Doesn't it seem extraordinary that the distance from Shanghai to Kwii-choo-fu is 1150 miles & that we took 16 1/2 days to do it - Thats an average of only about 69 miles a day - But heres the little time table C. has made out

Shanghai to Hankow	*600 miles*	*3 1/2 days*
Hankow to Ichang	*400 miles*	*3 1/2 days*
Ichang to Kweifu	*150 miles*	*9 1/2 days*
	1150 miles	*16 days*

The last part of course was far less than 69 miles a day - The last 150 miles in 9 1/2 days is slow eno' travelling in all conscience & yet this is the only way of getting into the country - The Chinese are indeed extraordinary people. Its very interesting to have been here & to have seen them & their ways. I am so glad we came. Its an uncommon sort of thing to do too which is always nice - I don't expect we'll find that many other people have been up the Yang-tze in a house boat - tho' many will probably have been to Japan! Do give me the news of Muriel - I long to know how she is "getting on" as they say! I wonder if you have seen her or if anybody has been to stay with her yet. Also how are Tookie & Dod & "the rest" - I expect Mog is just the same as ever this year. I don't expect she'll ever be any different now. I do hope you have been riding Flirt & liking her. You don't know how your account of Irish, the first day you were out (& the only day I've heard about, mark you) made my heart beat with excitement - I felt as tho' I was going to ride her myself. I'm afraid we will never have such a splendid mare as she is. She really is exceptional - at the price - but perhaps Harry might give me a mount on her once in a way - if our own horses were at a low ebb - The more I think of horses the more I long for next winter! The next Sunday you go to the stables give them all extra love & kisses from me especially to the Lady Love & Her Honour's Ladyship - Bless them, tho' they'll be so greedy & eager for food that they'll probably pay no attention but just you make them listen - It really is touching the way C. loves old Tyke & Bighead. He talks of them constantly & is much looking forward to the letter you said you'd write him about them - It will be a terrible problem when they get too old for work. An old horse is only a luxury for rich people & not for those of limited means - And now my child I think I'd better stop this letter - I'll probably be able to write another to be posted at the same time as these 2 so that it will take you a perfect month of Sundays to read them all! If we do get to Ichang on Sunday & get letters it will be exactly a month since we got the last at Shanghai when the steward brought them to us in the middle of the night. It seems like centuries ago - The black bearded man sends you his love. Do you know he really looks most imposing with a beard & so handsome! It does away with the extreme squareness of his face! tho' he doesn't much like it when I tell him so! & says "What ails a square face!"

Bless you forever my child

Toujours à toi

D -

1909 -

January 1st Friday - Started this morning at 7.30 on our downward journey & owing to a strong head wind made very slow progress & only got as far as Wuchan by 5-30 when we tied up, the captain saying that the wind was too strong to go on. Another thing which delayed us about an hour & a half was the breaking of one of the yuloes. It went with a tremendous crash as tho' the whole boat had smashed! We had to put into the side while they spliced it in some way - In a way it was lucky for us as we were able to get out & have a good walk - We came down several small rapids! Its not so alarming as one wd. think except when the boat gets into a whirlpool & swirls round madly! The crew yuloe & row for all they're worth & its soon over. It has been very cold today with the head wind getting into the cabin thro' the 101 holes & chinks with which the boat abounds - To make matters worse I broke one of the windows - the beautiful painted vase of flowers! - however the boy nobly gave us one of his windows out of the kitchen, which doesn't fit very well but certainly its better than nothing. It has a white bird of sorts with its beak wide open apparently trying to catch a blue butterfly, painted on it! A great work of art! The crew have had a hard days work today yuloeing incessantly & are now making up for it by snoring loudly next door as I write - "The Squeeze" has a nightmare every now & again & talks wildly in his sleep (or seems to!). We have had a fire going all day - We haven't come nearly so far as we ought to have done but the captain still swears he can get us to Ichang by Sunday.

January 2nd Saturday - We have had a long & hard day's yuloeing, starting about 7-30 a.m. & going on till 6.30 with never more than 3 or 4 minutes rest at long intervals. It is apt to get on ones nerves, the incessant singing & noise that accompanies it - not one second of quiet! We thought at anyrate at night they wd. be worn out & thankful to rest but not a bit of it, as soon as we stopped, they talked & wrangled amongst themselves the same as usual which I hope shows that it cant be such hard work - or at anyrate that they don't feel it, as one wd. suppose. We took till about 3 o'clock before we were thro' the Washan gorge. We have had no walk today or exercise of any sort but writing letters, reading, piquet, patience & meals have enabled us to get thro' the day quite successfully!

January 3rd Sunday - At 11 o'clock last night just as we were going to sleep blessed if they didn't all get up & start yuloeing again!! It was dreadful! They went on till 2 in the morning, rested till 7.30 & then began again keeping at it all day without ceasing. (It is now 7-30 & they have not stopped yet) The captain is evidently determined to get us to Ichang tonight but it is not possible & its cruelty to animals besides. We came down the big Shin-Tau rapid this morning! It was most exciting as we neared the top & then plunged down into the roaring torrent! It didn't take long to get to the bottom! They have to yuloe for all they're worth in a rapid so as to keep control of the boat & be able to steer her - As we sped down the Pa-dun-ze rapid about 3 o'clock we caught sight of the only other house boat the same as our own that we have seen, waiting to be tracked up! We flew to the window & waved frantically & were soon answered by more European wavings! We were too far off to make out who they were, but they were probably missionaries & evidently Americans for they were flying the Stars & stripes! These are the first white people we have come across since leaving Ichang - with the exception of the Customs man who came on board the first day - At 9 p.m. we got to the custom's house on the other side & the men got ½ an hour's rest while the custom's man - an Irishman with a most charming & friendly tyke - came on board & had a "crack". Luckily there was just eno' whiskey left to give him a drink! As soon as he had gone, on we went once more in the same old way till we at last got to Ichang at ¼ to 1! The men had worked practically without a stop for 18 hours! Instead of throwing themselves down as soon as we stopped & going straight off to sleep as one wd. have supposed, they talked & jabbered for another hour. My pity, which had been roused all day for them was turned to wrath - It did seem so unnecessary!

January 4th Monday - Got up very late in consequence of our disturbed night - Mr. Ross came down, having seen that our boat was in, while we were taking down our curtains & making other preparations for leaving the Kwadza - He took us up to his house where we are going to stay till the Kiang-Wo sails probably sometime on Wednesday. We found bundles of letters waiting for us but none for me from N.J.D. which was most disappointing & unaccountable however they'll come in time I suppose - After "tiffen" we went upstairs & had a glorious bath & clean up - rather necessary after 14 days in a house boat! A "lady" came to tea - There are quite a lot of foreigners in Ichang & scores of missionaries - So far as we have seen they are a dreadful crew - The Ross' are by far the nicest as they at any rate are quite natural & simple - After tea we had a walk in the Chinese grave-yard! There are good paths all thro' it & it apparently is the chief promenade of the residents of Ichang! It covers an enormous amount of ground & certainly is not a place of any great beauty - tho' interesting - The Chinese put the coffin down on the ground & cover it with earth, they don't dig a real grave so the consequence is the whole place is a mass of hillocks about 5 or 6 feet high - Chinese die by the 100 so one wd. have thought they wd. be more economical of space however they think nothing of uncovering an old coffin to bury a new one so I suppose it doesn't matter - The most of them have a rough stone with some writing on it stuck into the side somewhere but it is a very different place to the Kirk yards at home - We came upon a string of miserable looking little pack ponies with great heavy sacks on their backs, tottering along under the weight - Chinamen have no idea of looking after animals & imagine they have no feelings & dont even feed them properly so the consequence is one never sees anything but the most wretched looking ponies & dogs. Oddly eno' they think a great deal more of birds & often have them in cages & look after them well. These poor little pack ponies had muzzles on to prevent them eating by the side of the road as they w^d. otherwise do & at the end of the journey they are expected to find their own food which must be difficult considering that the whole country is as bare & brown as it can be -

<u>January 5th. Tuesday</u> - The Ross' are all that is kind & hospitable & can't do eno' to make us comfortable - The entertainment provided for today was to go to the American mission to see a Chinese boy's trade school which they have started there - It is a sort of D^r. Barnado's & an excellent thing I s^d. think - The missionary & his wife were just as American as they c^d. be - Ever so many other "ladies" dropped in at intervals - My word, but I'm thankful I haven't got to live here amogst them all! They all seem so very full of their own importance too - The Ross' have 3 of the most enchanting grey & white pussies. Great fat friendly things with loud <u>loud</u> purrs - Two of them tie themselves up in a knot together in the same chair in the most engaging manner - There is also rather an innocent little boy of about a year old. I'd like to know what sort of language he will speak - With a Chinese amah - or nurse - talking Chinese, the other servants talking pidgin English - which by the way is the most fascinating language! - & a pure Scotch mamma & papa it will be rather an odd mixture!

<u>January 6th. Wednesday</u> This afternoon C. & M^r. Ross walked to the top of "The Peak" - On the opposite side of the river to Ichang there is a range of hills, the highest of them - about 1000 ft - being The Peak - M^rs. Ross & I followed, crossing the river in a sampan & joined "the gentlemen" - as M^rs. Ross calls them! - & we went for a walk into the country in the valley behind the hills - It was most interesting, as hitherto our experience of China has been bounded by the banks of the Yang-tse. There are <u>no</u> roads in China, the only means of getting about being rough little footpaths with hardly room to pass anybody - There was any amount of agriculture on each side in, what in summer are paddy fields but at this time of year they plant them with cabbages, beans, wheat & we even saw a field of onions! These paddy fields quite remind us of Ceylon built in terraces just as they are there, but there of course the resemblance between the two countries ends - We passed a soap tree - Large pods grow on the tree & the Chinese use the seeds inside as soap. Unfortunately there were none actually growing - M^rs. Ross tried to ask an old woman who was sitting in front of her cottage peacefully smoking her pipe if

we $c^{d.}$ get some but the old lady sprang up in a perfect panic & scuttled into the house as fast as her poor little pegs of feet $w^{d.}$ carry her & shut & barred the door in an agony of terror so we had to give it up - Its very funny the way some of them are still frightened of a foreigner or imagine that they have an "evil eye" - We took a sweep round & came back to the river again at a place with a name which sounded like Annie-miao ($w^{d.}$ be rather a nice name for a puss!) There was a Chinese temple here which we visited - An old priest came to show us round first giving us each a cup of the vilest tea which we had to make some sort of attempt to sip - They are quite satisfied as long as you taste it which is a mercy - It $w^{d.}$ have been an impossibility to have drunk the whole of the filthy stuff! The temple itself is a dirty barn like place with a mud floor & grubby dingy gods all round sitting on sort of altars with an extra big grand one in the middle - In the chief place there was an enormous great gong or drum on one side & an equally large bell on the other both used when they are worshipping & the noise they make on these occasions is I believe appalling! In front of all the gods are iron bowls in which they throw little bits of lighted paper also places to put "joss sticks" which they also burn thinking that in some way or other they are doing honour to the gods - It was anything but an impressive place being squalid & dirty & not at all a fit habitation for gods -We came home down the river in a sampan, rather cold as it was about ½ past 5 & one of the men broke his oar about ½ doz times & had no more idea of mending it than a cat altho' it was quite a simple matter - After tea we packed for we have to go on board the Kiang Wo tonight as she sails at day break tomorrow morning - We are really quite sorry to leave the Ross', they have been so very kind & hospitable - Its a very great question whether we'll ever see them again but perhaps when they get their holiday in 6 years time they will pass thro' Carlisle on their way to Stranraer or Perth when we most certainly $w^{d.}$ go & see them - They came on board with us at about 10 & sat & talked till 11! $M^{r.}$ Ross is a tremendous little "gasser" but a most intelligent <u>thorough</u> Scotchman so one doesn't get bored with him! At last he got to the end of his tether & they left with much hand-shaking, regrets at parting, thanks for hospitality & hopes of meeting again!

c/o $M^{r.}$ Ross, Ichang, China

6. 1. 08

*My own belovéd child, you must be the first to know the news - darling, you can guess it - Your twin is going to have a baby! I can't grasp the fact myself yet & can do nothing but laugh at the thought! You just don't <u>know</u> how pleased I am tho' there's no doubt its a pity it didn't wait a little longer but, in the meantime I'm just as well as well can be & there's no earthly reason why I $s^{d.n't}$ continue so. It is exciting, isn't it? Fancy <u>**me**</u> with a baby! I sit by the hour & think & think. I only knew for certain yesterday when C. got the missionary $D^{r.}$ to come & see me - I began to sort of feel not myself the day after Xmas & since* *then was in a pretty good stew, being so ignorant (naturally!) of these matters so we thought it was best as soon as we got to civilization for me to see a D^r. Of course he had nothing to do or say except that I mustn't over-do - he said certainly continue our expedition - Its a perfectly natural thing & being a good strong woman there's no earthly reason why I s^d. feel ill - In the meantime I'm as right as rain so don't you worry about me dearie - You are pleased, aren't you Ninnie V? It'll be your first god-child & what a ripper it will be. It shall have black hair & blue eyes! It will arive the end of July - I always thought I'd loathe it & be terrified but apparently not. Its wonderful darling perfectly wonderful - C. is as excited as I am & we make all sorts of plans for the future - I was dreadfully shy at first - as you can imagine - but am getting more used to the idea now & love talking about it. I know I shall just love it & so will C. tho' I expect we shall both get thoroughly sick of the little beggar at times - & so will you! I wonder, is it really necessary to give the nurse a holiday on Sunday afternoons , the way Ollie does? but perhaps it will be different & you'n me'll like "wurling" my baby's "toach" - Yes, its possible we may, tho' I know at present the prospect makes you shudder! Oh dearie I am so very very pleased, you can't think but you can gather that from the tone of this letter I know. We've always been very fond of children & got on well with them so I'm sure we shall love young Salkeld - Write to me instantly my child to: Hotel du Wagon Lits, Pekin, China - & put via Siberia as large as you can write it in the left hand top corner (none of your nasty little niggles now) or it will go round by sea & take weeks instead of a fortnight - You're a naughty naughty girl as you must have omitted to do this when writing to China as when we got to Ichang C. had 7 letters from his mother & I had none from you except the old one at last come on & caught us up from Colombo - I had one from Bryde addressed by you without via Siberia & also one from Olly so those two must have come that way by accident as they always send them round by sea unless you're very particular & underline it several times so print it child, anything sooner than give me such a dreadful disappointment again - If it hadn't been for the Colombo letter I don't know what I s^d. have done but I won't distress you by telling you more & rubbing it in - Its over now & I'll get them all in time - Write to Pekin till further notice - which may come by the same post as this or a few days later. Heavens child in all this rigmarole & excitement I've never told you that we shall be home a month earlier! The D^r. thought it w^d. be better to get home the end of March instead of the end of April as by that time however well I am I shan't be feeling much like travelling so my child there's not much longer now - C. hopes to get a day on Tyke & we might even be in time for the P^t. to P^t. if its late! Doesn't it bring it close dearie? I do so long to see you - Lor we'll have more than ever to talk about. I'm going to write to you to Houghton too in-case you're there for they shan't know at Comlongon & Holm Hill before you - And now you've got volumes of diary to read which will take a month of Sundays to read so I must stop. You mustn't think I'm frivolous about the subject. Its just that I'm so dreadfully pleased - Goodness knows its a responsibility I quite realize that.*

Yrs forever & ever

D -

[Daisy also wrote a very similar letter to Nina at Houghton. She stresses: *You mustn't worry about me dearie whatever happens. I really am most awfully well except for feeling a little sick in the evenings. Here I am thro' the first 2 months without knowing it...*]

<u>January 7th. Thursday</u> - On the Kiang-Wo! It seems like coming home to be in her again! All the officers greeted us as old friends especially the chief engineer who beamed & gripped us by the hand! We are the only passengers on board so have the saloon to ourselves, thoroughly comfortable round the stove - There has been nothing to see all day but mud banks & dull grey skies & it is cold & raw outside so it is very tempting to get up a jolly good fug & stay indoors which we have <u>not</u> done - We have been for 2 walks pacing up & down on the upper deck like caged bears!

<u>January 8th. Friday</u> - Another very disagreeable day which we have spent almost entirely writing letters - Early this morning before we were up we got over the dreaded Sunday Island without sticking! This part of the river seems so tame after seeing the gorges & rapids & is ever so much wider & I think dirtier - The chief engineer - who name is McKinnon - is the most innocent man! He took us to his cabin today & showed us a photograph of his family. Father, Mother, brothers & sisters & told us all their histories! We make a funny party at meals - The captain & 2nd. officer English, the 1st. officer & chief engineer Scotch & ourselves - Sometimes conversation is rather difficult & there are long pauses which they don't seem to think it necessary to break but as a rule we chatter away most amicably - They are all such nice men which makes it easier - We are anchored for the night at the mouth of the Tung Ting lake -

Hankow, China

10. 1. 09

My Minty, just one more line must I inscribe to you to go inside C's letter to let you know that your sour Nook letter & Ireland one I got last night & never was so pleased & delighted in all my life - They had been all the way round by Hong Kong & forwarded here from Pekin but "never mind now the train's gone": - I've got them & am perfectly happy. Lor child but how I did love them & do. We got in about 5.30 so C. went off to see if there were any & I waited, without any excitement because I just knew there wd.n't be any but lo & behold back comes the man in no time with these 2 & one from Car (with Via Siberia on it, clever girl) & several from his mother for himself but her letters are too unaffording for words. About The Oaks meet all she says is that you had a "nice hunting run" & that "the Twin" & she rode back to Holm Hill together after it - Now whats the good of a little scrap like that? but no matter, in time I shall have your proper account. Such a dreadful day of rain I never saw. C. went to church this morning but we thought it wd. probably not be very *good for me to get wet so I didn't go with him - I was sorry as I s^{d.} like to have gone this morning - perhaps we'll go this evening if its any better - which I don't think it looks like being - I have a kind of feeling that I'd like to go & thank the great Head of the Universe for bestowing such a blessing on me - Oh I do hope I shall make a good mother - It won't be for the want ot trying anyway if I don't -*

Blessings on you my own Twister - Will you write & tell Miss Lamphier & give her my best love. We've always told her everything at once & this is such a great event I feel I'd like her to know immediately -

Yrs forever & ever D -

I have laughed madly over your Irish visit, for all the world like Christina Mc.Nab! I am simply dying to hear more. Parts of it must have been beastly tho' I feel sure we'll have a "good laugh" over it when I get home! -

January 9th. Saturday - A dull cloudy day & very cold; so, except for a "constitutional" which we forced ourselves to take up & down the deck (with the usual crowd of staring Chinamen who come up in flocks to look at me!) we sat in the saloon all day & stoked the stove! We have got in 2 wicker deck chairs so can make ourselves quite comfortable. We got to HanKow after 5-30. C. went ashore to see if there were any letters & joy of joys brought back quite a bundle! We are going to stay on board this boat till Monday night when the "Loong Wo" starts for Shanghai. They are both tied up to the same pontoon so it won't be far to take the luggage - in fact it will seem quite a waste of time to bother to pack!

January 10th. Sunday - A perfectly horrible day - Poured with rain without ceasing - C. went to church in spite of it but I really cd.n't! We wrote letters all afternoon for tomorrow's mails & at 4 o'clock went to tea by invitation with the Dunnes (the Jardine Matheson people) - Mrs. Dunne is rather a dreadful woman, very gushing & just as "com" as they're made. He is not quite so bad but they're neither of them a patch on the dear Ross'! The school girl daughter was there with very red kitchen-maidy bare arms & her hair almost hidden by the enormous black bow with which it was tied, also a very cock-sure irritating young man! After tea the girl played a "piece" on the piano, loud pedal down all the time very halting & feeble - A dreadful performance but she was quite pleased with herself & Mamma simply bursting with pride! We were glad to escape at last so as to be able to go to the evening church but had to promise to return to tea tomorrow! The captain of the Kiang Wo has his home at Hankow so he is living on shore but we still have the chief officer & engineer on board & have many a long "crack" with them! Such nice Scotchmen.

January 11th. Monday - A much nicer day today tho' very cold - Spent the whole morning shopping & going to various shipping offices etc: trying to find out about steamers & such like but they don't seem to send very "brainy" people to their Hankow offices so we c$^{d.n't}$ get much information, tho' of course it will be alright when we get to Shanghai. Hankow is a highly civilised place after what we have been used to lately. It seems quite funny to be back in it all again. We had to go to tea again with the Dunnes - M$^{r.}$ Dunne was too busy to put in an appearance & the girl was out so we had the full benefit of M$^{rs.}$ to ourselves! After dinner we said "goodbye" to the Kiang Wo - A most touching farewell! M$^{r.}$ Duncan nearly broke every bone in my hand! We shall probably see them again at Wa-hu as they are going to follow us there with some of the Loong-Wo's cargo - With the river in its present low state the Loong Wo can't get over some of the bad places between this & Wu-hu with a full load but at Wu-hu they can take it all so we will have to wait there for the Kiang Wo & transfer it all - The gangway of planks built on pontoons leading from the ship to the bund has been a seething mass of coolies loading all day accompanied by the usual yelling & shouting. It was really a matter of some difficulty to make ones way thro' them especially as there was quite a "sea" running so that the whole concern was heaving about as tho' in a monsoon! It was about 200 y$^{ds.}$ too & terminated in a flight of steps - This boat has more passengers than the Kiang-Wo amongst them being a honey-moon couple! He plays the piano & she sings! Too painful for words as the poor lady is not blessed with a beautiful voice - even when speaking & <u>such</u> a laugh! It is a first rate boat - the best they've got on the river & is most comfortable -

<u>January 12$^{th.}$ Tuesday</u> - We got over all the difficulties quite safely last night tho' we passed another boat stuck & we ourselves I believe just touched - We had stopped at a place called Ta-tung & this was Captain M$^{c.}$Niel who had been waiting 5 hours for us & was in a thoroughly bad temper judging from the way in which he plunged up & down the passage calling at the top of his voice for a boy & swearing like a trooper - at everybody in the boat apparently - for not being up to receive him! At last he roused a boy & together they made the most dreadful noise with his luggage, hauling & banging it about. He said afterwards he hadn't realised what a dreadful hour it was & was so cold & tired & frightfully annoyed at not getting assistance at once that he forgot everything else! He is such a nice man & very good company - We are very glad to have him on board - tho' he needn't have made so much noise about it! We have been all day at Wu-hu waiting for the Kiang Wo - It was <u>most</u> annoying tho' it really doesn't so very much matter to us as our boat to Japan won't go till Sunday or Monday so it gives us quite a big margin. The Kiang Wo is a much slower boat but at last she arrived about 5-30 - Almost before she'd stopped alongside the coolies began to discharge her cargo into the Liang Wo - Of course it took some hours to do & I s$^{d.}$ think it must have been after 11 before we started again. There is an army D^{r} on board - quite a nice young man - who sits at our table & so does Captain M$^{c.}$Niel so we are quite a pleasant little party! The saloon is only heated by hot pipes which is an abominable way of heating a room

- I far prefer the stove we had in the Kiang Wo. All Jardine Matheson's boats are "Wo", the name of the firm itself being, in Chinese "E-wo" - Colder than ever to-day & trying to snow.

January 14th Thursday - Another cold day but nice bright sun - We were going hard all day & got to Shanghai at about 10 o'clock. It was too late to go ashore so we just slept on board & inspite of the fact that they were unloading cargo all night slept soundly! It is very sad to think that our Yangtse expedition has come to an end. I sd.n't think it is the least likely that we shall ever be here again - It has been perfectly ripping & I think somewhat out of the common which is always rather nice!

S.S. Loong-Wo -

14.1.09

"Smelly" dear!!! we get to Shanghai tonight & will probably have missed the mail but just in case we dont I must send you a line. You will be glad to hear that I am as well as well can be, perhaps even better than I was when I last wrote which is saying a good deal! I sometimes feel as tho' I can hardly believe that there's anything the matter with me I feel so well - I'd no idea that people were ever as well as this tho' I suppose May & Dhu Dhu were - We're so used to seeing poor Tookie & Dod feeling so bad & dozens of other people one can think of who get really ill but really barring occasionally feeling slightly sick - which passes off generally as soon as I eat - there really is nothing the matter with me now & long may it continue - I suppose there's nothing to prevent it continuing all the time now as long as I'm sensible & hang it all I am that I think "as regards" my health, knowing that it is a far too precious possession to be tampered with in any way - C. realizes all this too so I think between us it stands a good chance of being a strong healthy child - Don't you think a mixture of C. & I will make a dreadfully innocent baby or even if its only like one of us it won't be bad looking - tho' I says it as shouldn't! I think it wd. be rather nice if we teach it to call you "auntie". I always like to hear the Broadhurst boys call Mog that & it makes a distinction from all the other aunts - We are having quite a lively time in this boat with Captain Mc.Niel! In the diary I've told how he came on board at 3.30 a.m.! The first thing I heard was shouts of "Boy", "Boy" for about 3 mins: as loud as he cd. yell walking up & down the passage in a perfect frenzy of rage & then muttering to himself, finally in desperation, in a loud angry voice almost crying with passion "G— d— these people, why are they all asleep?"! How we have laughed over it since! Of course we were all asleep at 3 o'clock in the morning! He is rather like a child, keen & natural & impulsive - the sort of man Sholto wd. like & evidently he & James were great friends - I wonder if Mog has ever heard of him? A thorough Scotchman, tall & red haired, with at present a beard, high cheek bones & quite the shabbiest clothes I've ever seen but what can you expect after 9 months shooting in the heart of China? We will have to send our luggage home from Shanghai when we get there & before we leave for Japan, for it to get to London the same time as we do - There's no doubt we brought far too many clothes with us & won't miss them a bit

when they go home. The truth of the matter is one wants next to nothing & are far happier without a lot to pack & unpack at each place - We are only allowed the very smallest amount on the train without paying enormous excess so, of course want to take as little as possible as we'll hardly want anything till we get to London & there we'll find the luggage awaiting us - I'm going to get some combinations & flannel shirts in Shanghai & will live in my Bertie tweed & thats really all I want unless of course if the Lampsons want to take us out in Tokio, in which case I have got my blue serge - not that I can meet the band but perhaps Mrs. Lampson will be able to help me to get a bit of elastic put in it - My tweed band is perfectly alright still but then it always was miles too big. I wish I knew how long it is before one has to have ones clothes altered - Perhaps it wd. be better to get a costume with a big sack coat that will do one all the time now & send home the serge one wh: as you will remember is not made for this job being cut away & tight fitting - I'll just have to ask Mrs. Lampson. Oh dear, oh dear how frightened I am of the old N.D.L. boat! Won't it be vile returning to the old Germans - I just know I'll be sick - I've lost every bit of faith I've ever had & will be thankful when we've done with the sea - Poor little you being sick five times in that short time - I've never thrown quite so often as that & am heartily sorry for you! Lord what hell it is! & I've got to face it again - They say from Shanghai to Nagasaki it can be very bad but courage child courage & don't think about the return journey! I wonder if you were sick on the way back too? I do hope not. I suppose we shall be about a month in Japan so that you won't have time to write there at all but continue to write to Pekin till further notice (Don't forget Via Siberia, Via Siberia, Via Siberia!) There is such a nice dog on board who belongs to the Captain, a sort of large fox terrier with yellow spots on its face - Not the least like the Pippet & yet a most engaging person. I do hope the dog will be pleased to see this twin, this twin will be so pleased to see the dog! How well one knows the agony of leaving her to go to Houghton but I'm sure its over very soon for her. Well, well Dalston was the last day I've heard about - When we get to Yokohama I trust there will be budgets waiting but unless you put via Siberia I'm afraid there won't so I mustn't think too much about it. I wrote to Dod Lampson some time ago telling him we arrived at Yokohama about the 25th. so I hope he'll ask us to stay with him for a few days tho' of course the problem of clothes wd. be somewhat difficult to tackle. Its no use taking my black evening dress as I sd. never get into it (you know it always was on the tight side) & yet it seems hardly worth while getting another just to wear once or twice & besides there wd.n't be time to have it made so we will just not be able to go to dinner parties & the only "dressing" I will be able to do will be Olly's "blows" & black skirt which of course is not exactly smart mais, nous verrons - Well, my dearest child I must now cease! as it will soon be time to eat. This boat keeps rather saner hours than some of the others lunch being at 12-30 & dinner at 7 - goodbye for the present & best love from the T.B.

Toujours à toi

D

By the way what a pity my letters have arrived with the envelopes torn - I'll not have to *put so much in them in future & yet I thought they looked strong eno' - Jardine Matheson provided the big envelope I sent all the last lot in & it was made to fit & sealed up by a most obliging Portugese clerk - I don't think it can have burst. I always send them to Comlongon tho' I trust you're more often at Houghton because I feel that from there, wherever you are they can be forwarded -*

A truce, stop writing child Enough - Once one gets wound up how one does ramble on to the other chap

Yrs forever & beyond -

Astor House Hotel, Shanghai

17. 1. 09

My child, one line before we leave Shanghai just to let you know "where all" to write to until we meet once more. The tender to take us on board the "Lutzow" starts at 5 o'clock. It is not 10 past 2 so there is less than 3 hours & then —! How I dread it but its ridiculous to begin in this mood! Its just possible that I shall be perfectly well. (Don't you believe it!) We dined last night with Captain Mc Neil's cousin & his wife (he is staying with them). Such nice people tho' we were bored almost to tears at having to go - The party consisted of host & hostess an Indian army man & his wife, such a dreadfully irritating woman who talked 19 to the dozen & such utter twaddle, dear Capt. Mc Niel & ourselves. Its really very entertaining meeting new people - Mr. Mc Neil took me in & I liked him extremely but in the drawing room afterwards I must say I was somewhat bored with the two ladies! C. enjoyed himself very much I think. Its rather a good thing to go "out" occasionally - Oh! another guest was Capt. Wright, the army Dr. we met on the Loong Wo. We have struck up quite a friendship with him & took him with us in our cab. Such a nice little man - He came with us to church this morning - We went to the Cathedral. Excellent singing & a splendid sermon on Education - Religious v. Secular - It was most interesting. It will be difficult for me when the baby gets to an age when you must teach it something but by that time perhaps I'll know a little more about it myself. In the meantime I really enjoyed the service - I don't know whether I attended much to the prayers or really prayed them but I was interested in it all & felt some good of it all - I shant forget the Shanghai Cathedral - It was as tho' the clergyman was preaching straight at C. & I - My goodness but its a big trust we are being given. It makes one feel one ought to try ones best in these next 6 months to fit oneself for the task - I'm getting so used to the thought now. I hope you are too. Just at first it was most upsetting in its suddeness wasn't it? I am still very well tho' of course occasionally feel a bit sick which is nothing - Probably other people wd.n't even notice but of course "unaccustomed as I am" I feel anything tho' I promise you its really nothing & I've absolutely no cause for complaint! We called on the Landales yesterday but were told by the boy "Missie lying down - getting new baby"! So we didn't get in! We knew she was going to have one - Its a girl so she now has 2 girls & a boy - I am sorry not to see her again. She's a nice woman. I must write to her from Japan - C. is going back there this afternoon to try & see Mr. Landale, just for civility & I am to meet him at the tender. Its perfectly ridiculous I know but I don't really <u>*much*</u> *like being left! Its so much nicer just to go along with him & have no sort of worry or anxiety of any kind but of course I don't say so, for its really perfectly childish & must be suppressed at any price! Its simply pouring with rain. Most dreary & unpleasant. Lets hope to goodness it won't do this in Japan - wdn't it be dreadful?*

It does seem extraordinary to think that while I'm writing this you don't know anything about young Salkeld & he's 2 1/2 months on the way already! Upon my word child I wish you were nearer or better still that instead of letters I was going to see you yourself - in the flesh - in Yokohama when we get there on Saturday! Thank heaven its only Mon: Tues: Wed: Thurs: Fri: & we land once more Sat: evening! Aurevoir chérie - Love from the T.B. & you know how much from me is contained in this foolish unsatisfactory epistle

Yr forever & beyond D -

'Young Salkeld' (Daisy and Carleton's first child, Catherine) in their car at Wreay Syke, near Carlisle, their first home

<u>January 15th Friday</u> - It seems quite like coming home to be in Shanghai again! & <u>so</u> civilised after being up the river - We went first to the Astor House Hotel where the porters & boys greeted us with smiles & bows - How they remembered in a big hotel like that where they see hundreds of people who are always changing I can't think but they say Chinamen <u>never</u> forget a face even after years - I went back to the Liang Wo with a cab to get the luggage while C. went off to get information about our boat, to see about sending home baggage etc: & didn't get back till lunch time. I, in the meantime unpacked - After lunch we visited more shipping offices to try & make out our way back from Japan but anything like the stupidity of the clerks never did I see! They didn't seem to know anything, even about their own

lines - It seems a peculiarity of clerks out here - they are quite useless & so different to any one wd. find in London; however C. managed to get a certain amount of information out of them & the rest can be done thro Cook at Yokohama (they haven't an agent at Shanghai which seems ridiculous) The rest of the day we employed packing the boxes we are going to send home by themselves - It is much warmer here than up the river & today the sun has been shining -

January 16th. Saturday - A summons to the telephone this morning when we were having breakfast! Captain McNiel, who is staying with a cousin of his asking us to dine tonight - Impossible to refuse tho' bored to death at the thought of turning out especially as they give one such a good dinner at this hotel! Finished packing & shopped in the morning - Some of the shops are quite good tho' somewhat expensive. It poured with rain in the afternoon so we went in a tram to call on the Landales - She has just had another little girl so we cd.n't go in, however we had done the right thing by calling - Shanghai in the rain is not a nice place - It seems to get muddier than any other town I've ever seen - Captain Wright, who is staying at this hotel was also dining with the McNeil's so we all went together in the same cab - an extremely draughty victoria with the usual scuttling pony - Almost all the cabs have 2 men on the box, the "footman" one skipping on & off by the wheel in the most terrifying way - We had some difficulty in finding the house & seemed to drive miles to get there - It was quite a dinner party - Mr. & Mrs. McNeil, Captain McNeil, an Indian army man & his wife - Jakes by name, Captain Wright & ourselves - It was quite enjoyable except that Mrs. Jakes was the most irritating woman I've ever met! She was American with the most dreadful voice - We didn't get back to the hotel till 12 o'clock -

January 17th. Sunday - We went to the Cathedral this morning - Quite a big red brick place packed with very smart "London-y" looking people - The music was very good & there was an excellent sermon - It poured with rain all afternoon - Before going on to the tender - which started at 5 o'clock - C. went to call on Mr. Landale but just missed him as he came to call on us! However he came to see us off which was very nice of him - It took rather over an hour to get out to the Luctzow - She is just exactly like the Goeben & Bulow but almost bran new - There are very few passengers. Only 3 Europeans besides ourselves & about ½ a dozen Japs - We didn't get dinner till after 7 - quite an unheard of hour for these boats! We have got a splendid 4 berth cabin so have really got room to turn round in -

6
Japan

The Oriental Hotel, Ltd., Kobe, Japan

January 22$^{nd.}$ 1909

My belovéd child, This is my first from Japan! What next I s$^{d.}$ like to know? Manchuria, Siberia, Russia, Germany before I'm done! I am thankful to tell you that C. has just gone off to the old Lützow to pack up & then we are done with German boats for ever & ever I trust - We are going on from here to Yokohama by train tonight - I felt I simply c$^{d.n't}$ bear another day of the Lützow & C. was nearly as bad so thank heaven we decided to abandon the brute. I have had a loathsome time since leaving Shanghai - I w$^{d.n't}$ have a "life on the ocean wave" no, not if you offered me millions. I have done nothing but lie either in the "Damenzimmer" (ugh horrible German word signifying "ladies room" as by the way you might possibly guess!) or on deck, just like a toy while my poor old C. loafed about as dull as dull & attended to my wants in his usual angelic style - so sympathetic & not the least irritated, tho' it must have been maddening to see a great lump of a helpless woman - & no cause for it either for there was really very little motion - The long & the short of it is, I am the very rottenest sailor & not fit to go to sea! I'm afraid there is no diary to send for I simply have not been able to write it, however I'm afraid it won't be vastly exciting when it does come. It has been horrid weather. Rain most of the time & hopeless dull grey everywhere so the Inland Sea - which is supposed to be one of the sights of the world was most disappointing - as well as the fact that we came thro' the best of it last night in the middle of the night - such a pity especially as, as soon as we (went) thro' the straits into the Inland Sea proper (look at a map) it was like a mill pond & I speedily came to a state of mind in which I c$^{d.}$ have enjoyed it - We were at Nagasaki the night before last & went ashore to dine but the dinner is all I can tell you about for it was raining so hard that the streets were deserted & flooded with rain so that we saw nothing - Theres nothing like rain for utterly & completely spoiling a "day out" from a Primrose League trip to a tour round the world - They say it ought to be fine in Japan at this time of year so lets hope it will soon "take up" - I'm so excited at the prospect of getting to Yokohama tomorrow & finding your letters awaiting me that I can scarcely contain myself - Your Irish one was the last so can you wonder? By the way I was much excited at seeing a photograph in a Black & White of Lord Dunleath & another of Lord Arthur Hay! Unfortunately one can't see their faces! This seems a nice clean town, very different from a smelly Chinese one - There is no time to see anything of it now but we will be back again before leaving Japan - The people look so nice in their kimonos & mounted on curious sort of pattens to keep them out of the wet & only kept on by a strap thro' the big toe - Lord how amusing!

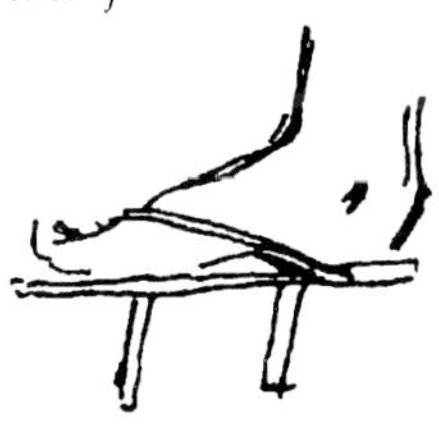

A French Monsieur et Madame of the very chicest place themselves in position to receive their guests! Une reception!

"Bonjour madame, vouz alley bien?" & all the rest of the Jargon! I love the french language but it seems strange to hear it in Kobe! Ah, the ladies have now retired. To wash their hands think you? - or what?!!

I can't tell you much about my health dearie considering how sea-sick I've been - When one has that fell disease one knows nothing else! Possibly young Salkeld made me worse & yet I don't know - anyhow it doesn't matter now. Thank heaven it is over - I wonder how your health is my child - You never mention it & I'd like to know for you know I left you in a pretty rocky state. The next letter will really be a good one - These last two have been rotters I'm afraid & I can't continue this much longer either as we are shortly off to catch our train. Lord but it will be a releif to be in a nice steady train instead of a beastly bobbing ship - There were only 5 European passengers in the Lutzow 2nd. class "concluding" ourselves 2 of whom were getting off here so now that we have gone too there will only be one poor wretched youth - There were 6 Japs too to begin with but I think they'll be all left too by this time - One of the Europeans was a Russian - Such an extraordinary man with a perfect hatred of Japs & English. He was far from complimentary in many of the things he said chiefly abusing English food & saying how cd. a man be romantic on eggs & bacon for breakfast & such like stuff which was quite amusing & none of us wd. "rise" - he was quite interesting too sometimes & says he is coming to see us at Harbine when we pass thro' - he is going there himself - Well dearie I must now cease. This is foul writing paper I'm afraid but no worse than the stuff you used for your first letter so now we're quits - I do hope you're having a good time à la chasse - Embrace every nose severally from me - Bless you forever & ever my child & blessings also from the T.B.

Toujours à toi

D -

9 weeks next Tuesday will see us in London & a very few days after in "the North" - Such a nice name for the Border country! C. is going to write for tickets at the Gaiety the night after we arrive. Its an old custom of his to go to the Gaiety immediately he arrives!

January 18th. Monday - The boat sailed this morning at about 6.30 - Our fellow pasengers consist of 2 Englishmen & a Russian, 5 Jap men & one little Jap woman in kimono who smiles incessantly - Only one of the men wears a kimono & he somewhat mars the effect by adding a Monte Carlo hat & brown boots! The Russian is most talkative (talks all European languages!) & tries to get a "rise" out of us all by abusing the English, their food etc: Nobody will rise & we only sit round & laugh at him as he is really quite amusing - He thinks it is no wonder we are an unromantic people as we eat bacon & eggs for breakfast! I wish to goodness they did the same in Germany! The food on this boat is just as German-y & disgusting as it was on the others tho' certainly quite clean - I have not been very happy today & have spent my time reading with much firmness lying on a sofa in the "Damenzimmer". It is too annoying - Why am I such a vile sailor?

January 19th. Tuesday - Another miserable day for me! Best not to talk about it too much! We arrived outside Nagasaki at 5-30 p.m. where a Dr. came on board & spent ages fussing & examining - He certainly didn't "examine" us very much - To count us over & make sure that we were all there seemed to satisfy him - Nagasaki I sd. think ought to be quite a pretty place but apart from the fact that I was not exactly in a fit state to admire the "Beauties of Nature" it was pouring with rain & everything looked grey & dull & miserable - We went ashore in the N.D.L. launch for dinner - We accosted the first person we met to enquire where there was a decent hotel - It happened to be a most charming Scotch woman who showed us the way to the Belle Vue Hotel, all of us paddling along in thick mud & umbrellas up - It was raining so hard that we cd. do nothing but sit in the hotel - a funny little place - & after an excellent dinner went back to the Lutzow.

January 20th. Wednesday - Talk about the beauties of the Inland Sea! Well, I'm afraid I am not in a position to judge for it was too rough for me to do anything but lie in a deck chair & pray for the end! As a matter of fact it was such a horrid day, pouring with rain & thick mist that there wasn't much too look at even I'd felt inclined - All one cd. see was that there were any amount of islands with trees on them dotted about & looming out of the mist - We got to the straits of Shimonoseki at about 5.30 & got into the Inland Sea proper. Here it was gloriously calm, like a duck pond & I cd. have enjoyed the scenery but unfortunately it got dark so one cd. see nothing!

January 21st. Thursday - We got to Kobe at about 12 o'clock this morning & after another Dr.'s inspection went on shore - It was such bliss to be on shore & the hotel was so comfortable & the lunch so good that we decided we wd. go on to Yokohama tonight by rail & leave the old beast of a Lutzow to follow with the luggage! A glorious plan! C. went back to the boat to pack a bag & after tea & writing some letters we went by the 6.38 train from the Sannomiya station (Sleeping car & diner) - Of course we had no time to see Kobe but we shall be back here on our way thro' Japan - The people look charming in kimonos & mounted on curious looking sort of pattens - They're like little stilts & are grand things for keeping them out of the mud tho' they look dreadfully uncomfortable & if not used to them I'm sure one wd be bound to sprain one's ankle at every step - However they all get along in them splendidly & everybody uses them even to those who wear European clothes & bowlers!

January 22nd. Friday - We had a most comfortable night last night made doubly so by the fact that we were not on the Lutzow! The trains aren't up to ours but still they're quite good & we were able to sleep a certain amount tho' of course there's always a lot of shouting & banging when they stop at a station which is disturbing - We had breakfast in the train & got to Hiranama which is the station for Yokohama at 8-26 - We had been recommended to go to the Club Hotel so selected the Hotel porter with that name on his cap who put us into rickshaws & with our luggage in another off we set thro' the most dreadfully muddy little streets - tho' otherwise clean with nice little houses & shops - The rickshaw coolies are splendid men & splash thru' the mud in heroic style. They are all small with the best developed legs I've ever seen! & <u>such</u> ugly faces!! The streets were full of children going to school, all the little girls dressed in the brightest of kimonos, the boys not quite so gay & <u>all</u> with pattens on - I saw one take a terrible toss running up a slope (I knew it w$^{d.}$ happen!) but he didn't seem to mind even tho' his books & "piece" flew out of his bag into the mud! We stopped at Cooks on the way to the Hotel & collected 28 letters! Immediately we got to the Hotel down we sat to read them! Quite a business, but a most delightful one for all that! It took such a long time to get "thro'" with them that there was only time for baths before lunch & after that a long visit to Cook to make our last final arrangements - We found the usual splendid young man - that Cook always seems to employ - full of information & apparently as much interested in the trip as tho' he was going himself! This morning we heard the most awful row going on the room next to ours - voices raised in anger & abuse. A disgraceful "scene" until we discovered that it was a rehearsal! The Hotel is full of the Baudman Theatrical Company & two of them were evidently "running thro'" a scene! They look quite a good class of company - We must go & see them one night before we leave -

The Club Hotel, Ltd., Yokohama Japan

January 22$^{nd.}$ 1909

Petite, tes lettres! tes lettres!! Oh dear how I love them. how I <u>revel</u> in them - they're just A1 darling - Heavens how I wish mine were ¼ as good but as you cant get your own letters perhaps you think mine are quite good! Anyhow my child if you love them anything like as much as I love yours I'm quite content. No, but really honestly my dear they are simply rattling good letters (& always are) I got 2, one written from Houghton before Xmas & another from Comlongon just after - I really don't know which I like best! And there are others to come yet between the last I got at Hankow & the first of these 2. Don't you fret dearie, I don't mind a bit that they haven't come regularly. They're so absolutely glorious when they <u>do</u> come, that they're worth waiting years for! Go on sending them <u>via Siberia</u> whatever happens & you won't go wrong - Tuesdays, Thursdays & Saturdays from London - You <u>naughty</u> girl to go falling into ploughed fields - How you w$^{d.}$ have frightened me if I'd seen you! That run from Holm Hill must have been <u>bliss</u>! Oh lord how well I can imagine it all - <u>how</u> I wish I'd have been there & yet of course if I'd been at home I s$^{d.n't}$ have been riding in my present condition so I s$^{d.}$ have missed it anyhow - The p.c's taken at The Oaks caused us <u>intense</u> excitement & interest! You & the old love (& my habit I think?) caused me to "cry out" when I first saw it! And then the Kinmount & Cumberland Hunt balls - I always love hearing about these things! Ha! Ha! Ha! You & Parker M.F.H.!! What next I wonder! I bet you & Mog had a "good laugh" over it! I heard *from Mog & Helen of how everybody was saying that nobody looked better than N.J.D. & I can well believe it - Clever child to get a green dress - DayNin always did look nice in green! The old accordion pleateds "came out" at a Cumberland Hunt ball as far as I can remember didn't they & they poor dears cost but a few shillings - £6 is a lot of money doubtless but not for a dress & think what a lot of trouble & worry it will save you instead of that eternal "furbishing up" of old dud? It is now 2.50 & The Lutzow is only just in. We saw her coming from our table at lunch - the old brute! C. has just gone with a man from Cook to see about the luggage. It is all packed ready to go from here by P & O - After he has done this we are going for a walk & won't be back until too late to add to this so I will leave it to go into the next diary & letter & "close" now. C. has today signed the lease for Wreay Syke from June 1st. for 3 years! Isn't it thrilling? Just think of the furnishing my dear - wont it be the deuce of a job? We shall have April & May to do it in (except for the first 2 weeks of May when C. will be out with the Yeomanry) & then there'll only be 2 months of waiting for "little Willie" or whatever you like to call him! (Pon my word it wd. be rather a neat little name wd.n't it? What shall we call him? Its a great question - he certainly shan't be called "for" somebody unless perhaps Tom after his great great uncle Colonel Tom - Its such a nice name - C. likes Lancelot but its too "flowery" I think & reminds me of Tennyson! My health is perfect - I'm even better than I was - Aren't I a lucky dog? As soon as I left the boat I recovered the sea sickness & am right as a trivet - My clothes get smaller & smaller for me every day however the dressmaker is coming to my assistance in letting them out - Doesn't it really seem too extraordinary for words that a twinnie is in this state - The oddest part being that one gets so used to it - Perhaps you'd better tell Helen (if you haven't already) on pain of death if she repeats it to anybody - I dont think she wd. if put on her honour & it might hurt her feelings if she never found out till we got home. She wrote to me such a nice letter - expecting you & so looking forward to having you Bless you my child an 100 fold*

January 23rd. 1909

Observe that this is the next day! There is a theatrical company in the hotel! I had just settled down to go on with this in the drawing room when in bustled a man saying he was afraid they wd. disturb me as they were going to rehearse but I cd. stay if I liked for they didn't mind! I was sorely tempted to remain but didn't as I thought I sd. never get on with this but came next door where it is nearly as bad for the walls are thin & we can hear everything! One woman doesn't know her words! "Welcome, welcome to old England" says a man "Ah, what can I say?" from the woman & a little later on evidently calling "off" "Here, what you are doing with that supper" & the rotten reply of "Coming Father, coming". As if the girl wd.n't have said "Alright , don't get excited"! I wonder how the Greystoke play went off & I do hope you enjoyed your visit & that they weren't too dreadfully noisy - You sd. be more able to cope with them than you were last time anyhow - dearie, I'm sure its best that you sd. have a full time - (You become a real "Society Girl" indeed! Impossible) - tho' of course its difficult & beastly that I'm not there for you to "tell about" it to but I will be very soon so cheer up my dear & then we'll get out each others letters & go thro' them systematically I think talking about the things as they come or else we'll get into the deuce of a muddle! Yesterday I went & ordered myself a new costume. It was necessary as I had to send home my serge after all & had nothing but Bertie's tweed. Its very dark, sort of grey with a faint purple stripe & a "suggestion" of green! Good lord, how dreadful it sounds but don't be frightened its really very nice - I bravely took the woman into my confidence as to how I wanted it made - luckily she understood at once so all was plain sailing & now I must see about something in the nature of a hat to wear with it. At present I've nothing but the tammy I got in Shanghai, all the others going home as they were totally unsuitable for winter wear. On the way home we stop at St. Petersberg & pass thro' Warsaw. Its a lovely day today, bright sun tho' apparently a strong wind - We haven't been out yet but are soon going me to the dressmaker & C. to the Lutzow to get the luggage. She is not in yet but soon will be - Then either today or Monday we get our final orders from Cook. He is making out various different routes for us to take to get to Pekin, Mukden etc: Needless to say I am all for the one which takes in the least sea! There's one way which only means 12 hours but that means heaps more train which of course is more expensive but no matter (The rehearsal - "The Scarlet Pimpernal" is waxing fast & furious! They are acting it tonight - On Monday they are giving "The Flag Lieutenant" - If we are still here it w^d. be rather nice to go to that but in the meantime I have written to M^rs. Lampson at Tokio & they may want us to go there which of course we'd do as soon as possible - we haven't very long in Japan as we will have to leave about the 17th of Feb: so as to fit everything in - I can't tell you much about Japan yet as we haven't seen much but this afternoon we intend "taking a walk" so after it I'll be able to tell you more - Oh dear how lilly that pip is - W^d. that it were here. I saw the very neatest fox terrier yesterday ever I saw in my life - perfectly square with spots -

C. will be back in a minute & I must "go upstairs" before his return so as to be ready.

Yrs forever & a day D -

C. loved your p.c. & studied it with great attention!

January 23rd. Saturday - A lovely sunny day with a fairly strong wind which was rather a good thing as it dried up the streets splendidly - The Lutzow was due in at 12 o'clock but didn't arrive till after 2 which kept us hanging about waiting for her to get our luggage off etc: When she did come C. went on board & found M^r. Lampson there! He had come over from Tokio on business & hearing that our boat was coming in (he knew we were on her) went off in the launch to meet us, but of course we had left her in Kobe! He had tea with us & then we all went in rickshaws to a place called Noge Yama, a hill just outside the town where there are many Shinto shrines & a splendid view of the town & harbour - We ought to have seen Fugi-Yama too but clouds hid the top - The drive there - about 1/2 an hour - & back was perhaps the best part of the expedition. The streets are so neat with their little wooden houses & the most fascinating shops I ever saw & the funny little Japs bowing & smiling away at each other in the most courteous way. The very children give each other a lovely bow from the waist when they meet! Its all so delightfully clean & unsmelly, in this respect far superior to China. Mr. Lampson went back to Tokio & we to the hotel -

January 24th. Sunday - We went to church this morning & on the way there had our first sight of the great Fuji-Yama away in the distance - It certainly looked very fine, covered with snow & gleaming in the sun - After lunch we went by train to Kamakura to see the great Buddha there - We started well by missing the train! much to the agitation & regret of one of the porters! Luckily there was another train going from a different station so we bundled back into our rickshaws & had a dash for that - & caught it! The train took not quite an hour, thro' highly cultivated country, chiefly rice fields with low wooded hills, a great many of them evergreens with brown grass & rushes - Neat little houses are dotted about in exactly the right places with trees of precisely the right proportion & shape standing beside them! Kamakura used to be the capital but is only a little sea-side village now, tho' it has got an electric tram & an hotel - The way to the Buddha goes thro' the village - it stands in grounds of its own surrounded by some very fine old trees with smaller - either plum or cherry trees, at present of course with no leaves on them - The entrance is thro' a great big gateway with images of frightful looking monsters on each side & then up a flagged path with the god sitting at the end of it - he is a most impressive sight, made of bronze, a sort of greeny grey colour - He is 49ft. high 97ft 2in in circumference - His face is 8ft 5in long, his eye 3ft 11in, his nose 3ft 9in, his curls, of which he has 830 are 9in. long & the circumference of his thumb 3 feet! He is hollow inside where there is a small shrine with candles burning - In his back are 2 windows which give light to his inside - He is really very fine & dignified sitting there with his head slightly bowed & his eyes cast down - so majestically calm & quiet - he is called The Diabutsu & dates from about 1252 - he used to live in a temple but this was destroyed ages ago since when he has remained alone in his glory - We climbed up a little hill behind him & got a good view of the town & bay & then went on to the Hase no Kwannon a temple to the Goddess of Mercy - The entrance to this was rather nice up flights of steps with regular trees of single camelias, some of which luckily were in flower also an orange tree with enormous oranges on it! The temple is just like a large open shed with numerous gods & goddesses more or less grotesque & hideous all round & at the back "on the payment of a small fee" as the guide books say, there is a sort of inner place with an enormous image of the Goddess of Mercy - It is pitch dark there so one only sees her dimly by the light of candles - She is made of lacquer gilded over & stands 30 ft 5 1/2in high! After this we went to the hotel & had some tea & then caught a train back to Yokohama - At this hotel we were waited on by little Jap girls - Very polite & bowing in all directions but not particularly pretty! It was quite dark when we got back, a lovely star light night with a new moon - The streets are very badly lighted but each rickshaw has a Japanese lantern which more or less lets them see where they're going I suppose - The harness which the horses in the carts wear is the most primitive I've ever seen. There's no leather, nothing but ropes & strips of bright coloured cloth - The pads are sometimes enormous high wooden things or else just a thick pad of cloth - They have sort of little quilts on their backs & others fastened on underneath them - to protect them from the mud - I suppose! Its very funny; one w[d.] have thought amongst their other & many modern & up to date appliances they w[d.] have introduced proper leather harness.

January 25[th.] Monday - Had a dreadful time this morning trying to telephone to the Lampsons to let them know that we go to Tokio tomorrow - The telephone in this country is even worse than at home for one gets interrupted by excited Exchange people talking in Japanese & they don't understand you when you try to explain that you are not "thro"! Most complicated & confusing! After a visit to Cook when all arrangements for our future - (till we arrive in London on March 30[th.]) - were finally settled we strolled down a street with the most fascinating shops - It began to rain so we had to return to the hotel, perhaps just as well or we s[d.] have been tempted to buy up the whole place - The rain continued hopelessly all afternoon - Too beastly for anything - of course it made it impossible to do any sight seeing - Lets hope it is not going to continue - There is quite a nice little sitting room in the hotel which we have practically to ourselves - In fact the only time anybody has even come into it was when the Theatrical Company politely turned us out as they wanted to rehearse there!

The Club Hotel, Ltd., Yokohama

January 25[th.] 1909

My child, another letter from you this morning & such a ripper - Written from Comlongon all about Greystoke. I'm so glad you had such a good time there, as you seem to have done - What rippers they must all be. I'm longing to know them better. Fancy you getting such pals with Millie Lowther. Last time you thought she was a sort of "calf" didn't you but after all you were'nt in a state to make any new friends just then were you? & the fact that you did like her this time & were amused with all the shouting & yelling just shows me how much better you must be in body & soul - It is nice that you're such a "success" at Greystoke - We've always longed to know them properly & knew we'd like them - Its just pouring today - or rather this afternoon - Too "file" for words but lets hope it won't last. We go to Tokio tomorrow - We c[d.n't] go this afternoon as my clothes were not ready - My "costume" is going to be quite nice I think but I have very great doubts of the hat - It had to be made as anything they had were too dreadful for words - It is a sort of mouse coloured toque with purple wings - Oh lord doesn't it sound dreadful? but how w[d.] you like a woman to put a bundle of straw with a feather on your head & you've got to decide alone whether it can ever possibly look anything like a hat when at the moment it might simply be anything? It is going to cost 37/- too whats more - So hideous or comic or what not I've just jolly well got to wear it - It is to come tonight so before long I shall know my fate! One can't get nice plain becoming things! Our expedition to the Great Buddha yesterday was delightful - My dear, such an impressive thing - perfectly huge & so dignified - C. walked all the time - it wasn't really far - but I had a rickshaw which came along behind & I got in when I felt so disposed - Its seems dreadful for me to be in this feeble sort of state but of course its better to give in & I am most sensible I can assure you - It does seem extraordinary to think that you don't know anything about it yet - as I write - Nobody knows in fact except C. & I & Mrs. "Bax" the dressmaker but I suppose in a day or two you'll hear & what will my Ninnie V. think & do I wonder? I shan't hear from you, on the subject - till Pekin - It seems years to wait till then - C. is "even now" with Cook making final arrangements for our getting there - I think we are to go across to Fusan (only 12 hours from Moji & at night so that's not so bad!) & by rail thro' Korea to Seoul, from here 2 days sea (just must be faced) to Dalny & "thence" by rail via Mukden to Pekin - I think it will be very nice seeing Korea & am looking forward immensely to Pekin. I like Yokohama very much. It is so nice and clean - To my mind the Japs are infinitely superior to the Chinese - a Jap is as clean as one is ones self. Chinese live in filthy hovels while - Goodness only knows what I was going to have said for at the "juncture" in came C. with 2 letters from you!!! I nearly swooned with joy! Nov: 27th. & Dec: 2nd. been to Pekin all the way round by sea, forwarded to Hankow & then here. Now I think I have got the complete "Set". Nov: 27th. is from Comlongon just after you got back from Ireland & Dec: 2nd. from Comlongon & Houghton just before Broadfield - which I haven't heard about - so perhaps thats another letter thats on its way (oh I do hope so). I just perfectly love your letters - And to think that you think them dull - I was perfectly engrossed reading about your evening clothes & then you began to apologize for mentioning them & I laughed aloud! Talking of clothes - my hat has come & I'm afraid is dreadful - too small & horrible "tight" - Never mind, after the Lampsons we shan't know a soul & after all quite nice women sometimes wear awful hats & besides perhaps it isn't so dreadful! I shall try & get time to take it back in the morning to see if they can "fake" it about a bit otherwise I might have a go at it myself. Wd. that Spookie were here! She'd soon fix it! It will be what I have on when you first see me so don't take an awful scunner at me the way people do in books when they see other people for the first time after their faces have been mutilated in an accident or something! I'm awfully glad you & Mrs. Sulkeld are such good friends She writes C. the most hopeless letters you can imagine - Heaps of them but absolutely nothing in them & not worth 2½d. 2½d. forsooth! not worth ½d. - She just hasn't the gift - Of course its alright about the Oakes & I'm sorry she was distressed - I felt it was all "Louis" & I daresay it will be better in the end.I'm awfully glad you & Helen are going to look at Wreay Syke some day & of course you'll tell me all about it - I am looking forward to seeing the Lampsons tomorrow - I'll have to tell Mrs. L. of my "condition" I think or they'll want me to do too much perhaps - I don't think she'll notice it for herself yet tho' my waist certainly is enor-

mous - I don't know <u>how</u> to tell her - It will be most embarrassing & yet I think it w^d. be better to do so. Don't you? Silly question unless you answer by telepathy for I shall see her tomorrow morning almost before this letter has started but I like writing to you as tho' I was talking - This is what I like about your letters. They're real "talks" - In this hotel there is a quite nice "Ladies drawing room" which C. is allowed to smoke in & which we have practically to ourselves (except then they came & turned us out to rehearse!). We draw up arm chairs on each side of the fire & if it wasn't so dreadfully "hotel-y" we really might be in our own house - Heavens what experience of hotels I'm getting & before we'd scarcely ever stayed in one! The Temperance at Castle Douglas or The Woodbank being about the limit! I rather like hotels. We criticize freely & like some much better than others - They're very expensive here - in fact travelling in Japan <u>is</u> expensive worse luck but that just cant be helped. I do wish M^r. Salkeld w^d. stump up a bit better especially now we're going to be a "family" but I'm afraid he wont being so dreadfully pigheaded & I daresay £1200 will be alright, anyhow I'm not the woman to complain - not me - I've too many of the blessings of this world to be thankful for to worry myself over <u>that</u> & when I get happy letters from you my own belovéd Twist my cup of happiness is full to overflowing - I am going to write to the Young Brother for Edouard de Reszke's address - We might <u>possibly</u> be able to see him which w^d. be a great lark & anyhow I must write to the kid. Clever little boy. <u>Him</u> Chorus Master forsooth! What next I s^d. like to know? He's a perfect little marvel that child & him only 22. I only hope - as C. suggested - that the others won't be jealous of him - And yet where theres real merit. I dont expect they will be. My dear I can't think why you dont go & hear - Surely you c^d. do it & get back the same night? It w^d. be such a lark but of course he's left by now. I'm so glad the Big one is finishing your picture. I had a dreadful feeling that he never w^d. Is there a good place for it in the drawing room at Wreay Syke? I think to have the room a sort of browny yellowy grey to match it w^d. be rather nice with green do you think & perhaps a good pink cushion or two? I think furnishing is the most difficult thing in the world & I feel inclined to paint a picture of it so as to get the right tones! Pon me word thats rather a good idea - And now my child I must cease this epistle - Blessings on you - It is Monday Evening so at home it is about 10. 30 in the morning & possibly at this moment you are climbing into the motor to go to the meet if the Broadies have come home but if not going in the Murrell Hill conveyance. Give Helen my love & tell her I'm going to write to her soon, also love to all the rest of the family - Tell Selby his letter to C. has just come & is much appreciated (He also did not put Via Siberia hence delay) C. thanks him very much for it -

I wonder what the D.F.H. ball was like & if dear old Albert was there. Dear me, what an escape that was, when I now know the real thing & I honestly believe I w^d. have done it. I'm sure I s^d. for I always expected & made myself think it was inevitable - To think of it!

Aurevoir Chérie

Toujours à toi D.

I've got "writers' cramp" or something in my wrist from this letter!

January 26th Tuesday - We got away from Yokohama this morning by a very slow train at 12.40. We stopped at every station - It was a lovely sunny day - The hills in the distance with snow on them looked beautiful - The country thro' which the train runs is very flat just here - It is mostly rice fields in which the water stands 2 or 3 inches deep so that it looks as tho' there had been a flood. There are any amount of neat little wooden houses spotted about. Each one is like a little picture! We got to Tokio in about an hour & drove to the Hotel Metropole in rickshaws - Tokio seems to be a most confusing town, numberless small streets neither named nor numbered & dozens of little bridges over canals or creeks - After lunch, armed with a map we found our way to the Lampson's hotel where they had left a message to say they wd. be back at 5 o'clock so we employed our time by a walk in the Park. Of course at this time of year it is very brown & bare tho' rather nice in spite of that, with a pond with a fascinating fountain in it, in the middle! There was also a large open space where they were playing football & hockey. We became engrossed watching the latter - little Japs tearing about in the most energetic manner! Then we went back & had tea with the Lampsons at their hotel & sat for a long time talking & comparing notes - It was very nice seeing them - Mrs. Lampson seems to be enjoying Japan very much - They move into their house tomorrow & we are to go & have lunch with them - We walked back to our hotel - rather creditable to find the way in the dark for the streets are shockingly badly lighted inspite of the lights - few & far between - being electric - There are just dozens of trams. They follow each other at the rate of one a minute about!

January 27th Wednesday - We started off this morning about 12 to find our way to the British Embassy to have lunch with the Lampsons - On the way we passed the Imperial Palace which is enclosed by high walls & many moats. Nobody is allowed inside the Palace or the Gardens tho' there is a kind of park just inside the wall where the public may go but it is really nicer outside the wall for fir trees of the most lovely shapes grow all along the top & are reflected in the moat where quantities of wild duck &, I believe geese - tho' we didn't see any - swim about as tho' they were tame ones, tho' they really are genuinely wild - The Lampson's house is inside the Legation compound & we had some difficulty in finding it The woman at the gate gave us long directions how to get there which were quite useless as we didn't understand a word she said! After lunch we went in the Lampson's carriage - a most ridiculous old ramshackle shay with a pair of innocent shaggy horses, a coachman & a "running groom" who every now & then leapt off the box to run on ahead & clear the way, shouting & pushing the people aside, really rather necessary sometimes in these narrow little streets - We had a most delightful drive to the Ueno Park where we got out & visited a temple - It stood amongst a lot of very fine old trees & had a splendid avenue of great stone lanterns leading up to it. All temples have these stone lanterns which are presented to them as sort of offerings. There was a lovely gate way most beautifully carved & then up a few steps was the temple itself which looked rather small & insignificant after so much grandeur - We didn't go inside as it means taking off ones shoes but they are always open in front so one can see a good deal - This was a very nice one with beautiful carvings painted & gilded but all toning in with each other & not the least gaudy - We then tried to see the tombs of the Shoguns (one of the early dynasties) but in spite of M^r. Lampson trying his best to explain to the coachman (who doesn't understand English) in his best Japanese - which - as he has only just begun to learn it - is very shaky! we didn't get in - The principal gate was shut & we c^d.n't find out if there was another so had to give it up! After this we went & had tea in a real little Japanese tea house in the middle of the park surrounded by cherry trees of which there are masses - They must be quite lovely when they're out, It is most tantalizing that they aren't - There is no grass which seems rather a pity - Under the trees it is just the bare earth - We sat on cushions on the floor of the tea-house with our feet outside & a girl brought tea & sort of sponge cakes which were quite good - The tea itself was just like hot water with a slight flavouring of hay & was a sort of pale green with no milk or sugar & was drunk out of cups with no handles. They brought out boxes of burning charcoal for us to warm ourselves by, these being the only kind of fires they have - At the end there was much bowing & polite goodbyes - M^r. Lampson airing his Japanese with great success. We paid a short visit to another temple & went & saw a panorama of a battle fought 300 years ago. A most wonderful & realistic production which we got to by a pitch dark passage & stairs! A Jap explained it at great length but we were none of us any the wiser except M^r. Lampson - & even he didn't always understand! After this they drove us back to our hotel - Tokio gets more confusing every time one goes out I think! It is very large & a perfect network of little streets - We looked down on it from one place in the Ueno Park & it looked a perfect maze of roofs - None of the houses (scarcely) are more than one story high & <u>very</u> small at that - There are countless wires overhead, telephone telegraph & trams by the score - They look out of place somehow above the funny little houses -

Metropole Hotel, Tokio

28. 1. 09

My child, I now take up a perfect devil of a pen to inscribe you a few lines "along with" some diary - Possibly I won't have time to write the latter up to date as we have had a "big" day today visiting temples this morning & shortly going out again to meet the Lampsons & go with them to a Geisha singing & dancing show at the Theatre - It was so nice seeing dear M^rs. Lampson & "Dod" - She asked after you & has several times talked of you - she is an <u>awfully</u> nice woman I think & so friendly & cannot get over the idea of she & I meet-

ing under such very strange circumstances! It is odd certainly - I enjoyed my day with them yesterday so much. They are so delightfully keen to see & do everything & so interested & pleased - There certainly is heaps to do & see - I love Japan & think the Japanese are charming - They have such nice manners & are awfully nice to have anything to do with in the way of sight-seeing - They're always laughing too which is rather nice! A man from a silver shop has been showing us all sorts of nice silver things produced from a bag & is now packing them away. We had offered him £1 for a selection, which he does not consider eno' - He'll probably give them to us for that in the end - The only plan is to pretend you don't want them & they generally give them to you for what you offer in the long run. I'd be sorry to miss this lot. Such a dear little model of a stone canteen like they have in all the temples, an awfully pretty chain & 4 charming hat pins with dragons & poenys! It's dreadful! when they come & press these things on us we invariably fall heavily but C. is holding out firmly this time for £1 or nothing! We are going on to Nikku tomorrow & back to Yokohama on Sunday or Monday & after that I know C. has made you out a most elaborate list of all the places we go to till the 30th of March!! I wonder if you will come up to London to meet us. It wd. be nice dearie but of course we shall only be there a day or two staying at Lowndes Sqre. so you'll have to see if you can possibly fit it in somehow or other. If Shosh was up cd.n't you go to him? The hat you will be glad to hear is not so dreadful as we thought it was! In fact I'm beginning to think I look rather nice in it & C. says he likes it now that he has got used to it but it was such a Shosh seeing me in a hat again after first wearing nothing but a topi & then a tammy! I've simply never had on the black hat with the blue & the pink only once at Naples & now they are on their way home! If ever I do this kind of thing again I'll know much better what to take & what not to. There was snow when we got up this morning but thank goodness it has gone now & it is not nearly so cold. I haven't had an opportunity of telling Mrs. Lampson about young Salkeld, perhaps she knows without being told & yet I don't think its noticeable yet - She's such a dear I sd.n't mind telling her a bit tho' I'm afraid she'd tell Ciss Ruthven who wd. tell other people & so on, however I don't think I mind, like the others do. Everybody must know in the end & if it pleases them to gas about it now, it doesn't hurt me - especially when I'm not amongst them all. I long to know if you & Mrs. Salkeld have spoken about it & what she says! I don't expect she'll half like being a grandmother! She certainly doesn't look like one! I am still as well as I can be, perhaps better even as I don't feel sick hardly ever now - Isn't it a mercy? (Hang! the man won't take £1 & he stuck out for 11 yen & C. wd.n't give him the extra one - I think a great pity but its just possible he will come back) - This is quite a nice hotel but not so chic as the one the Lampsons were at & consequently much cheaper therefore we don't mind that it is not so swagger - it is made of wood which makes it abominably cold especially in the evenings otherwise its alright - The temples which we visited this morning were perfectly lovely - I shall try & explain them in my diary tonight - shan't have time now I'm afraid. I do wish you cd. see them. Shiny black lacquer floors, lovely red lacquer altars, gold lacquer pillars & the most enchanting carvings of birds & flowers painted most exquisitily - Everything in such excellent taste that it makes ones mouth water & I long *to be able to go there over & over again. The big entrance gate was a real "thing of beauty & a joy forever" - An immence thing of red lacquer -*

Gave one this sort of impression but I must get a photograph of some of these beautiful things. Its the only way even if its only a p.c. Its next door to impossible to explain these beauties to you but I can tell you they're something like & all so "chaste"! It was quite awe-inspiring to be standing there amongst such beauties. Oh dear! how I'm getting "tied up"! And now I must stop as it is time for the theatre & this must be posted now or never. Bless you forever & ever my child. Best of love from the T.B. (I won't say like Winnie Irwin that he gets more "devine" every day because I don't think he does!)

Yrs now now & always D -

The Club Hotel, Yokohama

February 1st. 1909

Petite, we have just got back from Nikko to find 2 of your letters waiting for me. Such rippers. The oldest was the last of the lot without "via Siberia" has the Oaks day Ennim & Car's ball. I think it "completes" the set. I am really quite sorry! I have enjoyed having them dribbling in like this so I do hope you have ceased to bewail - as I've no doubt you did when I first wrote in the heat of disappointment - for its perfectly alright now & I have got them all & the fact of them being old doesn't detract from their merits one whit - The 2nd. letter is written on Jan: 9th Curthwaite (poor child) Barrock (again, you naughty girl you are not to fall about like that, I'll not have it) & you were going to have Dalston Hall the following day. I simply yearn to see your hunting diary with me on the opposite side. What a splendid idea. It will be so fearfully interesting looking at it together! My diary this time is like a guide book I'm afraid - I wonder if you can honestly enjoy reading it? As the purser on the Bülow used to say "How is that pos-i-bul?" But yet of course I know it is & that you love reading every word I write, the same as I do yours & the longer the better. Whats the use of being a twin if one doesn't know that? Bored with my diary? why you might as well expect me to be bored with your letters! Nikko was too cold for words but I just loved it never-the-less. C. is sending you a p.c. of the best gate there which with the help of a magnifying glass & my description you may be able to understand a little how perfectly love it is - You might possibly think that it was too full of detail but that somehow doesn't seem to matter. As a whole - in the distance - it all takes its proper place & when you get up close you nearly go mad with the beauty & delicacy of the detail & want to study it as close as you can get - Isnt it a mercy I am so well that I can appreciate it all to the full - I don't think I cd. enjoy it more even if I was perfectly alright - I am alright but of course there is a difference & I'm not exactly my "usual" - naturally - Nikko is supposed to be good for furs so, having been pestered by a woman to go to her shop we went there one afternoon but there was nothing - only cat rabbit monkey badger etc: There was white fox at £5 a

The Nikko temple

skin which I might have got perhaps (2 or 3 of them) with wedding cheques but I didn't know if they were good or if that was cheap so I'm just going to wait for London & get something there. Much more satisfactory. Its impossible to get things in these kind of places when ones so ignorant. Don't you agree? In the end to get out of the shop we bought a pair of minute slippers made of orange puss which shall be "its" first pair of slippers! C. was very scornful & thought me quite mad but it was better to spend 1/- on them than pounds on something we didn't want, so I was firm & they are such dreadfully innocent affairs! Theres no doubt that the Yalla Yin must eventually be a pair of slippers. He w^d. look perfectly bewitching & be so comfortable. I'm very glad you're showing my diaries to M^rs. S. I was immensely amused to hear how you & Madcap tore her habit! It must have been dreadful for you. In one of her letters to C. she said she was going to get a new one because "the old one was beginning to look better on a dull day"! she didn't say it had a hole in it! As you will notice we are back at our old hotel again but are probably going on tomorrow or if not, next day to Myanoshta. You've no idea what a man C. is - He's worth dozens of maids & does all the packing & unpacking - won't let me do a thing - forbye of course all the arranging & paying etc: There never was such a man! I had a letter from Madge tonight but before it happened as the letter had been round by sea also one from our Mum - I never "got telling" M^rs. Lampson about young Salkeld - There was never an opportunity. I w^d. like to know if she noticed. Barring the fact that my waist is very large I really don't think I'm very different but of course if she remembers the former size of my waist then she probably did guess - not that it matters. How I love to think of you having good days like at Ennim. Oh dear, oh dear, is there anything like a good day's hunting - Madge had a day with Muriel & writes "anyone who can hunt regularly can't have much to grumble at" - She's right, to a certain extent, isn't she? Anyhow while its actually going on nothing else in life seems worth 2d. I do hope you'll have some with Charlie's hounds. My dear w^d.n't it be thrilling? Also with the D.F.H. "Allie" is a rotter if she doesn't ask you -

2. 2. 09 - Broke off here to go to bed. There is a tiresome female staying in the hotel who uses the sitting-room that we have had all to ourselves last time. It means C. can't smoke here & theres nowhere else to go except an uncomfortable "common" room where the other men smoke dreadful cigars & tobacco - I don't like a room thick with different smelling smokes! We have settled not to go to Myanoshta till tomorrow. Somehow theres a good deal to do here - For one thing this is the last place where there is a Cook! You've no idea what a useful man that is. He always knows a great deal more about the railways, ships etc: than the companies do themselves & of course gives one an unbiassed opinion as to which are the best hotels to go to etc: Oh dear I wish we were made of money There are such heaps & heaps of lovely things that one longs to buy but its no use we must resist. As it is how we're going to furnish when we get back goodness knows but "sufficient unto the day" I hope there'll be a sale somewhere near Carlisle. That must be a better cheaper way of getting chests of drawers etc: than buying new ones surely? It w^d. be rather fun to attend a sale & bid for fenders & the like! You & Bryde once did it at Summerhill didn't you & got splendid things for a "mere song"? I'm certain thats the way to do it - tho' beds, curtains carpets & those kind of things of course must be new - Happy thought - how about B's furniture for a servant's bedroom? I expect he'd be glad to get rid of it! Ninnie dear, there's no doubt about it - it will be nice when we are really established at Wreay Syke. There'll be lots of times when C. will be in Carlisle or shooting or something & then you'n me'll be "à deux" in the old way, only better for it'll be like when Harry & Mog used to leave us at Houghton but with the difference that the servants & everything will be mine & we can just blooming well do what we like with them! And when C. returns we'll both be very glad to see him I'm sure for he is an extremely nice person "I'll do insure you" -! Comment va la petite? Of course when you write from Houghton there is no news of her which is sad for I love hearing about my dog - You don't know how I revel in news of the horses. I do hope you have had a good time with M & H away & you with 2 horses to yourself. Theres a mail in tomorrow morning so I am "looking" for another letter. This will go tonight so I'm afraid I won't be able to let you know if I do get one. And now I think I'd better stop. This is merely "rambling" & tho' pleasant reading - at least I know I love when you "ramble"! - its not very profitable. C. always insists upon addressing anything of his to you to Houghton as he feels so sure you will be there. So you are generally I expect (& hope) & yet I feel Comlongon is safer especially with the Broadies going away etc: Well this budget will take a bit of reading! I hope you won't get it on a hunting morning. Theres never really time to read letters properly - at least those from the other chap.

Well, goodbye dearie once more. Best of love from the T.B.

Yrs forever & ever Amen D -

January 28th. Thursday - This morning we went to the Shiba Park to see the tombs of the Shoguns - We got there by tram, the Japanese clerk at the hotel giving us many directions & a paper with the name of the place written on it in Japanese for us to show the conductor, so we c^d.n't go wrong. The tombs are in the Park - The entrance is thro' the most magnificent red lacquer gate-way - An enormous place with pillars & carvings - Immediately in front is a temple but we didn't go into this one - a priest (at least we supposed he was one) led us to another temple which is supposed to be the best where another priest met us & showed us round - This was the Mortuary Temple of the $6^{th.}$ 12th & $14^{th.}$ Shoguns - They are all built on very much the same plan - First a gateway leading into a courtyard filled with stone lanterns, then another gate way into another courtyard where there is a large bell on one side & a trough of water on the other where they wash their hands before praying, then yet another gate which leads by a covered way to some steps, where before going up one has sort of covers put over ones shoes (otherwise one $w^{d.}$ have to take them off). Up these steps is the Praying room, a most beautiful place, black & gold lacquer, quaint paintings of dragons, a perfectly lovely ceiling & best of all, all round the walls at the top the most beautiful carvings of flowers & birds, in wood, painted - Cherry blossom with parrots, hydrangas & birds of paradise, poenys & pheasants etc: etc: Perfectly fascinating - Then came another place called the Meeting room with the most glorious black lacquer & gold & beyond that the shrines, each with a red lacquer altar in front & numberless gorgeous decorations but we were not allowed to go up close, nobody but priests being allowed into this holy of holies - The whole effect is quite exquisite - perfect colouring & such good taste - Behind this temple are the tombs. Each one has a flight of steps leading up to it, one was made of bronze with lovely bronze gates most beautifully carved with dragons etc: The others were of stone & not quite so fine. Each one has a smaller temple or oratory in front of it - The exteriors are apparently very fine too but to protect them they have an outside wall of black boards so one can't see them - From here we went to the Temple of the $2^{nd.}$ Shogun - It was very fine too, the chief features being the enormous gold lacquer shrine & the lovely red lacquer altar - The black lacquer here was beautiful too, delicious shiny black like a looking glass - The floors are all made of this but they are almost entirely covered with matting - Then we went to the Octagonal Hall which contains the tomb of the $2^{nd.}$ Shogun - It is composed of the largest & most magnificent specimen of gold lacquer in the world inlaid with enamel & crystals - a perfectly lovely thing. Just outside the tomb are two large stones with the most exquisite & minute carvings on them - By this time it was getting late so we had to leave, going out again by the same beautiful red gate - I shan't forget the Shiba Tombs of the Shoguns in a hurry & wish we had time to go & see them many times more. Its almost impossible to take it all in in one visit & there is heaps more that we $c^{d.n't}$ even attempt - The priests who showed us round were such nice little men who spoke quite good English & had the most excellent manners & laughed a great deal! This latter is a sign of great politeness in Japan which is apt to be somewhat startling till one knows it! (For instance when the waiter comes to tell you that what you have ordered is all finished, he bursts out laughing in your face!) We got little peeps of gardens enclosed by walks amongst the tombs & temples but unfortunately one is not allowed in - All round about there are any amount of fine trees, firs & other evergreens also cherry trees, wistiria etc: If only they were in flower! At 5 o'clock we sallied forth once more to go to the Japanese theatre - They are giving a series of performances for the Italian Earthquake fund - M$^{r.}$ Lampson & a Miss Clive were there waiting for us - It was a <u>real</u> Japanese entertainment - Weird was not the name for it! The first item was positively painful! Three little geishas sat on their heels perfectly motionless & sang - if it can be called singing! - to the accompaniment of 2 other geishas & an old man playing on the national instrument which is something like a banjo with 3 strings & played with a flat piece of ivory - They were all dressed alike in black kimonos with gold or silver obis (or sashes) & sat in a row on a low red platform with a bright green fir tree painted behind them. They went on for hours & it was most painful! The next thing was very much the same except that 2 Geishas also in black kimonos came & danced in front of the "orchestra" - The next was more elaborate as there were 2 rows of "orchestra" - one raised above the other - with some dreadful drums added to the instruments & the Geishas who danced in front wore the most gorgeous kimonos - They have their faces painted white with a dab of red on their lips & in style & everything else look exactly like their own pictures - which I have always thought were impossible! Their background was plain gold & black & the whole effect was most Japanese-y & curious - Everything they do has a meaning & the song which goes on all the time is explaining it all - in fact it is a play - but of course we c$^{d.n't}$ understand it - When they are supposed to be off the stage they just kneel down with their backs to the audience! The last part was still more elaborate but we c$^{d.n't}$ stay as it was getting so late -

<u>January 29$^{th.}$ Friday</u> - This morning we went to say goodbye to the Lampsons & went to Nikko by the 2 train from the Yeno station - We got lunch here - European food in a Japanese house & oh the draughts! The place seemed to be made of glass & none of the doors or windows fitted besides a large pane of glass being broken behind our heads. Japs are so used to being cold that I suppose they don't feel any extra little draught! The journey took 5 hours stopping at every single station - The country was flat with a glorious range of snow-covered mountains - Fugi amongst them - on the left hand side. Oddly eno' there were parts which reminded me forcibly of the Long Plantain! Fir woods with brown grasses & what looked like beech seedlings with the dead leaves still on them, just exactly like woods at home tho' the resemblance ceased abruptly when one saw a rickshaw going by or passed some houses which certainly are not the very least like Margaretsfield! In parts there were miles & miles of rice fields looking very bare & desolate - Some of the more precious trees have their trunks wrapped up in straw & look too comic for anything - like very attenuated hay stacks! When we got to Nikko it was quite dark & fearfully cold - Snow on the ground & freezing hard. We put on all our coats & came up to this hotel in rickshaws. They are <u>not</u> cold weather "vehicles" by any manner of means! We each had 2 men & 2 others arrived as we neared the hotel to assist at the last part which is up hill. The little street up which we came from the station is lighted with electric light! Some of the little shops have it in too where it

looks most out of place! Our reception at the hotel was like a scene at the Gaiety! The front door was brilliantly lighted with electricity - On our approach the door was flung open & out streamed 2 girls & about 1/2 a dozen men who ranged themselves in a row & bowed down to the ground to welcome us - We stepped out from our rickshaws, assisted on all sides & entered, bowing to right & left! Most impressive!! We are the only guests at the hotel as this is really a summer place but they all bustled round, tripping over each other in their efforts to serve us & in a very short time provided us with an excellent dinner - There are no fire places, only horrible charcoal stoves so it is very difficult to keep warm especially as none of the doors or windows fit!

January 30th Saturday - Colder than ever today, goodness knows how many degrees of frost but a nice bright sun so that it really is warmer out of doors than in the hotel - We spent the morning at the Mausoleum of Teyasu (he was one of the Shoguns) - We thought the Shiba temples were fine but this is 10 times more beautiful - It stands in a wood of the most beautiful fir trees (crytomerias) & really passes my powers of description - The approach to it is up an avenue of cryptomerias with a huge stone Torii at the top - a torii is a Shinto gate-way something like this

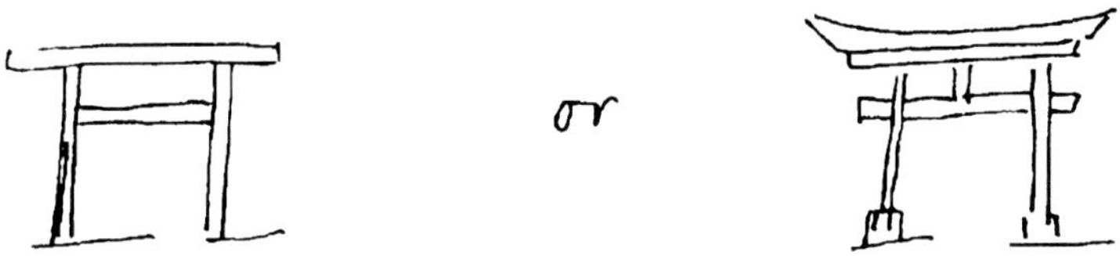

One sees them all over the country -

Inside the first courtyard there was a most gorgeous pagoda lacquered & painted in most harmonious colours - Up a flight of steps there was a fine gate - Gate of the Two Kings - It was chiefly made of red lacquer & had 2 enormous & hideous red monsters, one on each side - The carvings & decorations are chiefly lions, tigers, elephants, poeonies & bamboos. A delicious mixture! Thro' this gate there are 3 sort of treasure houses also beautifully carved & painted - On one side stands a huge conifer tree which Teyasu was "in the habit of carrying about with him in a flower pot" (the Guide Book) which gives one some kind of idea of the age of the place, (17th century) Near the tree is a stable with the horse which carried Prince Kita-ShiraKawa in the Formosan campaign of 1895! A truely innocent fluffy beast who pawed the ground for us to give him beaus which we purchased from his lady attendant! The stable was beautifully carved - monkeys being the chief subject - but had no door & was dreadfully draughty I sd. think - Japanese horses stand facing outwards - on pillar reins, their manger being a small box secured by 2 chains one from each side - Next there was a huge granite holy water cistern with a beautifully decorated roof supported by pillars - Then another building containing a library in the same sort of style - Then some more steps with 2 huge crytomerias at the top, one on each side leading into another court yard where there was a large bronze bell, several lovely bronze candleabra, a huge bronze lantern & a bell tower & a drum tower one on each side in gold red & black. On the left there was a small temple the inside was supposed to be very fine so we had to take off our shoes to go in & horribly cold it was too (forbye having holes in my stockings!) but it was well worth it - After this we went up another flight of steps to the most beautiful thing I've ever seen - A gate called the Yömei-mon - The fence on each side is carved with birds & flowers - perfectly exquisite. The columns are painted white with a geometrical pattern. One of them has the pattern carved upside down on purpose in case the flawless construction of the whole thing w[d.] bring misfortune - there are carvings of dragons & unicorns & other wierd beasts - The colouring white, black & gold with faint touches of colour - From the inside it is just as fine. In fact, as I said before it is the most beautiful thing I've ever seen - Thro' the gate there is another courtyard with 3 more buildings much the same as the others & then the last or Chinese gate another "symphony" in white black & gold tho' not so fine as the Yömei-mon except perhaps the actual gates themselves which are wood painted white with plum trees, dragons & bamboos carved on them - the carvings left the natural colour of the wood - After this gateway - at last - comes the oratory itself a large room most beauifully decorated with a lovely ceiling - On either side there is a sort of little ante room with lovely carved wood panels & gorgeous ceilings - Behind is the Stone Chamber - so called because the floor is of stone instead of lacquer as they usually are - (I dont know which is the coldest to "stockinged feet" not much difference I think!) Behind beautiful gold & black lacquer doors are the Shrines but this is the holy of holies where nobody is allowed to go, but anyhow they can't be <u>much</u> finer than the things we had already seen! This finished the temple but there was still the tomb - To see this we passed out by an archway over which was carved the masterpieces of one of thier greatest artists - "The sleeping cat"! A black & white spotted cat with muffed paws. closed eyed & smiley mouth! It may be famous but it is not up to much!! We climbed about 20 steps to get to this blesséd tomb all amongst the cryptomerias. It is made of bronze shaped like a pagoda surrounded by a stone wall with a fine carved bronze gate - There was a lot of snow lying about which I think added to the beauties of the place especially as the sun was shining - Its impossible to do it justice in words, it must be seen I think to be realized. Its the mixture of black & gold (a great part of the gold being beautifully worked brass) that is so fine - As a whole it is perfect & in detail it is perfect, So what more can one desire! In the afternoon we walked down to the town of Nikko, the road - which we had come the night before in the dark - leading by the river Daiyagawa over which is the famous sacred bridge made of red lacquer & looking very fine as seen from the other bridge, used by ordinary mortals a little higher up, with a background of dark browny green cryptomerias with snow covered mountains behind - As we walked down the street the people flew out of their shops inviting us with smiles & bows to go in but we kept steadily on with vain promises of "later on - perhaps - if there's time"! till we got to the Fine Art Exhibition where we were met by the most charming man who showed us round - I can't possibly describe all we saw there - Suffice it is to say that there were specimens of lacquer, bronze, china, cloisonné, etc: etc: etc: both old & modern, all beautifully arranged, some of them for sale - Needless to say we fell!

January 31st Sunday - This morning we went for a walk along the river to a place called Gamman-ga-fuchi where there is a row of about 50 stone images sitting on the opposite bank. They were rather difficult to distinguish being of the same colour as the rocks & half buried in snow. Along the road were any amount of pack ponies being led along in strings - There are also rails on which they run trucks drawn by enormous bulls. Such very nice people, fat & well fed - a great contrast to the ponies who are very "weedy" - When we got back we went to see the other temple - a Buddhist one - Tuemitzu's - It is not nearly so fine as Teyasu's & we were sorry we had not left the best to the last. We sd. probably have thought this one much finer if we had not already seen the other - It was much gaudier & not nearly such fine workmanship - In the afternoon we finished off the "sights" of Nikko - at least those which we have time for - by looking at the outside of another & much smaller temple & a curious sort of pillar called the Sorinto which was erected to avert evil influence & stands on a little mound. It is about 42 ft high & is made of copper - black - with brass ornamentations - Not a thing of any great beauty. Then we went to the house of our friend of the Exhibition who had invited us to see the fine new shop which he is building where he is going to set up for himself. He had already got a lot of things collected which I'm afraid was what made him invite us however in spite of not buying we parted the best of friends His funny little dog greeted us with the greatest joy - He says it always loves foreigners as it is a foreigner itself! We're hardly given a moment's peace in this hotel with people coming to implore us to go & see their goods - "not to buy, oh no, just to look" - so likely! Its really rather a bore & they are so persistent & come again & again! The other "sights" of Nikko are waterfalls & a lake but they are all practically snowed up at this time of the year so we can't go & see them - We can only do the temples by keeping to the paths cut in the snow - The ground underneath is like rock - Nobody comes to Nikko at this time of year so we are seeing it under unique circumstances! We have such a nice little girl to wait on us - She slops about the room in her funny heel-less slippers, makes little remarks occasionally, warms her hands by the stove & sniffs in the friendliest way! Japanese people have quite the most charming manners. The servants in this hotel are quite embarrassing in their attentions & will hardly let us do a thing for ourselves & bow & smile whenever they pass!

February 1st Monday - We left Nikko for Yokohama this morning by the 10-25 train - we walked to the station as it is really too cold to go in rickshaws - Our departure was as imposing as our arrival! The entire household turned out on the front doorstep to see us go & the "goodbyes" & bows & smiles on every side were a sight to behold! We felt like royalty & bowed & smiled with the best of them! It was a perfect day, rather wasted in the train except that the country with the distant hills was certainly looking its best - We had to change twice, the 2nd time being at Tokio where we had to change stations which means going from one end of the town to the other. We managed it most successfully in a tram & had time for some tea - Horrible stuff - Why is it railway tea is always undrinkable? We got to Yokohama about 5 o'clock & are back at the same hotel. This time, instead of a Theatrical Company there are 2 "Trick Cyclists" staying here! A man & his wife - very American! It is much warmer here which of course is not to be wondered at considering that Nikko is 2000 ft above the sea.

February 2nd Tuesday - Spent most of the morning at Cooks buying our last batch of tickets, also a few "shoppings" including darning wool which is forever in use (or ought to be if it isn't!) In the afternoon we tried in vain to get photographs of the Shiba Temples at Tokio - we went into dozens of shops but they had nothing but horrible coloured things so we had to give it up - A great pity as we have got such a splendid collection of them - something of every place we have been to! We were chiefly in a street called the Benten dori where there are the most fascinating shops - We cd. hardly get along for stopping to look at things! Beautifully carved ivory, china, silver, silks, embroideries & 101 other lovely things -

The Fujiya Hotel, Miyanoshita, Sagami, Japan

February 4th 1909

My child, we only got here last night & have not been out yet but the post goes at 12 & this must go then if it is to catch tomorrow's mail. I expect you'd rather have a scrap than nothing therefore I scrawl a "line". This is going to be a very nice place I think especially as the rain has ceased & the sun is shining - a lovely day - We are sitting in a sort of glass balcony bathed in sunshine! Perfectly ripping. This is such a nice hotel. Our room might be "the spare room" of a private house & all the other rooms most tartey - The baths certainly are miles away but when once one gets there --! marble, let into the floor so that you slip down into it - Wooden walls with sliding panels - real Japanese style - but no locks! ha-ever - There are only 2 other people in the hotel so the chance of being "surprised" is remote - Such a nightmare of a rickshaw drive as I had up here yesterday in the rain! Bumping & crashing along - Truely painful - I have always envied babies in perambulators but I don't now - not a bit & I see that it is positive cruelty to animals to take them up rough roads! I am determined that I shall walk down if it is anything like decent weather - A rickshaw wd. want to run down the hill with me & that wd. be worse than toiling up even!

C. thoroughly enjoyed his walk & plunged along in the rain & mud! I longed to be doing the same - I do walk - quite a lot - but that w^d. have been too far & too much of a climb I think - The other people in the hotel are, I think "honeymooners" & such dreadful creatures - especially the woman - very very flashy darling! I am much excited about seeing the plum blossom which is out. They have got it stuck about in vases all over the hotel - Perfectly enchanting arrangements - From where I am sitting I can look right away down a valley to the sea, twinkling away in the sun - I love Japan & only wish we c^d. stay longer - It will be too sad leaving on the 17th. - Some - d-a-a-y we might come back again & do all in our power to collect sufficient pence for you to come too - W^d.n't that be lovely? The letters hadn't arrived yesterday before we left Yokohama but if there were any they will be forwarded here so theres still hope. I have been altering my tweed skirt so as to be able to wear it here - My waist is just abominably large - How extremely annoying that you are no lighter. Give it up child, give it up - its no earthly use for you & I to try to be light - It is evidently "not to be" for anything thinner than you were when we left I've never seen - to look at you might have been 7 stone - & I suppose you're the usual "few lbs over 10"!

Best love to M & H. dear things - I love to hear of them - not to mention all Cumberland news. Remarks by M^r. Cropper make me grin with pleasure, accounts of people's horses also! Oh I adore your letters! And now I must cease or this won't go. "Whither w^d. you rather" a scrawl like this or wait for a long one till the next mail?

Best love from the T.B. -

Yrs ever & always

D -

February 3rd. Wednesday - We left Yokohama today by the 1-14 train & got here (Fujiya Hotel Miyanoshita) at 5 o'clock - It was raining so we drove to the station in rickshaws with the hoods up - Not comfortable when your hat is too high to get in & you have to sit with your neck bent the whole time! We went as far as Kodzu by train & then had an hour in a tram which whirled us along thro' the country & villages in fine style for an hour till we got to Yumoto - It was pouring with rain all the time which was a great pity - We saw any amount of orange trees in gardens simply a mass of fruit also a lot of plum trees in blossom but they didn't show up to advantage in drenching rain. All the children seemed to be coming home from school each one under an enormous Japanese umbrella with their kimonos tucked up out of the mud & of course with "getas" or pattens on! Miyanoshta is 4½ - or supposed to be - miles from Yumoto - C. walked but I had a rickshaw with 2 men - The road leads up one side of a valley - Hills on each side & a river rushing below - It is up-hill practically the whole way & must be perfectly lovely but there was so much mist & rain we c^d. hardly see anything & the higher we got the dencer the mist became - C. enjoyed his walk very much & by taking a short cut got to the hotel shortly before I did - I'm not sure that I enjoyed my drive so much! The road was a perfect disgrace - full of holes & stones & the rickshaw springs not of the best therefore it was rough to say the least of it & it went on for over an hour! I was glad when at last we got to the hotel! It is 1300 ft above Yumoto - which is sea-level - so no wonder it was a stiff climb - I felt so sorry for the poor coolies but they're fine muscular little men & used to it I suppose - A covered rickshaw is a very dull mode of conveyance - You can see nothing except the men's back & the road just in front which is not very entertaining! I took my hat off or it w[d.] have been unendurable! This seems a delightful hotel - So well got up & most comfortable with a charming little Jap proprietor - he assures us that this rain is most unusual & that it is sure to clear up. Lets hope he will prove right for I am sure it ought to be a lovely place & if it continues to rain of course it will spoil everything - There are only 2 other people in the hotel but I don't think we shall see very much of them - I hope not anyhow, judging from their appearance! Before leaving Yokohama we made friends with an elderly spinster lady in the hotel - A tremendous "gasser" but most interesting & a great traveller - She has been to every country except Formosa & is on her way there now! Her name is Gearon & she knows the Herries' (Carlaverock) -

February 4[th.] Thursday - The mist had quite cleared by the morning & it has been a lovely day with bright sunshine tho' a cold wind - We went on 2 walks, one before & one after lunch exploring the various roads & paths - This is a lovely place - The village & hotel are built on one side of a thickly wooded very steep valley at the bottom of which runs a river dashing over great big stones & rocks with every now & then a very pretty waterfall - It has any number of smaller streams running into it which all make waterfalls - such is the steepness of the valley - Japan grows a great many evergreen trees - great big ones - I don't know what they are - besides fir trees, bamboos - (wh: always remain green) - camelias (with occasionally some flowers on them & growing as "forest trees"!) & a great many other ever-greens so that the effect - when the sun is shining - is almost like summer, & much nicer than if it was all brown & bare - Cryptomerias are a most beautiful bronze brown which mix very well with the green. The tops of the hills are very bare & brown & in places where they are burnt - quite black. We passed thro' several small villages - The inhabitants take no notice of us - except perhaps to give us a sweet smile & bow from the waist - which we return! C. is getting quite a good Japanese bow! Miyanoshta is famed for its hot springs. Every now & again we came across really hot water bubbling out of the ground! At one place there was a regular burn of it plunging down into a deep pool from which a cloud of steam rose! All the hot water in the hotel comes from these springs - It is never necessary to boil or even heat it - They have the most splendid baths here. Marble ones sunk in the floor, you turn the tap & the water comes boiling out! Its difficult to realize that there is not a furness or a kitchen boiler at the "tither en'" to cause it! There are cold water streams too or else it might be rather a bore! Sometimes the two will rise within a few yards of each other - It is a most curious sight to see a burn of really hot water with steam rising from it come dashing down the hill!

February 5th Friday - Another lovely day - Bright sun & frosty. We walked in the morning & afternoon again, the same as yesterday & devoured the new English magazines which arrived ("The Sketch" for Dec 30th etc:) - Two more females & two men arrived at the hotel so we are not quite such a select (?) party! It is really a huge hotel & is always packed during the summer - We are given our meals in a small room adjoining the real dining-room & are waited on by 2 charming little girls - The women of this class always wear dark kimonos the only colour being their obis & in the opening at the back of the long sleeve one gets glimpses of bright colours from the numberless coloured kimonos they wear underneath - This is a most comfortable hotel - one of the best we have been in yet - the proprietor tells us he was in England 6 years so he evidently learnt there how to make English people comfortable - His wife is a charming little person who speaks the most perfect English with the proper English intonation - She has never been in England so I don't know how she has learnt it - Surely not from the average English speaking tourist!

February 6th Saturday - Yet another lovely day spent in the same way as the 2 preceeding ones - The nicest walk is up the valley by the side of the river - It is a very pretty river with the cleanest water - The garden at the back of the hotel is the most fascinating place. It has a little stream running thro' it which has its banks carefully lined with stones at artistic angles with plants growing amongst them & little trees & bushes at intervals - There are miniature bridges across the burn which ends in a waterfall & a little pond in which gold-fish & trout swim about! The whole thing of course is artificial but the effect is charming - It must have been such fun laying it out!

February 7th Sunday - Today we went on a most delightful expedition to Hakone - It is 6½ miles away right over the hills, 1000 ft higher than this - We started off at 20 past 10 - C. walked all the way but I had a "chair" - (Just an ordinary wicker chair on two stout bamboos, with 4 stalwart little coolies to carry me - on their shoulders!) A curious but very pleasant mode of conveyance! - I feel sure it is like riding a camel! The men all walk in step with rather a slow swinging stride & the motion is really most comfortable). We cd.n't have had a better day. The views were perfectly lovely, hills & valleys - The road wound up & up till at last we reached the summit from where we cd. see the sea & the far far distant shore on the other side. After getting to the top we had a bit of flat to the village of Arhinoyu where there are sulphur springs - Oh my! the smell! Rotten eggs not in it! However, we soon left them behind & went down-hill till we got to the Lake of Hakone - Then we went thro' a lovely grey stone torii & down a fine old cryptomeria avenue by the lake-side till we got to the village of Hakone where we had lunch in the hotel. It was a glorious walk! Some parts were planted with cryptomerias of different ages, Some of them still quite tiny & not looking at all "happy" at that height, with snow lying about. In other parts there was a perfect jungle of little bamboos - in fact there was plenty of variety - The road was perfectly disgraceful, as apparently all Japanese roads are - Hardly more than a track with huge cart ruts & holes & stones - we passed a lot of carts both going up & coming down - They certainly don't load them very heavily, if they did the horses simply w$^{d.n't}$ manage to get along at all - as it is they toil up stopping many times - They are very small & lightly built too & don't look the least suitable for such terrible hills & atrocious roads. Very often the coolies took short cuts along precipitous little stoney paths. This was rather uncomfortable as of course they c$^{d.n't}$ keep such good step & the two men at the back seemed to be miles lower than the two in front & they grunted & puffed till I felt a perfect cad! Of course I walked parts of the way every now & then so as to give them a bit of a rest. They were such nice cheery men & so attentive, tucking me into the chair but their English was very scanty. They pointed us out several things of interest on the way - Some monuments erected to 2 brothers of ancient fame, some funny little images carved in the rocks by the side of the road & best of all an enormous image of one of their gods - "Jizö" - carved in a block of stone, sitting rather far back from the road in a little clearing. A most impressive person, all alone out there with little Joss-sticks burning in front of him, his lap heaped with stones which in some way or other are meant as offerings - the Hakone Hotel is very "Japanese-y" built at one end of the lake, looked right up to Fugi wh: unfortunately we c$^{d.}$ only just see on account of the clouds. All the same it was a heavenly day. A cold wind with a lot of snow lying about but a lovely bright sun all the time & beautiful clear atmosphere - After a most excellent lunch waited on by rather an elderly lady who made up for her very imperfect knowledge of the English language by laughing a great deal & smiling incessantly we were invaded by another woman & a girl with enormous packs on their backs, which they insisted upon unpacking for us to see the contents - Some very nice things - all made - they said - at Hakone. After much haggling we bought some rather nice cushion covers made of some sort of Japanese material made of half paper, half cloth & then we started on our home ward journey with many bows & "Siyönaras" (goodbye!) - We went there in 2½ hours & came back in 2¼ - In spite of its being down hill the chairmen can't get on much faster - in fact I s$^{d.}$ think at the very steep bits it was harder work going down than up. They walk along inside the poles one just a little behind the other, as there is not quite enough room to go abreast. Every now & then they change on to the other shoulder in the neatest way, all at the same moment at a signal - We passed a most delightful & simple contrivance for getting fire-wood down from the top of a high hill to the bottom - They had rigged up a wire which must have been about $^1/_4$ of a mile long at the top of which they started a small bundle of freshly cut wood - it came down the wire getting faster & faster until it arrived at the bottom with a tremendous bump! We saw 2 or 3 bundles coming down - It was most fascinating to watch & must have been a glorious sensation for the wood - if the end had not been so very violent! We got back at 5 o'clock, quite ready for tea.

February 8th. Monday - This morning we went up a glen to the place where the Hotel hot water comes from - It was very narrow with the burn dashing down far below in a series of lovely water-falls. In places the hot water came out from amongst the rocks at the sides with clouds of steam rising from it! You've no idea how extraordinary it looks - It is taken in bamboo pipes to the hotel & has a sort of salty mineral taste - This afternoon we went up another & smaller glen - This one was thickly overgrown with bamboos & cryptomerias - The burn was very dry so part of the way we found it made the best path! There don't seem to be many birds here just now. Only crows, jays & I have noticed a very pretty little blue bird & a brown one with orange on it, besides a large flock of bulfinches - & of course the homely old sparrow! but that one meets all over the world apparently! It was another lovely day today - Hard frost. They don't seem to have a thermometer but there must be a good many degrees judging by the icicles which hang down from all the waterfalls & cover any branches or twigs which can be reached by the spray - We have to leave here very early tomorrow morning to catch the only good train to Nagoya - We will have to get up at 5-30! Not a very cheerful prospect but there is no other alternative!

The Fujiya Hotel, Miyanoshita, Sagami, Japan

February 8th. 1909

My child, voici encore! We have been having a fine old "laze" at this place. There is not much to do unless to go walks & I of course don't feel like doing very much in that line especially as this place is made of hills which stump me at once but its rather nice to be having a sort of rest & as the hotel is very comfortable with jolly good fires & ripping arm-chairs why not benefit by them? We have a walk before lunch of about an hour & another after perhaps a little longer on the flattest roads we can find, cold frosty air but delicious sunshine & the rest of the day "put in" a quantity of talking & reading the illustrated papers (seductive things at the best of times!) not to mention eating! Lor how I eat! You'd be quite shocked - I am myself but I remember the way Olly used to eat under the same circumstances & comfort myself with the hope that it is but natural (which I honestly believe it is) - anyhow I seem to want it all & don't "rise" with the beastly "over-eaten" feeling, so I suppose its alright. Yesterday we had a ripping expedition to a place 6 $^1/_2$ miles off which I have described in the diary - We both enjoyed it immencely - C. strode along in fine style making my little chair coolies look like dwarfs! I did quite a lot of walking too & was car-

ried the rest of the way! A curious sensation but really quite nice tho' one can't help having the feeling that ones a great heavy lump - The roads are something like the Boot lane at its very worst & in places much worse - You really have no notion how bad they are. Its so funny that they s^d. be, in this otherwise highly developed country - but then it is full of these kinds of contrasts - We've got to get up tomorrow at 1/2 past 5 to get to Nogoya - The only decent train is at 9.30 & it takes 2 hours walking & tram to get to the station, forbye having breakfast, paying the bill etc: etc: (we won't really have to get up at 1/2 past 5 but its just as well to think we've got to! Don't you know that feeling?) - We only settled to go to Nogoya yesterday. There is a very fine castle there for which one has to have a Permit from the Embassy - We asked Dod Lampson to send us one for the Imperial Palaces at Kioto - where we had meant to go straight to - & he sent us one for Nogoya also so we may as well stop - as it is on the way - & use it. I'm really sorry for your sake that we keep altering our plans as I know how annoying it is to imagine a person doing one thing when they are doing another all the time but its difficult to stick exactly to what one originally arranges. Of course the worst part of it is it causes such delay in the way of receiving letters. For instance Cook imagines we are going to Kyoto straight from here & will forward our letters there so we shant get them till 2 days later but no matter. They are such a joy when they do come that as I said before they're worth waiting years for - By the way my dear if you haven't already done it, get hold of Harry's Chinese & Japanese photograph book - Its probably full of the places we've been to. I was just thinking the other day that it w^d. give you a much better idea of the places - As to me I am longing to get to Houghton so as to look at them! Dont you know the way one loves photographs of places one knows? We took 2 rolls of film to be developed the other day & dashed if the whole lot were not fogged. It was really too annoying - We have been most careful of them, only taking the very important things, as films are so beastly expensive & really the p.c's one buys so good, so it was really most disappointing. The elephants in Ceylon & some of the quadza & her crew, 20 in all - I can't think why the camera was leaking as it appears to be alright - Theres some fate against my photography - I think I must give it up for good! It seems so sort of ungrateful to Olly who lent the camera that they s^d. be failures but pon me word its not my fault. I am sending you a "pick-sure" out of a little guide book - It is the beginning of the

Cryptomeria Avenue at Hakone

Hakone Lake and M^t. Fuji

cryptomeria avenue leading to Hakone which I tell you about in the diary & if you look very closely you will see the torii thro' which we came (see the diary!) on the left behind the trees you see the lake - the other one C. sends to you with "a little kiss"!

We didn't see Fuji as well as therein depicted but it is the view from the hotel nevertheless - I have sent Helen a p.c. of this hotel. Ask her to show it you. Its rather nice. The amount of work we'll have when we get home sticking all our p.c's & photographs into a book is appalling but it'll be rather a nice job too "commencing" with one of the old Goben & a collection of Gibraltar! I wonder if you will be at Murrell Hill when you get this. Give them all my love if you are - You know its very flattering & touching the way they all love DayNin. Isn't it? Oh my dear, I'm getting so dreadfully excited about coming home. It really will be thrilling. We talk about it many many times & think about it by the hour! Do lets try not to go mad! I know perfectly well we will but I suppose we'd better try not to! C. is reading my diary before I send it to you & will correct the spelling. As if it mattered ('s if I cared!). He also critisizes sometimes which is a thing I'll not stand - I can do anything I like to him now which is splendid as he is frightened to retaliate in case he hurts me! He is very sorry that the tennis court at Wreay Syke is not big eno' for tennis as he says he w^d. love to play with you this summer - He thinks you w^d. beat him but somehow I think different - what do you? You'n me never shone at tennis tho I was the best! You're the best golfer tho' that I will admit - I long to see your new bag - Time you had one - The post is going as I live

Y'rs forever D -

February 9th. Tuesday - We got up this morning in the dark at ½ past 5!! We were by way of having breakfast at 6 but apparently Japs have no idea of time & its quite impossible to hustle them so by the time we'd finished it was ¼ to 7 - Our tram went at ¼ to 8 & one can only just walk the distance in the hour! We had decided to walk as really rickshaws on these roads are perfect misery, so off we set with portmanteau & canvas bag on a hand-barrow with 2 coolies & the other bag & a small wooden box which we have got (a provision box of Captain M^c.Niel's which he most kindly gave us & in which we put our purchases!) tied on each end of a bamboo over another coolie's shoulder - It was very nice at that hour of the morning (it generally is when once the awful wrench of getting up is over!) Of course it was pouring with rain when we came up so we were now able to see all that we had missed - it reminded us forcibly of some parts of Scotland - The hills & fir-trees & the river gushing down below in a very rocky bed - We had a great "flap" at the end as we thought we were going to miss the tram! The coolies tore on ahead with the barrow bounding from stone to stone! It was luckily down hill all the way - & we caught it alright - which was the main thing! It took about an hour & a quarter to get to Kodzu where we had ½ an hour to wait for the train, which we spent in going on to the beach & having a look at the sea - It was rather misty - not a particularly nice day - We got into the express train with a dining-car which got us to Nogoya at 4.16 - It was very full which was rather a bore - These trains have long corridor carriages with the seats down the sides, not divided into compartments, which is not nice especially as all the men smoke - With the help of lunch at 11 & tea at 3 (which as we had had breakfast at 6 was just about right!) we got thro' the journey alright - We got splendid views of Fugi every now & then, towering up behind the other hills & covered with snow - We are staying at the Nogoya Hotel - not a very nice place but we shall only be here one night - We were pestered as usual by these tiresome shop people who come into the room & insist upon giving us their card - They won't go away either & refuse to be snubbed inquiring into the length of our stay etc:!

February 10th. Wednesday - Immediately after breakfast this morning we went off in rickshaws to see the Castle - We had a permit which Mr. Lampson had sent us which we had to show to the sentry at the gate before he'd let us pass. The Castle is surrounded by a perfect maze of high walls & moats - with water in them! - A guide took us round - The Castle itself is built in the style of a pagoda 5 stories high, white-washed & with 2 gold dolphins on the roof - It is an old fortress but is not used for anything now. We climbed 120 steps to the top where we got the most splendid view of the town & surrounding district - Perhaps the most interesting thing being the barracks which are all round the Castle where cavalry, infantry & artillery were all drilling - Attached to the castle is a sort of palace where the Emperor occasionally comes - It was just a suite of rooms without a stick of furniture in them, opening one into the other. The Japanese never have furniture, just cushions to sit on & a vase of flowers! The walls of these rooms were all painted with the quaintest pictures - One room had tigers, the next musk-cats & so on the nicest was pheasants & cherry-blossom, also a door with a large cock scratching its head! The actual rooms which the emperor uses we were not allowed to see. After the castle we went back to the hotel & had lunch & then caught the 1-10 train to Kyoto - It was quite the slowest train that ever was & took 5½ hours to do the 94 miles stopping at every single station - We came thro' a lot of snow & rice fields by the acre which aren't very interesting at this time of year - Yesterday's journey was much more interesting as we were coming thro' orange groves simply laden with fruit & tea plantations! The latter caused us great excitement as we have not seen tea since Ceylon! It was like meeting old friends to see the stumpy little bushes again! They're not so large or prosperous looking as the Ceylon ones tho' - The drive from the station to this hotel (the Kyoto) was long & thro' a perfect maze of the worst lighted streets that ever were! Electric light certainly but of the very feeblest description -

Kioto Hotel

10. 2. 09

Petite, one line (literally) with this small portion of diary or it will miss this mail. On arrival here last night I found the "Last of the Barons" awaiting me - in other words the last of your "all-the-way-round-by-Suez" letters - the one about Broadfield & a bit out of Browning at the end - My belovéd, you must have been rather in the blues I'm afraid but it was ages ago so I hope those feelings dont come so often now & that you are looking forward to our settling down at Wreay Syke as much as we are ourselves - Whenever we talk about it you come into our plans - C. has even decided how we are going to sit at "table"! It is to be a round table & he is going to have one on each side of him! I'm afraid he insists upon calling you "Smelly" I dont know what we're to do to prevent him! But really honestly my child we're all going to be just as happy as possible together. I just know we are & I do hope you know it too. Heavens girl its getting exciting! Not much more than 6 weeks now! I wonder if you'll come up to London? It w^d. be nice & yet unsatisfactory too of course with us staying at Lowndes Sq^re. & you at Bedford Sq^re. We arrive on Tuesday evening & will go north - to Holm Hill I suppose if they're there - on Friday or Saturday as C. wants to hunt Monday - If M^rs. Salkeld is worth 2^d. she'll ask you to come too but she's very bad at thinking of these things - Isn't it awful when one begins to make plans? There's no getting to sleep at nights at all! As soon as we've got Wreay Syke measurements we'll have to be off to London again & do as much as possible before the training - (Consult a calendar & you'll see there's jolly little time) -

And now my twinnie I must cease I will write you a real decent letter on Saturday. Its better to have a good many when one can post 3 times a week don't you think or I wonder if you'd rather have one budget once a week? Futile to ask a question now - By the same token I'm longing to hear if you hunted in Herefordshire. How perfectly thrilling if you did! Oh lor how I long to be "a horse bag" again. It'll be such ages before I am. Ha - ever its lucky for me the summer's coming.

Bless you for ever & ever my own & best love from the T.B.

Toujours à toi

D -

February 11th Thursday - Pouring with rain all morning so we didn't go out - A grand opportunity for me to do some necessary sewing but lets hope its not going to last - It cleared up in the afternoon so we went to try & find some shops as they are supposed to be extra good in Kyoto, but we failed to do so! This is the most extraordinary town - Miles & miles of streets exactly alike - It is very old & built entirely of wood, one storey high - Every house is a shop so where all the people live goodness knows! After the rain the streets were inches deep in mud but as all the people (without exception) go about in "getas" it doesn't matter to them as these "getas" raise them 4 or 5 inches from the ground - We wished we had got them on too tho' I'm sure they'd be very difficult to walk on to begin with! This is a very comfortable hotel with a most charming & obliging manager. The only thing is the electric light which is perfectly vile & has a dreadful habit of suddenly dying down till its almost dark & then shooting up again! They have their own engine so possibly its the "Shaw" of the establishment being funny!

February 12th Friday. A lovely day so off we set in the morning to see temples! It is appalling the amount of things there are to see in this place. We shall never manage them all & will be so confused at the end! We went first to the Kiyomizu. It is built on the side of a hill - The street leading up to it was composed of shops with the most fascinating earthenware toys, to be had for a few pence so we came away with soldiers & a lady in a kimono etc:! The temple is quite unlike any we have seen before being very plain with stone pillars & bare floor. Being built on the side of a hill it has to be supported by a wonderful sort of scaffolding made of great beams of wood. The roof is made of bark, layers & layers of it pressed down, about a foot thick. Behind this principal temple are several others dedicated to various gods & all very much alike. Between two of them is a shed with 100 stone images of "Jizö" - People whose children are dead go & tie the childrens clothes round these image's necks - It is a most pathetic sight! The view from up here was glorious, the whole of the town & surrounding district being very clear. After this we went on to the San-jü-qen-dö, the temple of the 33,333 images of Kwannon, the Goddess of Mercy! This is the most curious place - It is a very long building, rather dark & barn-like filled with gilt images of Kwannon standing in tiers one above the other - There are 10 rows of them with 100 images in each row - Each image has dozens of hands & as many heads & each one is different! At the back there is a gallery with some more more or less delapidated images - Altogether, as its name denotes there are 33,333 images of Kwannon in the building! There are also a great many beggars outside all clamouring & whining for money - This is the first time we have been bothered with beggars in Japan so we can't grumble - After leaving this we went to the Daibutsu or Great Buddha which is quite close - It lives in a sort of white washed hall & is not nearly so fine as the Kamakura one - It is only a head & shoulders, rather roughly & badly carved in wood It is 58 ft high & 43 ft across the chest. Its eye is 5 ft long & its mouth 8 ft 7 in! There is a sort of hen-ladder stair-case round the wall up to the back of its head which we scaled! but it was all rather dark & gloomy. On leaving the Daibutsu we saw an enormous bell 14 ft high which weighs 63 tons - It has a wooden beam at the side to sound it with - After this we hailed 2 rickshaws & came back to the hotel for lunch - We had found our way to all these places entirely by the map, in spite of repeated invitations to take rickshaws from the coolies who have regular "stands" at the corners of the streets - In the afternoon we went to see some cloisonné works & most interesting it was too. Everything has to go thro' 12 processes & it is slow & finicky work - The outline of the design is laid on with the finest of wire & then it is filled in with enamel & baked & polished - We saw the men at work & were then taken to the show-room where they had the most lovely things - Of course it is all most abominably expensive (the best things always are) - The man who showed us over spoke English - While we were looking at the things they gave us tea, their nasty tasteless Japanese wash but we had to drink it. Oh w[d] that we were millionaires! We got away from this place with some difficulty & then weakly went "just to look in at the window" of a porcelaine shop! Of course it ended in our going in here too! It was very nearly as seductive as the cloisonné! It was after 5 o'clock before we managed to leave! They arrange all their things so well in these shops, everything looks its very best & makes one long to buy!

February 13th Saturday - Very cold today with occassional slight snow-showers - Armed with our Permit we went to the Imperial Palace & Nijo Castle this morning - They are both very fine especially the former where the throne is - It is quite a plain lacquer chair inlaid with mother of pearl on a raised platform in the middle of a large hall, with a canopy & curtains of red white & black over it - This & two low red lacquer tables & another chair for the Mikado in another room are literally the only bits of furniture in the whole palace, which is very large with dozens of rooms & miles of corridors with sliding paper windows - All the walls are painted by famous artists with the favourite subjects of tigers, bamboos, cherry & plum blossom, birds etc: etc: The nicest of all were wild geese, quite beautifully painted - The feet of one in particular was a perfect masterpiece & just done with a few touches - The paintings are all on the lower panels - Up above it looks like white wash & all the wood-work is plain cyprus - It is rather severe but impressive - Anything like the cold, in the palace, I've never felt! No solid walls at all & no artificial heat of any kind - Nijo Castle - or palace - was very much the same sort of thing but perhaps richer - All the paintings were on a back-ground of gold-leaf but I don't think that was much advantage - Some of the ceilings were very fine & all the brass fittings were most beautifully chased - Here the Shogun's crest, of 3 sort of ivy leaves, was to be seen everywhere while at the other palace it was the Mikado's - a 16 leaved crysanthenum - The floors in both are all covered with rush matting, padded so that they are quite soft to walk on - Of course we had to take off our boots but I'm glad to say they provided us with sort of bags to tie over our feet so it wasn't so very cold - Whenever we visit these places, palace, temple or whatever it is, we have to write our names in a book! In the afternoon we went to a silk store - too seductive for words!

Kioto Hotel

13. 2. 09

Mon enfant, C. has just pointed out that by the time you get this there will only be 3 more weeks!! Est ce possible? I have enjoyed myself - & am enjoying myself - more than words can say but lord how nice it will be to get back - I'm simply yearning to see you again twister! I got a letter from you yesterday morning - from Comlongon just after the hunt ball - My dear, I was so glad to hear about dear old Albert. Such a relief to know that he doesn't mind now & that he is in such good spirits. I'm glad he enjoyed reading my diaries - Its quite impossible to find time to write to people except to you & occasionally Mum especially now when we are so much on the move - Kioto is a perfectly fascinating place. Just to walk about the streets affords endless entertainment, what with the shops & the people & "one thing & another" - Its all so typically Japanese & we are always the only Europeans to be seen whereas at Yokohama & Tokio they swarm. The cloisonné & the porcelaine yesterday my dear, & the silk shop this afternoon! Really pon me word its too much & the poor 10th. Commandment takes a very back seat. Such gorgeous things - I've never known such temptation before & didn't know the desire to possess cd. be so strong! We have bought £6 or £7 worth of things here & must now cease or the money will give out. We are packing the things in a wooden box that Capt. Mc. Neil gave us & sending them home by P & O. They will arrive after us - It will be exciting unpacking them. Amongst other things there are some charming "ornaments"! A 2 ½d. cavalry soldier which C. loves. It is distinctly comic. He absolutely declines to give it to his son & indignantly declared that it wasn't a toy! I got a "dress length" this afternoon. If you cd. have seen the silks & embroideries etc: which the man heaped in front of us! They were so expensive tho'. In the end I got a gauze - creamy - with wisteria embroidered on it in silk - It was about 35/- & will be a "dream"! Really I don't know what the likes of Spookie or Muriel wd. do in such a place! I am able to do a lot of walking & am none the worse for it. Whenever I get tired we hie up a rickshaw & I am tooled along beside C. who puts his "best foot foremost" & fairly makes the little coolie run to keep up with him. it is a very good plan as it gives C. exercise & me a good "rest" - I am so glad you got 3 letters of mine running from Hankow & Ichang - I like getting them unexpectedly in a packet like that. As you say one fairly "swoons" with the joy of it! Of course you ought not to have got them like that & when C. heard it he said furiously "Then that damned Dunne never sorted them"! I sd. think it more likely that the Chinese post had something to do with it for it is very rocky, also the Japanese. My dear how tiresome about Irish & Flirt being lame at the same time but apparently it didn't matter & by now they are both doubtless all right - you don't know how I love hearing about them. It makes my mouth water! What a nice sensible man "Archie" Campbell must be to so appreciate the Blossom. Do you know my dear, Japanese cats have tails of about a couple of inches long & broad to boot. Personally I don't care for it.

Damn - the post has gone. They are going to send this down to the post specially so my child I must stop - Dash these posts - How annoying they are - Best love from the T.B.

Yrs forever

D -

<u>February 14th Sunday</u> - This morning we went to 2 more temples! The Hejashi & Nishi Honwaugi. They are both very fine but if the truths to be told we are getting somewhat "fed-up" with temples & none of them are a patch on the Tyesu one at Nikko - Of the 2 we saw today I think the first was the best - Its chief feature was its simplicity & its enormous perfectly plain pillars made of a lovely sort of brown wood - In the courtyard just outside there were a lot of pigeons flying about & little boys playing so it didn't seem quite so deserted as some of the temples do - It consists of 2 buildings connected by a gallery & is somehow unlike any other we have seen. The other one was a little further on & we didn't care for it so much. It was rather more ordinary with a lot of gold & black lacquer & painted wood carvings besides some paintings on the walls - The best was a pea-cock & pea-hen perched on a peach tree with white blossoms! The roof is made of bark about a foot thick - All the Kioto temple & palace roofs are like this - The priests seemed to be having some sort of a service in the Nishi temple when we were in - They were kneeling in a row in front of the shrine jabbering something in a sing-song voice as hard as they cd. go without seeming to draw breath! Outside there was a most magnificent old "icho" tree - We went back to lunch in rickshaws - We had walked to the temples in the morning - A walk in the streets is as interesting a sight as any, in Kioto I think - They are so full of life & so typically Japanese - After lunch we went in rickshaws to a garden called Kinkakiju. The coolies insisted upon our going to see a temple on the way! It was quite a nice one, rather small called Kitano Tenjin - There were rows & rows of stone lanterns leading up to it & also stone & bronze bulls. It took ages to get to the garden which was right out in the country - It is laid out in real Japanese style with a lake & islands with trees & stones in their gardens - "The Golden Pavillion" stands at one end of the lake - A sort of gilded pagoda. It looked very nice with the sun shining on it - Of course no garden looks its best at this time of year - It hasn't the least resemblance to a Western garden having no flower-beds or anything of that kind - The most curious thing was a pine tree trained to grow in the shape of a pink! Its extraordinary what the Japs will do with their trees, forcing them to take any shape they wish by tying up & massaging the branches when they are young - A tree being treated in this way is a curious sight!

<u>February 15th Monday</u> - Today we went to see the Geisha School - There were a lot of girls being taught to sing & play the Samisen & drum just as we saw them at

the theatre at Tokio. The classes were being held in different rooms & while one pupil was receiving instruction from an ancient female & making the most dreadful noises the other girls were cowering round the "hibashi" or box of burning charcoal which is the only fire that the Japanese ever have in their houses. Of course they were all sitting on the floor - It seems a dreadful waste of time to teach people to make such appalling noises! It is all so artificial & I believe takes ages to learn - They also teach them how to make & serve tea & to arrange flowers here but unfortunately these classes were not going on when we were there - We also went to the Maruyama Park, but this is a place to be seen when the cherry blossom is out - Today it was nothing very wonderful - it has been a very funny day today, foggy, almost like London in the morning, tho' it cleared up afterwards -

February 16th Tuesday - We left Kyoto today by the 3.30 train. We were sent down to the station in great state in the hotel "barouche"! It is the only carriage we have seen in Kioto & is a dreadfully innocent affair drawn by a pair of fluffy white horses, one of them a perfect baby by the look of it - The coachman couldn't drive for nuts but as there was a "runner" to go in front & clear all the people out "from under foot" it didn't much matter. We felt more than ever like royalty leaving the hotel in this way with the manager & all the staff - as usual - bowing farewells on the doorstep! We have had long talks with the manager who is a charming little man - We got him to give us the receipt of the hotel curry as it is perfectly excellent. The cook was brought up & introduced ("Captain, this is our chef"!) beaming all over & highly flattered - He wrote the receipt in Japanese & the manager translated it into English! The most delicious English too ending up with - "put some salt"! We got to Kobe at 5-14 & came to the same hotel where we had lunch after we had escaped from the Lützow! It is a very swagger hotel & I think is going to be thoroughly over-heated, with steam which will not be pleasant - The journey here was thro' the same kind of highly cultivated country that we have seen before. Scores of men & women working away most industriously - There are no hedges or fences of any kind so in a flat part one can see for miles -

February 17th Wednesday - There is nothing much to do or see at Kobe. It is a seaport town with large offices & houses in European style - We did nothing but send home our Japanese purchases by P & O, buy tooth-powder & tobacco & stroll about the town - It is very sad to think that this is our last day in Japan. It is a case of getting up at 6 o'clock tomorrow morning!

The Oriental Hotel, Ltd., Kobe, Japan

February 17th 1909

Well, my child, here we are back at this hotel & leaving Japan tomorrow - It is more than sad, I have enjoyed myself so much. On arriving here I got a letter from you! It was waiting "along" with one for C. from his mother in the sort of case place in the hall of the hotel

- The man took ages sauntering round with the key to unlock it. You omitted to send C. any message & in consequence hurt his poor little feelings! I was so intensely amused & interested in your letter - The Xmas tree & the village entertainments! It was just "to the life" & I giggled freely. Its extraordinary that you have managed to get so very little hunting - I wonder why, as you seem to have taken all possible opportunities & your aunt has not been what Mum wd. call "troublesome", but anyhow I hope you'll get in a lot from Murrell Hill & after the Broadies get back. Oh my dear wdn't it have been beastly if I'd been at Wreay Syke all this winter, unable to hunt. You see it began in November so everybody wd. have known from the very start. It really wd. have been very hard to have been feeling quite fit & living amongst it all & yet had to go dowagering about all the Season with Mog. Its certainly much better for me that it sd. have happened thus - It wd. have been awkward wdn't it dearie? I'm not sure whether my appearance in Cumberland when we come home won't give the show away - At present C. declares an outsider wdn't know that there was anything the matter, just a stout woman - that's all! I'm rather dreading the long journey - We'll practically be on the move continuously now untill we get home but that just can't be helped - Tomorrow we will be in the train all day, starting at 7 o'clock, on the boat all night (the lord preserve me from being sick) train again all next day until we get to Seoul. Here we'll get a rest - but dash it all, I forgot, C. made you out a programme of our movements so "all ye've got to do" is to take a glance at it. I don't know in the least how we're going to manage the Manchurian battle-fields - nor more does C. but I suppose when we get there we'll be able to find out. Of course the way to do it wd. be to ride & I was looking forward to it so much for of course now that way is out of the question. Kyoto was a very nice place "The Heart of old Japan" as the guide books say - but you know one does get rather tired of looking at Temples! I began to feel rather like the little American whose letter was found in the hotel blotter beginning "this morning we have been to 6 churches" (or whatever the number was) & this afternoon are going to 6 more! The worst part is having to take off ones shoes. It is such a bore & so cold. It isn't done as a mark of respect but simply because Japanese always take off their shoes on going into a house - You see they sit on the floor as well as walk on it so its just as if we were going to walk about on the chairs & sofas at home with muddy boots. Its all very well for them as they have socks with sort of soles to them but its jolly cold for us - & keeps me darn, darn, darning for one feels ashamed of having holes in one's stockings! C. is as bad as I am at hole-ing his socks & stockings so I have my hands full I can tell you, but I rather like doing a little homely job like that occasionally - By the way we hear that Mrs. Frank Dunne has got a daughter. It interests us vastly - at least it does me. I really don't think I much mind whether mine is a girl or a boy, tho' when there is a place & a', its probably better to "commence" with a boy! I'm really delighted that you're not fussing over Houghton trifles. You know we simply used to make troubles for ourselves that way, silly children that we were. I'm not fussing either but then as you say there's nothing for me to fuss about. C. is a very easy person to live with & I'm sure we shall never have rows or disagreeables. So far we have had nothing approaching a misunderstanding even. (Not like Frank & Olly at North

Berwick!!) And now I must have some lunch or I shall die of hunger -

Oh dear me - its getting so near the time of seeing you & talking to you that I don't know how to write or what to say! You've got the feeling too I daresay. I'm so glad you've got Bertie's Chinese photographs - I shall long to study them as I daresay they are places we have been to too - We will have packets of post cards & photographs to show you - You'll be such a nice person to show them to & we'll have them & the diary & all "to hand" & live thro' the last 6 months together & I shall want to hear every detail of what you've been doing - It will seem to you like talking of prehistoric times to bring up Paris & Ireland again but no matter - you just must! We're much annoyed because we've forgotten Wreay Syke - when we try & make plans we get hopelessly mixed by not remembering the place - C. is going to have all his things sent up from London, unpack them & see just exactly what he's got & then we'll be able to go to London armed with lists & buy for dear life - Won't it be appalling? Some things of course will be enjoyable but who $c^{d.}$ find entertainment in buying kitchen "utensils" & the like. I think the Grannie is sure to lend me her carriage - I do hope she will anyhow, as it $w^{d.}$ make such a difference. I am getting so excited about getting the first lot of letters at Pekin written after you all "knew about it" - I think I've got the last till then but after all its only a fortnight to wait now. I simply love your little holly calendar & many a time do I study it. C. can grasp dates in his head which is so wonderful - You & I were never any use without a date card firmly placed in front of us - See & prepare the dog's mind that the other twin is coming home - I do hope it will give me a warm welcome - I had such a rediculous dream last night when Olly & Car came to Wreay Syke on bicycles (Olly's was a perfect brute & made a noise like the old "Premier") - There was absolutely nothing in the larder - which was a little house like a temple on a hill - for we went ourselves to look so they just "cycled" away again! and now my child Ta-Ta for the present. You will probably get 6 more letters & then you'll get me & if you've never enjoyed yourself in your whole life before you will when I get at you!! C. refuses to send you a message as he says he is too hurt - He declares you $w^{d.n't}$ have done it if you'd been a man! There's no sense in that remark & I've told him so.

Bless you forever

Yrs now ever & always

D -

7

The return - via Korea - Pekin - Moscow

February 18th. Thursday - We got up this morning at 6 o'clock & went by train to Shimonöseki. There was only one 1st. class carriage (a long one) on the train & half of it when we got in was made up as a sleeper & the other half packed with people lying about on the seats! However by the time we'd had some breakfast the sleeper part had been converted into a day carriage so we weren't so very badly off after all in spite of there being about 11 grown-up people & 1/2 a dozen small children in the carriage! They were all Japanese with the exception of one Englishman & a South African "black", with some European in him, with whom C. conversed! It was a 13 hour journey! We didn't get to Shimonöseki till 8-30 & the distance is equal to from London to Ruthwell! It was an express train & didn't stop at every station but it was very slow - It is a very narrow gauge so it wd.n't be safe to travel at the pace our trains go - They did hurry up a bit at the end & it wasn't a bit nice! The whole train rocked furiously & going over the points at stations it was beastly - Japanese engines are rather little old-fashioned things made in Glasgow, Manchester or America & their rolling stock is very bad & shabby too - We had a mail van on in front just behind the engine, the axle of which went on fire. All they did was to pour water on it - It smouldered away all the time and at every stop there was the same game with buckets of water to put it out! They all seemed to take it as a matter of course & I don't think ever dreamt of changing the van! At Shimonöseki we were pounced on by a most agreeable little English-speaking railway guide, willing to assist us in everyway - There was 1/2 an hour to wait till the boat sailed which we spent tramping up & down the extraordinary long platform - 1/4 of a mile from end to end for we measured it! It was very nice after sitting in the train so long - At last the launch to take us off to the boat started & we left Japan! We got on board about 1/2 past 9 & promptly went to bed - A customs man insisted upon examining our luggage which was most annoying, poor C. having to hastily put on his clothes again & go with him. The boat was most comfortable & well got up. We were the only 1st. class passengers - her name is "Iki Maru" -

February 19th. Friday - We did a bit of a roll in the night, but thank goodness, even I didn't think much of it! We really had an excellent passage arriving Fusan at 8.35. We had breakfast on board & then they hustled us off to catch our train - No need to hurry considering there was 2 hours to wait & the station about 5 mins walk from the boat! Fusan is a funny little place evidently "growing" hard - It had been raining so walking about was not altogether pleasant as the mud was inches thick & very sticky - However the sun was shining so we sauntered about & sat on granite blocks which had evidently been collected for building purposes & watched the Koreans - In appearance they are quite the most comic people we have seen! They all wear white clothes. Very baggy trousers tied in at the ankle, a loose coat & -- a little black top hat tied under the chin with strings! Anything more comic you cannot imagine! At last our train went. This time we had the carriage to ourselves all the way except when a few little Jap officers got in & bowed & "carried on" with each other - as good as a play to watch them! Korea is a fine wild mountainous country, at this time of year as brown & bare as it can be - Korean houses are of the most primitive order, just little hovels built of mud & stones with straw roofs. In the distance a village looks more like a rick-yard than anything else! The first part of the journey was lovely as the sun was shining & the railway followed a river flowing thro' a wide valley with ranges of mountains on all sides - Top-hatted, white clothed men were to be seen all along the line carrying enormous loads on their backs by means of a very simple arrangement of forked sticks - The women also wear white, very bunchy skirts & put their coats - which are generally emerald green over their heads. There are no roads, only paths. We climbed miles up into the mountains, going very slow at times in spite of the enormous American engine which drew us & were for ever diving into tunnels - There seems to be any amount of rice cultivation in the valleys & some of the hills have been newly planted with pine but otherwise it looks a very poor sort of country with rocks sticking up thro' the soil in all directions - It got colder & colder as we neared Seoul which we reached at 8.35 being met by a top-hatted gentleman from the Astor House Hotel who c[d.] speak English & who conducted us to the hotel which was only about 3 minutes walk from the station - It was a funny little pot-house of a place kept by a French Jew who calls himself an Englishman! We had quite a comfortable room with a bath-room attached & went to bed very early -

February 20[th.] Saturday - I must have got a chill or something for I woke up this morning with a bad headache & quite unable to keep awake! so I stayed in bed all day & slept it off. Not a good way of seeing Seoul but otherwise the best plan - C. said it was bitterly cold out & I didn't miss much - It snowed in the afternoon so he didn't go out - Complications are beginning to arise about our boat! The one we meant to go by does not leave till the 26[th.], another that goes tomorrow has no 1[st.] or 2[nd.] class etc: etc: All this information we get by telephone from Chemulpo & it is not exactly cheering! however to go by train w[d.] be worse as it w[d.] mean 3 days in a 2[nd.] class carriage with no Diner, the nights being spent in Japanese Inns! All we can do is to go to Chemulpo & find out for ourselves -

February 21[st.] Sunday - I was feeling alright this morning so off we went at 12 o'clock by train to Chemulpo, armed with a newspaper parcel of food (for one of the telephone messages told us there w[d.] be no European food on the boat!) & an English-speaking Korean to act as guide. It took rather over an hour to get to Chemulpo - The first thing we did was to go to the office of the Osaka Shuseu Kaisha (the Company the boats belong to). Here the guide had an animated conversation with the Japanese clerk which he interpreted to us & which caused our spirits to rise! The boat w^d. sail that evening, there was 1st. class, also European food! With this good news we went off to the best hotel in the town to wait. The boat was not yet in but was expected any minute - Hour after hour went by & still no boat - The guide went back to Seoul & we were left to the tender mercies of a Jap "boy" in the hotel who was the only person who knew any English. There was a telephone in the place so we kept the boy ringing up the office for news of the boat but it never came in spite of plausible messages! The last was that it w^d. come in the night & start early in the morning - & we believed them! It was desperately cold & our room warmed by a tiny little stove however the food was quite good which was a great thing & the boy a perfect trump!

February 22nd. Monday - Up we got this morning, full of hope when in came the boy in fits of laughter with the usual remark "Not arriving", which meant that the boat was not in yet!! Suffice it to say that the bally thing did not "arriving" till about 10 o'clock tonight & there we were wait wait waiting in the pierceing cold & begining to wonder whether we were doomed to live the rest of our lives in the Club Hotel Chemulpo! We went to the bank for some money & there found an English youth in whom we confided our troubles! he was most sympathetic & urged us not to give up hope! Chemulpo is a funny little place, partly Japanese, European & Korean. It was frightfully cold. Everything frozen in our room this morning - out of doors, the sun was shining luckily & it was really warmer out than in, in spite of the pierceing wind - I expect it is a very nice place in summer as it is built on a sort of promontory with the sea all round, studded with islands. We have the funniest little room here which has to do for bedroom, sitting-room & dining-room!

February 23rd. Tuesday - The boat really came last night! & this morning we hurried down to the launch which was to sail at 9 o'clock - There we sat in a place like a rabbit hutch till 10-30! Just like the Japs! Apparently they can't do anything up to time, time being of no consequence in the East, so there they dawdled for an hour & a half, however we did eventually get away & went on board the Shimudagawa Maru - A tiny grubby little cargo boat! There are 4 or 5 Jap 1st. class passengers & an American & Englishman besides ourselves - The Japs have their meals first & then we have ours - It is not up to much but we can fill in the gaps with the food we brought from Seoul. Thank goodness the sea is like a duck pond & the little boat making splendid way thro' it - Our cabin is tiny & the berths just narrow wooden shelves with iron mattress & pillow but its not for long!

February 24th. Wednesday - Not so calm this morning so I made no effort to get up but stayed in bed till we arrived at Dalny at 2 o'clock - We had only taken 27 hours which was very good & we have every reason to congratulate ourselves on our crossing - It might have been so very much worse! The quay presented a very busy aspect & it was quite difficult to make ones way amongst the trains of mules that were hauling & struggling with heavy loads to & from the ships. A carriage from the hotel was waiting so the American, the Englishman & ourselves squashed into it & set off for the hotel which is about 2 miles from the quay - It was very cold with a tearing wind & clouds of dust so it wasn't easy to take in the sights around. Dalny gives one the impression of a deserted city - The Russians had started it on such a grand scale, fine wide streets with great big magnificent buildings, all abandoned & going to rack & ruin. The Japs can't afford to go on with them & if they did they are all most unsuitable for them to live in & not at all their style. Our room is in the "annexe" of the hotel. An awful bore as it means dashing across the road everytime we go there - It is not a very good hotel, bad servants & oh so over-heated - Enormous, red-hot boilers in every room & the windows not used to being opened -

South Manchuria Railway Company, Yamato Hotel, Dalny

February 25th. 1909

Chérie, such a time as we've had lately! You'd better read the diary & then you'll know. First there was interminable waiting at Chemulpo - Why is it so dreadfully irksome to be made to wait? I never knew anybody like C. He is so philosophical & never gets fussed - no more did I really tho' it was rather too much of a good thing - And oh, by the way, before that at Seoul I had one beastly day - It was "the cold" pure & simple for I now have a thunderer in my head but at the time I thought I had "the sleeping sickness" & such a racking headache & thirst & all the rest of the joys - It was too annoying for I saw nothing at all of Seoul. And then came the sea & down I went at the first ripple, sick twice & a racking headache lying on a shelf where there was just room & no more. Oh but how I loathe the sea - It really is hell to me & I think gets worse & worse each time but no matter we have done with it now except from Calais to Dover & that is only an hour so is a mere nothing, even if I'm sick all the way - My dear C. is such an angel on these occasions - There never was such a man, worth dozens of maids & so sympathetic! Today he has gone off to Port Arthur with the 2 men that were on the boat with us - The only way to do it was to "rise" at 6 o'clock & make a real day of it which we thought I'd better not attempt especially as we have a long day tomorrow to get to Mukden. He was very loathe to leave me but I insisted upon him going - to see Port Arthur was the whole point of coming here & I'm perfectly alright alone with you to write to in a dreadful little room called "the parlour" furnished in several shades of red with green satin chairs! In a very short time now we will be placing ourselves in the train for home - in fact by the time you get this it will be a case of counting the hours! Figurez-vous ma petite? one goes quite silly thinking about it, doesn't one? I have enjoyed myself so enormously all this time & yet I long for home & you my child & YOU to "tell about it" all to! I wonder if you are coming to London to meet us or not? Those are the kind of questions that are so useless to ask & yet one longs to know so as the little plans & stories one makes up in ones head may have some foundation to go upon - For instance, what is the good of imagining you coming *down to Lowndes Sq$^{re.}$ if you won't be in London etc; etc:? I somehow feel sure I shall be very tired when at last we do get home - sort of reaction - It will be so nice to sit still & be quite quiet for a bit - What shall we do when C. is with the Yeomanry? If Lord Mansfield is not at Comlongon it w$^{d.}$ be nice to be there don't you think or visit some of the girls or Houghton but <u>not</u> Murrell Hill I don't think, we're not left alone eno' there. No, I think Comlongon or Houghton w$^{d.}$ be best but that will be easily arranged later - I have hardly seen anything of this place yet as we didn't go out again after arriving yesterday at $^{1}/_{2}$ past 2 - we had lunch (I'd had nothing all day having "thrown" it all!) & then C. shaved & had a bath etc: while I snoozed & darned a pair of stockings & "recovered" myself & said thank God at intervals because we'd finished with the sea & then it was time for an early dinner & then I had a bath & so to bed & sleep - I must go out soon tho' - The sun is shining & it looks ripping but theres a strong cold wind which I found out coming over to breakfast this morning from the annexe - However jam on my tammy & put my scarf right over the lot & I'll do - Oh my dear if you c$^{d.}$ have seen our bed at Chemulpo! It was a small single one, just room & no more. You & I've slept in many a foul little bed but never have we been asked to sleep in such a small one as this was. And C. is <u>rather</u> bigger than you so you can imagine how comfortable it was, however its extraordinary what one can put up with when forced to & we slept like tops. And now I think I must go out & finish this after*

Well, I've been out & had a pleasant hour's walk amongst Japs & Chinese - I kept thinking how extraordinary it was <u>Me</u> parading the streets of Dalny as tho' it was the most natural thing in the world! It ought to be such a fine town, unlike any of these squalid Eastern towns - I think its very sad indeed that the poor Russians have been turned out by these Japanese who simply don't know how to make use of these fine big buildings & look lost in the great wide streets - Dod Lampson told us he is one of the sights of Tokio at present! He is followed by an admiring crowd, they've never seen such a giant & none of them come much above his waist! The "conveyances" in this town are a fair disgrace - Small victorias in the very last stages of decay drawn by a pair of miserable looking little ponies being slashed along generally at a galop in very great danger I s$^{d.}$ think of the whole concern falling to pieces. In spite of being weeds some of the ponies remind me forcibly of the black 'oss! I'd like to have a little carriage in which to drive him & the Heck. It w$^{d.}$ be such a lark - I am longing to see those 4 fluffy things again Just <u>think</u> of Pun's nose & the expression on his face. Its difficult sometimes to realise that he <u>is</u> a horse. I've seen some rather nice things here in the way of mules. They use them a lot & they <u>are</u> such nice looking things. Quite small & fluffy & harmless looking tho' I daresay they can be as disagreeable as possible sometimes. We are told that the battlefield of Mukden will be under snow so <u>thats</u> not much good. If it is we shall go right on to Pekin without waiting there more than a night as there will be nothing to do there & as cold as charity. We shall get letters at Pekin. Hurrah! You must feel that you have done nothing but write to Pekin! but no matter there'll very soon be no more writing - Well, so long childie in the meantime. I must post this & then have some lunch. Bless you forever D.

February 25th Thursday - C. went by train to Port Arthur with the 2 men who came with us in the boat & who are staying in this hotel. I didn't go as it was such an early start & my cold still needs a little "cooking". They had breakfast & lunch at Port Arthur & got back about 4 o'clock. They drove to the Museum where there were guns etc:, relics of the siege & only had time to see one fort. It is a place that to really study one wd. have to stay 3 or 4 days. C. said it was fearfully cold driving about. I found a "Ladies Parlour" in the hotel in which I was quite comfortable by myself reading & writing & walked in the big streets of the town.

February 26th Friday - half past 6 was the hour we had to "rise" this morning to go to Mukden getting there at 8.30. It was a lovely train, all American built, nothing but 1st. class & most comfortable. The only pity being that it was so slow. The Wigtownshire train wd. leave it standing! The line is so badly laid that it wd. not be safe to go faster - Whenever we stopped armies of coolies dashed at the train with dusters & brooms & carefully removed the dust from its beautifully varnished sides! They seem to be very fond of their train & determined to keep it spick & span! There was a guard of Japanese soldiers on board & others turned out at some of the stations - They have had trouble sometimes with Chinese robbers, hence these precautions - Soon after leaving Dalny the train passes over the battlefield of Kinchow - It was most interesting as we had the book & were able to locate the various positions of the armies (roughly of course) as we went thro' - It was most pathetic to see the numberless graves - At one place crosses marked the Russian graves & quite close at hand a Shinto Torii marked the Japanese - The country is wild & desolate to a degree & really doesn't look as if it was worth all that fighting - The stations along the line are all of Russian build & now occupied by Japs. In some cases the Russian name was still stuck up - It seems sad to think that the Russians had all the building of them, just for the Japanese to step in & occupy them - Some of the Russian houses about the stations were complete wrecks, caused by the Japanese fire - When we arrived at Mukden C. was hailed excitedly by a brother officer of his! A most unexpected meeting, tho' C. had seen his name in the hotel book at Port Arthur as having been there & knew he was somewhere about in the country - he was leaving in the train we arrived by so there was not much time for conversation, tho' they managed to get in a good deal in the short time! As soon as Major Shearman had gone we went off to the hotel - There was no carriage so we just had to go in rickshaws. There was a lot of snow about & it was pretty cold but nothing unbearable with thick coats & rugs - The hotel is miles from the station - It took us 35 mins to get there, thro' pitch dark bumpy streets & when we did get there it was a beastly place, however it was only for one night & we went straight to bed so it didn't matter -

February 27th Saturday - Up again at ½ past 6 (We're getting quite good at it now, with constant practise!) & off to the station again in rickshaws - It was a most interesting drive & rather like a scene out of a pantomime sometimes! especially at one place, coming thro' a gate-way in an enormously thick wall where we met a perfect procession of carts & wagons, evidently coming in to market drawn by the most motley teams consisting of ponies, donkeys, mules, & bullocks all harnessed together! It is the quaintest sight imaginable - & one we saw many times both yesterday & today - to see a great lumbering Chinese cart being drawn by perhaps a bullock & pony as wheelers with a mule & donkey as leaders with probably another moke hitched on somewhere or other to give a bit extra assistance! There are trams in the principal street of Mukden - which was the only one we were in - drawn by ponies - Men with red & green flags on sticks stand at intervals on the line, to keep it clear - The rickshaw coolie, who had our luggage unfortunately ran foul of one of these men who instantly fell on him in a frenzy of rage & began to beat him with the flags - The coolie - evidently a man of spirit - turned on him & they fought like dogs while the poor bag lay in the middle of the road! C. got out of his rickshaw & separated the men who luckily were not hurting each other, as their clothes are far too thick & padded for that - The great thing seemed to be to get hold of each other's pigtail & pull! No sooner had we started again, than a parting shout from the coolie brought the other man flying at him again with re-doubled fury, out shot the bag into the street again, & the same performance had to be gone thro', quite a crowd collecting to see the fun! C. having separated them again, this time we got away successfully tho' I'm sure if the coolie passes that way again tody, they'll have another go at each other! It really was very funny, tho' it might have been beastly! The train today was not nearly so comfortable as yesterday, however we had a sort of little loose box of a carriage to ourselves which was something - They are not properly shut in so anybody from the corridor can see in. There was one Chinese woman who took the deepest interest in me & came & stared in the most open way & infuriated me - I am not as peculiar as all that tho' she evidently thought so! There was a lot of snow the first part of the way which was very dazzling but we ran out of it in the afternoon & had nothing but miles & miles of brown, flat in parts & hilly in others, but always brown - Its a perfectly vast country, everything on such a huge scale - The train was in charge of an Englishman, the refreshment department under another which is an excellent plan, with so many foreigners travelling by it, tho' there were plenty of Chinese 1st. class passengers too - There was one very "big wig" with his wives (poor little painted things, hardly able to waddle & in the grandest of stiff silks & satins) & his ponies & carriage all on board. They got off in the afternoon at a station where there was a crowd to meet them & went off to the town in a regular procession - We were told he was the tax-gatherer. We passed several trains composed of open trucks crowded with Chinese coolies immigrating to the north for the summer where they can get work, returning to their homes for the winter - It was an extraordinary sight - There must have been thousands of them - They prefer travelling in open trucks to covered in carriages tho' how they can indure it in this kind of weather, day & night, I can't think - At about 10 o'clock we put out our lamp & settled down to sleep. I was quite comfortable but the seat was too short for C. to get properly stretched out. We got thro' the night wonderfully - It was very hot with the steam heating & we seemed to stop a great deal at stations where there was much shouting & yelling which of course was disturbing, but still when morning came we were quite fresh tho' coal black! Another disturbance during the night was, I regret to say, fleas! Perfectly beastly, but you can't expect perfection on a Chinese railway!

February 28th Sunday - We arrived at Pekin at 10 o'clock this morning, very glad to get out of the train - We walked to the hotel which is large & imposing as it is only 2 or 3 mins from the station - We first read our letters & then spent the rest of the morning till lunch cleaning - & I can assure you we were in need of it! Afterwards we went for a walk all amongst the Legations - this hotel is right in the middle of them. One can tell what they all are from the flags & the various sentries & soldiers about are a real study. The Cameron Highlanders are at the British Legation - They give them fur glengarries but that doesn't keep their poor knees warm! All the Legation buildings are very fine & new since the Boxer troubles, also the whole place round about very much opened out & improved since that time - It makes it much more like a European town than it was. The streets are full of Chinese traffic - everywhere great high walls with big gates shutting in various parts. A "classy" way for Chinamen to get about is riding on tiny little donkeys who totter along at a brisk pace with a rediculous pig-tailed man on their backs & a collar of bells round their necks which jingle the whole time - Their carriages are covered boxes on wheels, nothing more nor less, very clumsy at that drawn by a pony or mule - tho' some of them have European carriages & make an attempt at being smart. This is a very good hotel run by an Austrian - rather a pity as the food - in consequence is enclined to be "German-y" - Stewed pears with chicken at dinner tonight reminded us of the N.D.L. boats! Every nationality under the sun seems to have a representative staying here!

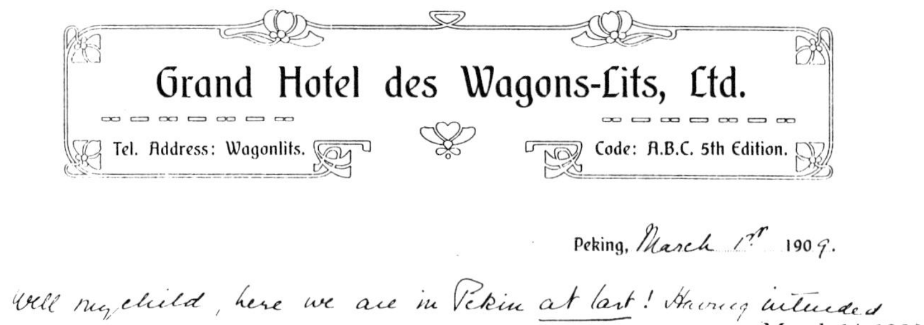
Grand Hotel des Wagons-Lits, Ltd.

Tel. Address: Wagonlits. Code: A.B.C. 5th Edition.

Peking, March 1st 1909.

Well my child, here we are in Pekin at last! Having intended

March 1st. 1909

Well my child, here we are in Pekin at last! Having intended originally to be here for Xmas we finally "land up" in March! Such a journey as we had to get here too - A whole day in

the train to Mukden, slept there in a horrid hotel (drunk manager, squalid & beastly, also another tiny bed!) then another day & night in the train. It was joy to get here at last, tho' its wonderful how the time passed. On Sunday night we start on 11 days & nights of it till we get to Moscow, but of course the most of that will be in the proper Trans-Siberian train - The worst part of our last journey was the fleas! I do hope we won't catch any more on the return journey! C. dearly loves the railway magazine you sent him. He w^d. look at it instead of at the Korean scenery but I think he has finished it now having read it from cover to cover! I found a letter from you waiting for me here yesterday from Murrell Hill - The one before I have not got yet as I'm afraid the silly asses have gone & forwarded that mail to Yokohama, tho' they were particularly told not to do so, however I expect it will return here before we leave & anyhow Cook in Yokohama knows just exactly where we are. Thats the worst of travelling about. One is apt to have ones letters delayed & muddled. It was disappointing as I wanted to know your first impressions of "the news" however I gather from your next letter that you're quite pleased! I'm still as well as can be & tho' of course I get tired in the train - as anybody w^d. - I soon get rested. I had letters from Spookie, Helen & Mog but none fron Mum or M^rs. Salkeld so they have gone the way yours have. I can see Spookie is pleased anyhow! & so are Mog & Helen tho expressed very differently. C. says he knows his father will spread it thro' the county quick eno' - I'm so glad he is so affable to you my child & said that about his 2nd. daughter-in-law! Its flattering for both of us isn't it? You seem to be really enjoying yourself at Murrell Hill this time I am so glad but its ridiculous to make comments on these kind of things when by the time you get this Murrell Hill will be a thing of the past & you will be at Houghton & I hope getting some good sport for you don't seem to have had a very good season taking it all round - Everybody seems to ride in Pekin - from the Chinaman on a minute donkey to a Legation lady of sorts who I saw this morning riding astride in the most up-to-date fashion! I love the ponies & mules here - the most of them are stout & well-looked after - Some of the ponies are real rippers - A great string of them are exercised in front of the hotel where we can see them from our window. I can hardly get dressed for looking at them! Its as fascinating as the parade at a horse-show or perhaps a circus considering that some of them are most fanciful being spotted in various tints! The Military Attaché here is a Lt.Colonel Willoughby of the Indian army. He introduced himself to us this afternoon - he seems quite a nice man - Tomorrow we must go & call on Dod Lampson's pal at the Embassy. Rather a bore as we feel sure it will mean invitations to dine etc & I've no clothes except Olly's old shirt & skirt which w^d. not be suitable! Most of the "sights" of Pekin unfortunately are some way out of the town & mean riding & staying the night in little Inns etc: which of course is out of the question for me but apparently one can hire a motor (at a fabulous price) which we are thinking of having for a bit of a tool round - It really is an awful pity I can't ride - I s^d. so love to mount one of these innocent looking ponies & go (on) some delightful expedition - ha'ever its no use thinking about it. I don't care much for rickshaws nowadays, they're so shakey & fairly joggle me up, so we only go in them now when absolutely necesssary. They'd be unbearable in this town I think as a great many of the streets are paved - & jolly unevenly too

March 2nd. 1909

C. got a letter last night from his mother in which she said you & Helen had been to see her but her letters are too unaffording for words. I do hope I'll get another from you before we leave here - There doesn't seem a great deal to do in Pekin but its rather nice to have a rest before we start on our travels - Just fancy 4 weeks today & we will be in London!! I am looking forward very much to Moscow & St. Petersburg & Berlin, at each of which places we "intend going" to the opera - I wish it wasn't such a devil of a way to get there tho' but I expect I shall get quite used to rattling along & the train stops every now & again for 1/2 an hour or so, so that one can get out & stretch ones legs a bit - But no going away from the platform for they have a pleasant little trick I believe of starting again before time! I must try & see Billy Maxwell of Munches I suppose - he is here with his regiment, but it is rather difficult to know how to do it. Ask him to tea I suppose & talk about Dumfriesshire! As far as I can remember he's quite a nice creature - I'm glad Mog & Harry had such a good time in Switzerland. What a tremendous party they were. I don't think Switzerland appeals very much to me. I'd so much rather stay at home & hunt - Oh my dear I'm so sorry to hear about the Lady Love. Its beastly when a horse begins to show such signs of age that one can no longer shut ones eyes to the fact. Bless her heart she has been one of the best & is so particularly "loveable" - there's no other word to express her - Well, my child I must now cease as this has to be posted - By the way, as you can imagine I was excited about Wreay Syke. Where the servants are to sleep is indeed a problem, but dash it thats the only house to be had so something will have to be devised - For goodness sake secure Maggie Little if you can. She wd. indeed be a comfort, but please thank Mog & tell her that Annie Hawkins at £38 is a lot more than we can afford - An awful pity as I sd. have loved to have had her - You won't get many more letters darling, another from here which will go in the same train as us - one from Moscow & another from Berlin will probably be all & then & then & then!!! Well, so long in the meantime dearie

Yrs forever & beyond

D -

I wonder if we'll see any change in each other - Its infernal cheek of you if you have as you say started a new face. Mine's the same old thing anyway tho' at present one cheek is covered with flea bites! Fondest love to the Pip, tho' you won't be with her I'm sure - The T.B. sends you his best love.

March 1st. Monday - Visited the bank this morning & studied "Chinese Life" in the streets & in the afternoon went into the Chinese city - It is surrounded by an enormously high & thick wall with a great gate in it - The stream of traffic passing in & out rivals Piccadilly! Such a curious & interesting collection of carts & horses, ponies, horses, mules etc: etc: mixed up with hundreds of rickshaws - It is not nearly such an objectionable city as Ichang! The street we were in was quite broad - & almost clean! - When we came out we went to the top of the wall which is about 20 ft. wide & looked down on the scene - It has been a lovely day, mild like spring - The worst of Pekin is the dust but we have been lucky so far in not having any wind to stir it up - The Military Attaché - Col. Willoughby - introduced himself to us this afternoon & is willing to do anything for us that he can He lives in this hotel so I daresay we shall often see him -

March 2nd Tuesday - This morning we went to the British Legation to get passports for Russia & to call on Mr Addison for whom we have an introduction from Mr Lampson - Each delegation has its own buildings enclosed by a wall in a sort of compound. The British is the biggest of the lot & was much increased in size after the Boxer troubles. The vice-consul (Mr Kirk) who gave us the passports was thro' the siege himself & was most interesting to talk to in the short time we were in his office. All the buildings in the old part are just as they were at that time but there are many other fine big ones added. We had to ask our way of a Cameron sentry at the gate. It was most refreshing to be answered in broad Scotch! We had lunch with Mr Addison who shares a house with another man & then went for a walk on the Chinese city wall & bought tobacco - It still continues to be lovely weather tho' one comes in with ones boots quite white with dust - If there was any wind I believe this is a dreadful place for dust-storms -

March 3rd Wednesday - Today we had a carriage & "did" 2 temples - The first was the Llama temple - Dirty & badly kept - The roofs of the various buildings are made of yellow porcelain tiles & inside are the usual images of Buddha & many old Chinese pictures, generally depicting the dreadful tortures to be expected in the next world for various crimes committed in this - There were some very fine vases & things of cloisonné ware very old & some good carvings in bronze but there is really not very much to see & one is pestered all the time by the priests, the most awful looking ruffians, begging for money! Hundreds of them live at this temple - they are all Llamas & must be the very scum of the country I sd. think. Priests are the only Chinese who don't wear pig-tails. The other temple was a Confucian one - the best part of this one are the fine old cyprus trees which grow in the courtyard. The guide (who we had brought with us) didn't take us into the temple as he said there was absolutely nothing to see. We then drove to one of the city gates (An Ting Mon) & went out a little way on the road to Mongol. It isn't a road, its just a sandy plain scored with tracks in every directions. Mules, ponies & donkeys struggling with heavy loads thro' literally feet of dust & sand (goodness knows what happens if it has been raining) strings of camels stalking along also heavily laden & an endless stream of men on ponies or donkeys, driving in mule carts or walking, all either going into the city or coming out thro' the one big gate. A truly wonderful & indiscribable sight. We came back by the same gate & drove back to the hotel thro' the Imperial City, which is enclosed by high pink walls, & past the walls of the Forbidden City, which is inside the Imperial City & besides the walls has a wide moat round it. The bodies of the Emperor & Empress are lying inside the Forbidden City in buildings on "The Coal Hill" which one can see above the walls - It is the only hill in Pekin & is an artificial one at that. All this information we got from the guide but don't know whether its correct or not for he didn't seem to know much about it - Pekin seems to be a very busy place simply teeming with life. I think the most interesting & nicest thing to do here is to walk or drive about in the streets observing it all - Our carriage today consisted of a victoria drawn by a pair of innocent fluffy white ponies, not much more than 12 hands high!

March 4th. Thursday - Shopping here is a work of some difficulty - The only European shops are "General Stores" where it is very difficult to get anything one wants. We went & watched them playing polo this afternoon on a very dusty ground just outside the wall which surrounds the Legation part of the town. The ponies are Chinese & the most of them very common-looking & badly shaped & none of them much over 13 hands but it must be a great thing for the residents here to be able to play at all. Billy Maxwell of Munches - in the Cameron Highlanders - came to tea this afternoon & Mr. Addison dropped in later so we had quite a tea-party! We have made friends with a naval Commander Hughes - or some such name - who is staying in the hotel so with Colonel Willoughby we have quite an extensive acquaintance here!

March 5th. Friday - Last night there was a terrific dust storm which has lasted with more or less violence all day - It is perfectly horrible - The sky is red with dust obliterating the sun, just like fog, & there is a high wind blowing which swirls the dust about in all directions, blinding one & getting right down ones throat - In spite of keeping the windows shut it is inches thick all over the hotel. These dust-storms are very frequent here at this time of year. We are lucky not to have had more as it is not a pleasant experience. We hardly went out at all - We bought furs this morning from a Chinaman who brought them to the hotel, with the assistance of our naval friend Capt: Heugh who is "knowing" in these matters - We have sent them home by parcel post. The great difficulty was to find some brown paper to wrap them in. They say it is an almost impossible thing to get in Pekin - however we managed to scrape up some - This evening we dined in the hotel with Col: Willoughby - He had a dinner party of 10 composed of more or less odd people! The American military attaché & his queer little sister & another American woman all talking with strong Yankee accents amongst the number. After dinner Col: Willoughby entertained the company by showing us photographs taken by himself of places all over the world in a sort of little magic lantern! It was rather like a Friendly Girl entertainment! the lamp went out & then the machine wd.n't focus (just like a magic lantern!) but it was quite a good plan & we all fired off suitable comments on each picture! Afterwards one of the guests - quite a boy - played the piano (an awful old brute) really very well - It was nice to hear some music again -

Grand Hotel des Wagons-Lits, Pekin

5. 3. 09

Eh bien ma p'tite, a few pages of diary & "a line" to help you thro' the dugs of the time - I expect it seems years to you but its incredible to me to think that in less than a month now we shall be home - This has been a very entertaining place. Not many "sights" but we know a good many people which has made it different to any other place. I have not enlarged on any of them in the diary but will do so now! The first we got to know was Lt. Col. Willoughby military attaché here, a very nice man who lives in this hotel - he has plenty of hair in front but is quite bald at the back of the top of his head! A peculiar effect to say the least of it. Then there is a nice old naval Commander - Heugh by name - who just came up & began to talk to us seeing, I suppose, that we were "real" people. Apparently he is a great connoisseur in curios, furs & other things that you can buy here & today assisted us enormously in the purchase of some furs - of which "anon" - he is a most amusing old thing & clever too I s^d. think - Then there is Billy Maxwell who came to tea yesterday & who jawed away 19 to the dozen - its funny when one remembers what a dreadfully shy boy he used to be. Do you remember a ghastly game of croquet you & I played with him & Lionel at Munches? They just w^d.n't - or c^d.n't - speák! Then on the polo ground yesterday another of the Camerons, seeing us standing there came over & spoke to us & informed us that there was a German a French & a Dane all playing - the rest being English, that they give from £5 to £8 for their ponies - & one can well believe it - more innocent mis-shapen people I've seldom seen! - & otherwise made himself agreeable. Then there is Dod Lampson's friend - M^r. Addison - A real "London" young man, very talkative, clever & amusing - his companion - M^r. Seeds - rather an aggravating weedy little specimen who tries to be amusing like Addison but doesn't succeed which is always so dreadful! M^r. Addison is trying to get permission to take a party to the Summer Palace before we go but I don't know whether he'll succeed - I hope so anyhow as I s^d. love to go. It is a great favour now-a-days to be allowed to go I believe & they make an awful fuss over it sending on officials to receive one etc: Tonight we are going to dine with Col: Willoughby - Just in the hotel dining-room but at his table instead of our own! He is going to have some other people too - a regular dinner-party! I don't mind so long as we have not got to go out to it - That w^d. be unbearable especially tonight for there is a duststorm raging which has been going on since last night - I never saw anything like it - perfectly disgusting - The whole air is <u>red</u> with dust, the sun being obliterated like with a London fog & with the high wind dust swirls about & gets into ones eyes & nose & down ones throat & makes everything simply filthy - We have been jolly lucky not to have had more of it tho' we shall probably have it now till we go, as they all say these storms last 2 or 3 days - An awful pity as it has been lovely here up to date. And now I must tell you about my furs! Captain Heugh said something about getting some <u>very</u> good white fox fur skins here for next to nothing so I got much excited & got him to ask some of the Chinamen who are always loafing about the hotel selling things, to bring some for us to see so this morning in they came with dozens of skins of various qualities. C. & I were rather *at sea, not knowing much about fur so C. boldly went to Capt. Heugh's room & asked him if he w$^{d.}$ be so very kind as to come & assist which he did with pleasure & was invaluable for the Chinamen who knew him & knew that he knew what he was doing & didn't try to "do" him for they knew they c$^{d.n't}$! We selected 3 lovely skins - 2 to make a "furr" & 1 for a muff & then there was a ripping squirrel fur coat, which Capt. Heugh said was a beauty so we took that too & then Capt. H. said what he thought was a fair price - far far less than what they asked to begin with - & they gave in with hardly a struggle! We got the 3 skins & the coat - of course not made up - for £11! The coat alone w$^{d.}$ be far more than that in London so we feel we've got a real good bargain tho' of course having them made up will make them "come" a bit more expensive tho' Capt. H. has told us of an excellent place to go to in London very cheap where his wife had some beautifully done - Lor! I shall be a swell & no mistake! I am buying them with wedding present cheques & shall have them made up with the same & if there's eno' over - which there will be - get a saddle! And now my child I must stop "for the nonce" (which I think means "for the present")- This letter will go in the same trains us which seems so rediculous but when we get out in Moscow it will go swirling on. The next opportunity for me to write will be from Moscow so it will follow this in a few days time. Best of love my Twister from the T.B. & myself*

Ever thine D -

6. 3. 09

I add this just to let you know that the dinner party last night was boring to a degree - After dinner a magic lantern entertainment! It was quite a good plan as otherwise we w$^{d.}$ have to have talked which w$^{d.}$ have been dreadful as they were not an exciting lot. Some of them are living in this hotel. I do hope we'll recognize them & not cut them. I'm not likely to, never forgetting a face, but C. might & it w$^{d.}$ be awkward.

Thank goodness the dust storm is over. We have heard no more about the Summer Palace so I'm afraid it must be "off" - Today, instead we are probably going to the Temple of Heaven! Doesn't it sound nice? Well so long dearie for this must be posted. C. always insists upon posting early - before the time they say - which is of course a good plan as one never quite knows how much to believe of what one is told in this benighted country -

À toi D =

Dash! C. just come in - booked to go to dinner with Mr. Addison tonight - Infernal bore -

March 6$^{th.}$ Saturday - Today we went to the Temple of Heaven - It stands in a sort of park with very fine old trees in it surrounded by a pink wall 3½ miles round. The temple itself is very impressive but in shocking bad repair, everything seems to be tumbling to pieces just for the want of care - such a shame - It is a curious place & totally unlike any other temple we have ever seen - It is a big courtyard surrounded by a wall with gates & in the middle a circular sort of platform with flights of steps leading up it made of white marble with balustrades & ornamentations of the same material - Everything has some symbolical meaning I believe & is very old but it was all Greek to us & we had a silly fat old guide who knew nothing & talked the very worst English The temple was quite spoilt by the colour - the wall being brick red with royal blue glazed tiles, bright green & yellow tiles being used to ornament some of the other parts. We meant to go for a drive after this but had to give it a miss as we had a brute of an old jibbing horse who w[d.n't] start under 5 minutes slashing & dragging (C. having to do the latter). When it did start it went at a break-neck pace thro' the traffic, the driver frightened to make it go slow in case it stuck up again - Of course the result was what might have been expected - we crashed into a rickshaw & upset it throwing an unfortunate Manchu lady who was driving in it into the street. She was not hurt. In 2 minutes we were surrounded by a vast crowd, policemen, coachman & rickshaw coolie all yelling at each other in a frightful state of excitement while we sat in the middle of it all unable to understand what was going on. At last, with the assistance of the guide we managed to make them understand it was the hotel carriage & nothing to do with us & they let us go on but it was rather beastly - As at any moment the old horse might have done a heap more damage we went straight back & "had it out" with the manager!

March 7[th.] Sunday - Packed & prepared for the next 11 days which will be spent in the train & started at 5.30 p.m.! We got a carriage to ourselves, cleaner & altogether more comfortable than the one we had coming - C. was much surprised by the man in charge of the train - who is always a European on this Chinese Imperial Railway - asking him if we were going straight thro' to Holm Hill! It turned out that 12 years ago he used to be in the parcel office at Carlisle & recognised C. before ever he saw the name even! He is a Scotchman from Ayrshire & his wife is now living in Annan! Talk about the smallness of the world! He came to our carriage & talked till 11 o'clock at night - he & C. having many mutual friends in Carlisle station!

March 8[th.] Monday - At 7 o'clock this morning we got to Shau-hai-Kwan where the train passes right thro' the Great Wall - We got up to see it. It is a wonderful construction - as wide as it is high - winding its way thro' the country & over the hills as far as one can see. It is in rather a delapidated state just at this place but I am very glad to have seen it for it is a wonderful sight - We were in this train till 6.45 p.m. when we arrived at Mukden - Here we had to change & wait about 2 hours - having collected the luggage & placed it in a heap in the refreshment room we had dinner & in a short time the Manchurian train arrived to take us to Chang-Chung. The Sleeper is arranged on the American system which is not at all a comfortable one - The berths are on each side of one long compartment with a narrow passage between & curtains in front of each - If you want to undress you must do it lying on your back in your berth with the curtains drawn, unless you prefer the public passage!

March 9th. Tuesday - At 1/4 to 4 this morning the horrid little Japanese car-attendants came & roused us all, so in the pitch dark up we had to get as best we cd. & have breakfast - at 5 we got to Chang-Chung where we had another change into a Russian train - Luckily the moon was shining which gave some light to guide our steps over the lines to our train, the luggage being shouldered by Chinese coolies. One has to keep a very sharp look out on ones luggage travelling this way - Heaps of people have had theirs stolen - One can't book straight thro' so at all these places there is a tremendous commotion - Everybody buying tickets with much bother - We got a coupé to ourselves in the train - There is no dining-car so one has to take little boxes of food from the Japanese train - They give one precious little so we bought some excellent bread at a station restaurant & drank some real Russian tea out of glasses sold by a charming stout Russian lady! It is so nice to see all these great big Russians after nothing but Chinese or Japs for such a long time - This is not much of a train, very shabby & slow with an extremely antiquated-looking engine. We got to Harbin at 4.10 p.m. Here there was the most wonderful man from the Hotel who seemed to speak every language under the sun & directed & assisted every body with their luggage etc: - & cheated them too right & left! I forgot to say that almost immediately after leaving Chang-Chung we got to Kwan-chen-zu where all the luggage had to be re-registered for some unexplained reason! At Harbin after we'd been to the Hotel to get our letters, bought the tickets etc: the Russian who we met on the Lützow came to see us. We had told him what day we were passing & he had remembered! He was most affable & at parting presented us with a bag of oranges! Most welcome, as you can only get fruit at a fabulous price on the railway - At 6.25 we left Harbin, had dinner, & went to bed. There was a great deal of confusion over the seats - We have not got the ones we booked but are quite comfortable in a coupé at the very back of the train

March 10th. Wednesday - Intensely cold all today - Every now & again the train stops at a station for 20 mins. or so & one can walk up & down the platform - the sun is shining brightly or, in spite of coats & mufflers, it wd. be quite unendurable. The Russians go about in huge fur coats & caps. The Chinese wear the thickest of padded clothes & I suppose manage to keep more or less warm - The country we passed thro' was very flat & uninteresting & all under snow - The train is very comfortable & the food good, but the amount of "extras" one has to pay perfectly appalling! At 6 p.m. we came to the frontier between China & Eastern Siberian - a place called Manchouria. Here we stopped 3 hours while all the luggage was examined - All the stuff in the van being hauled out to the Custom's Office - I didn't get out of the train as C. said it was too cold for words with the sun gone down & even walking up & down it was impossible to keep warm. The train is well heated

& it is possible to keep it ventilated which is a good thing, by opening the windows in the corridors - Those in the carriage are frozen fast & in spite of being double the inside one has a rim of ice all round it & no power in earth can open it. Our fellow-passengers are most pleasant & we are all the greatest of friends! One of them is a black & white puss belonging to a Russian lady

March 11th Thursday - The engine broke down last night for 2 hours so today we are making up time & only waiting 2 or 3 minutes at the stations so that there is hardly time to get out. There is any amount of snow about & the scenery much more interesting, hills, with fir trees & silver birches which look lovely in the snow with the sun shining on them. The stations are the funniest little places all built of wood, as are all the houses, a good many of these being just log huts - Between the stations one never sees a sign of human habitation & if the sun was not shining it wd. be the most dreary place. The engines burn wood here so the forest is very much cut all along the line with here & there acres of logs all neatly piled up ready for use.

March 12th Friday - We were woken at 6.20 this morning by the customs people who came fussing in to examine the hand luggage, why, goodness knows as it was all done on Wednesday at Manchuria - The whole morning we were going along beside Lake Baikal & perfectly lovely it was too. The lake of course was frozen & covered with snow with sleighs going about on it - using it as a road - (All the "means of conveyance" here are sleighs & they use the frozen rivers as roads.) It is very rocky all round the lake - The railway is a real work of art winding along the shore & diving thro' innumerable tunnels - We got to Irkutsk at 2.15 p.m. where one has to change trains - There was a tremendous commotion with everybody struggling to find places - The line is shockingly badly managed - They have a pleasant little habit of selling the places twice over - not to mention running the train a car short! However we were alright as C. nipped across & got our places before anybody else had time to claim them! One row went on far into the night, between a French lady with 2 boys & a Russian actress - The latter insisted upon getting into the former's carriage with 14 packages which filled up the place to such an extent that they cdn't go to bed! We got letters at Irkutsk & had time to have a walk up & down the platform - It is not safe to go farther . They start the train with 2 bells, then 3 bells 2 or 3 minutes after & off so one has to "look slippy" - This train is much the same as the last except that only one window in the corridor will open & they are all so frosted on the outside that one can't see out which is most tantalizing!

March 13th Saturday - Today we have been going thro' dense forests of fir & silver birch - Quite lovely, with deep snow & bright sun-shine - Its extraordinary the way the time passes - with plenty of books & papers to read, conversation with our fellow passengers, short walks whenever we stop, not to mention very lengthy meals, for there are only 2 waiters for the lot of us, it doesn't seem the least wearisome - By 12 o'clock the sun has melted the ice on the windows so that one can see out - the only thing is that it does get stuffy - The only means of ventilation is a window in the corridor which we are continually opening, only to have it shut 3 or 4 mins: later by the French woman who unfortunately suffers from the cold! Otherwise she is a very nice woman & gave me a cup of excellent tea this afternoon - made by herself with a spirit lamp!

March 14th. Sunday - Rather more open country here - We got to the junction for Tomsk this afternoon so we are now well on the way - There seems to be more snow here & in places we were going thro' deep cuttings in the drifts - it must be an awful business clearing this line after a heavy fall of snow.

March 15th. Monday - The engine broke down which delayed us some time in the night & then this morning one of the springs of our carriage had to be renewed, 15 men working like galley slaves for about an hour to do it. Also this afternoon we suddenly pulled up short amidst a certain amount of excitement, but we cd.n't find out for what cause tho' the guard explained at great length - in Russian! The country here is desolate in the extreme. Snow-covered plains as far as the eye can see.

March 16th. Tuesday - We got to Cheliabinsk this morning - The platform was swarming with Siberian emigrants waiting for their train with their wives & children & all their belongings - A most pathetic sight - Little do they know what a desolate country they are bound for. The Government gives them a certain small sum to enable them to get there telling them they're going to the most wonderful place in the world - & they believe it - Poor things - They travel 4th. class which means little better than cattle trucks - No windows & no seats. How they live thro' it goodness knows - Today we have been going thro' lovely forests. I never saw anything like the silver birches & they look so particularly well in the snow standing out white against the fir trees - At 3.25 we got into Europe! A big stone with "Asia" & "Europe" engraved on it marks the boundary -

March 17th. Wednesday - We passed a convict train today - The windows are strongly barred besides a guard of soldiers & the prisoners being chained to their seats so escape is practically impossible besides most certainly ending in death - Poor things - they are even more to be pitied than the emigrants - It is gradually getting much warmer & this has been a red letter day in that our window came unstuck & we were able to have as much air as we wanted & let the french lady "fug it" as much as she likes in the corridor -

March 18th. Thursday - The last day! Enormous tracts of flat snow covered country but much more inhabited than Siberia - We got to Moscow at 7.10 - where an American guide instantly pounced on us & conducted us to a grand motor bus belonging to the Metropole Hotel! The streets are covered with snow & simply swarming with sleighs dashing madly about in the most reckless fashion! The motor was a good deal <u>more</u> reckless & had no non-skids so why we didn't fly into the middle of next week goodness knows. This is a huge hotel - very comfortable & <u>very</u> expensive!

<u>March 19th Friday</u> - Moscow is a fine town with very wide streets & dozens of churches all built in more or less the same style - 4 or 5 little towers each with a cupula like an inverted top surmounted by a cross all covered with gold leaf, so the effect tho' somewhat peculiar is very rich & magnificent - two of our friends of the train had a guide & this afternoon most kindly asked us to go along with them & get the benefit of him too - We first went thro' the most sumptuous covered bazaar - a sort of glorified Burlington Arcade! - It consists of 4 streets each 3 stories high & has over 1000 shops in it! One of our friends bought an astracan cap in one & "a present for a lady" in another! From here we went to the church of St. Basil - It is the most peculiar looking place imaginable from the outside - Every one of its cupulas - of which I think there are 11 - are all different - the result is a most hopeless jumble - The inside is a regular maze - 11 little chapels gorgeously decorated with narrow winding passages leading from one to the other - More a wonderful than a beautiful place - After this we went to the "House of Romanof" where the Great Grandfather of Peter the Great was born & lived - It was a funny little rambling place with tiny low rooms full of very nice things & papered with either painted leather panels or lovely embroidery - The streets & pavements are very snowy & frightfully slippery so we purchased some snow boots & feel much safer & drier!

<u>March 20th Saturday</u> - This afternoon we had a guide & went to the Kremlin - This is a part of the town enclosed by a wall containing the Palace, barracks, innumerable churches etc: We went into 2 of the churches, the one where the Czars are crowned & another where the Czars used formerly to be buried - Anything like the richness of the decoration I have never seen - "Ikons" - sort of pictures made of silver gilt & encrusted with the most magnificent jewels

(The diary ends abruptly.)

Well, my girl, here we are in Moscow! 10 more days – (is it really true?) & we will be in London –

Hotel Metropole, Moscow

March 20$^{th.}$ 1909

Well, my girl, here we are in Moscow! 10 more days - (is it really true?) & we will be in London - Mon dieu - to think of it!!! First & foremost let us discuss plans (a one-sided sort of "discussion" but still). To begin with M$^{rs.}$ Salkeld is going to have us at Holm Hilll & can have us till the 14$^{th.}$ when she leaves but if she cant have you as well I shall just leave & go to Houghton. Another thing darling I think you must come to London to meet us. I have been looking forward to it so - I don't see how we c$^{d.}$ possibly be up in time for the P$^{t.}$ to P$^{t.}$ - I don't think I c$^{d.}$ arrive at 7 o'clock one night & start the next morning - I'm pretty feeble - more so than I was & I think it w$^{d.}$ just kill me - Dearest c$^{d.}$ you give it up to be with me those few days? If you go to At Alice I know she lets one do exactly as one likes & besides she'd understand fast eno' if we told her. C. will be dashing about doing all sorts of things & you & I c$^{d.}$ have a glorious time together so do do do come child. We'll be so awfully happy my dear that there will be no time for you to have nasty feelings - You must never never have them again. As to me being changed in the face - what bunkum - I'm positive I haven't changed in one single aspect - except for a large waist - so don't you worry about that. Apparently it takes ages to "show" so you needn't be the least frightened - Just you look out for exactly the same woman & you'll see her right enough! The hat of course may give you a shock but as a matter of fact I rather like it now so perhaps you will. As to whether you get asked to Holm Hill or not, sufficient unto the day & anyhow we will have had Wed: Thurs: Fri: & Saturday & you bet I'll manage something - The upshot of all this is -

Come to London -

I gloated over your little plan but it just c$^{d.n't}$ be - Do gloat over mine & do it like a good girl - The 11 days & nights in the train were wonderful. The time passed so quickly but lord I was tired on the last day - however I'd sooner do that a million times than come by sea - It was really awfully interesting & I loved the Siberian forests with nothing but snow wherever you looked. Moscow is a nice place too, tho' we haven't seen much of it yet. It simply swarms with sleighs - you never see wheels except on motors - Some of the horses are rippers drawn by prancing nags with very high hind-quarters & arched necks - Evidently Russian bred as I've never seen anything like them before. We're not going to St.Petersburg after all. They all say it will be so dreadfully cold there & we've had eno' of that in Siberia so we're going to Warsaw on Sunday night & spend a day there to see the de Reszke's then to Berlin & then if you please to Brussels!!! You see its all on the way so we will have Sunday & Monday there & start from there at the ladylike hour of 11 arriving Victoria 7.10! The opera is closed here - isn't it too sickening for words that we s$^{d.}$ just hit on the one week in all the year? I'm so vexed about it tho' I daresay I'm much better in my bed & resting, after that train - Of course we'll go in Berlin & Brussels - By Jove just won't we - By the way if you're coming to London remember to write for your ticket - Ashton of Bond St is a friend of C's so ask them to give you next door to us - dress circle -

or if impossible get 2 somewhere or other & we'll make Shosh or somebody else come & sit in couples -

C. is out this morning at the "Crédit Lyonais" (Ha, ha familiar name!) I cannot bear banks & the like - The atmosphere in them fairly does for me & I can now fully sympathise with Mog. How I wish you were here to bear me company. Letters more than ever seem perfect waste of time. And yet lor how I did revel in your 2 which I got on arrival here - At least we didn't get our letters till the following morning as the Office was shut. I stayed in bed for breakfast & as soon as C. was ready he went for the letters & I lay in bed & read till I was silly! They were such corkers - you really write a thundering good letter. I was trembling with nervousness when reading about Bo! Pon my word that is a child & a half - I'd just give anything to see him & shall whats more - We are having regular "pistolets" breakfasts here consequently I am dying for lunch. I wish to goodness my old man w^d. come in. I shan't let him go out by himself again in a hurry - I'm sure I know whats happened! He's found an English-speaking clerk & is having a long & confidential talk with him! He always does that! A very "common" man on the train who we made friends with gave us a letter of introduction to a friend of his here & we are expecting that he will turn up this afternoon to "show us round" - its rather a bore except that he will act as guide & save us having a professional one at 12/-! Moscow is horribly expensive & no doubt seems more so coming from "The East" where of course everything is much cheaper than in Europe. I just got a real good cold in my head in the train which was an awful nuisance as it didn't exactly add to my comfort but I don't quite see how it was to be avoided living in such appalling contrasts. You've no conception of the cold - out of doors - (We don't have anything approaching it at home) & then the train heated up to boiling point & to have air you had to have draughts so the result was inevitable -

Having got thus far in came C. with all the belated letters from you & Mum & Ollie M^rs. Morton & M^rs. Salkeld. The ones written immediately after you'd heard the news. My child I was so glad to get yours & to know what you think on the subject - Yes my dear it does enlarge the heart. How glad I am that you now realize that if I had a dozen husbands & 50 children it w^d.n't & c^d.n't make any difference to my feelings towards you. He is my husband it is my child & she is my twin - Its like the idea of the Trinity - I love you all wholely & yet you're each one separate. My child we'll share that little baby the same way as we shared the Dog - Oh what a lot I think about it. Quite calmly now too as tho' it was the most ordinary thing in the world which after all it is. Heavens, there are billions of babies in this world & yet we fuss as tho' this was the only one! Oh but it is - it is - Of course I'm glad you told Helen. I'm not sending you any diary as we will be home so soon its not worth it. You shall take it back to Eaton Place with you that first night if you like - the "sights" here consist of churches chiefly - Talk about a "bit o' money" - Some of the images are simply encrusted with the most lovely jewels ever you saw. My dear, I'm "too tired" to write any more - I'm so sorry as I s^d. like to tell you all about Moscow for it is a lovely place. Bless you my child - Love from the T .B. Forever & ever D -

Hotel-Bristol, Varsovie (Warsaw)

23. 3. 09

A week today ——!!!! My dear how I do hope that you have been able to "comply" with my suggestions in the last letter, for I have spent hours planning every moment - I have just sent you a p.c. to know if you're coming or not for if you're not the disappointment of looking for you at the station & not seeing you w$^{d.}$ be so intense - C. insists upon hanging out of the window! I tell him you won't want to see his ugly mug & I shall have the best place! We had rather a ghastly journey here from Moscow, starting with a night in the train & then a long long day - 2 hours late as there was a river in flood & we had to go round a longer way so we didn't get here till 11. 30 p.m. Gosh! I was tired -

added in pencil:

Central Hotel. Berlin - 25 - 3 - 09 -

I must just write you a few more lines & C. must finish the letter as my dear I regret to say I am in my bed - We had a nightmare of a journey yesterday to get here, I thought I'd got influenza at the very least but am miles better today - All the same C. got a D^{r} who says I am just tired & must have a rest of a day or two & then I shall be quite fit to continue the journey - Oh my word it will be nice to be back again & see your smiley face! I do hope you're coming to London & trust I'm not asking too much even from you - I am longing to hear about that - Do you realize that this is my last letter!

Bless you

Yrs ever

D -